ASIAN ORIENTATIONS: *Treasures From Honolulu's Oriental Art Society*

ASIAN ORIENTATIONS

Treasures From Honolulu's
Oriental Art Society

EDITOR: HOWARD A. LINK

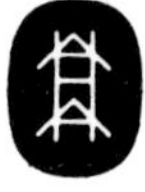

Organized by the Oriental Art Society of Hawaii
in cooperation with the
Honolulu Academy of Arts

Asian Orientations: Treasures from Honolulu's Oriental Art Society is the catalogue of the exhibition shown at the Honolulu Academy of Arts in the summer of 1985. The exhibition and catalogue were organized by the Oriental Art Society of Hawaii in cooperation with the Honolulu Academy of Arts and were made possible in part through a generous gift from Mr. Wing Tat Lee of Hong Kong and supporting gifts from members of the Society and community. Grants in Hawaii from Duty Free Shoppers Limited and China Airlines provided additional support.

Library of Congress Cataloging in Publication Data

Main entry under title:

Asian orientations.

    An exhibition held at the Honolulu Academy of Arts, July 11-Aug. 25, 1985.
    1. Art, Far East—Exhibitions. 2. Oriental Art Society of Hawaii—Exhibitions. I. Eyre, David. II. Morse, Peter. III. Link, Howard A. IV. Oriental Art Society of Hawaii. V. Honolulu Academy of Arts.
N7336.A85 1985 709'.5'0740996931 85-5486 ISBN 0-937426-05-9

Photography by Dan Wilson and Raymond Sato
Printed in Hong Kong

ORIENTAL ART SOCIETY OF HAWAII

The Members

Mrs. Grover H. Batten
Mrs. Samuel D. Berger
Mrs. E. F. Black
Mrs. John Bowen
Mrs. C. Wendell Carlsmith
Mr. James Charlton
Mrs. H. H. Ching
Mr. Kenneth Chong
Mrs. Patricia Cohan
Mrs. Judith M. Dawson
Dr. and Mrs. Robert Desowitz
Dr. and Mrs. Gene W. Doo
Dr. Zeng Yuhe Ecke
Mr. and Mrs. George Ellis
Mr. and Mrs. David W. Eyre
Dr. and Mrs. James H. Furstenberg
Mrs. L. A. R. Gaspar
Mrs. Bradley Geist
Mr. and Mrs. Windsor G. Hackler
Mrs. Fritz Hart
Doctors Clayton and Lynette Honbo
Mr. and Mrs. Mitchell Hutchinson
Mrs. Cecily Johnston
Mr. and Mrs. Richard Kimball
Dr. Eugene Knez
Mr. Henry Kramer
Dr. and Mrs. William Lau
Mr. and Mrs. George Lazarnick
Dr. Ernest K. H. Lee
Dr. and Mrs. Robert Lee
Dr. Howard A. Link
Mr. and Mrs. Warren K. K. Luke
Mr. and Mrs. Fred Martin
Mr. and Mrs. Melvin McGovern
Mr. and Mrs. Ferdinand Micklautz
Mrs. William Miller
Mr. Peter Morse
Mrs. Vatanee Navapan
Mr. Benji Nerio
Dr. Jack Paldi
Mrs. B. L. Sahney
Miss Sheela Sahney
Mr. and Mrs. Douglas Snelling
Mr. and Mrs. Garrett Solyom
Mr. Oliver Statler
Dr. Willa Tanabe
Mr. Charles R. Temple
Dr. William W. T. Won
Mr. Yung-fu Yang

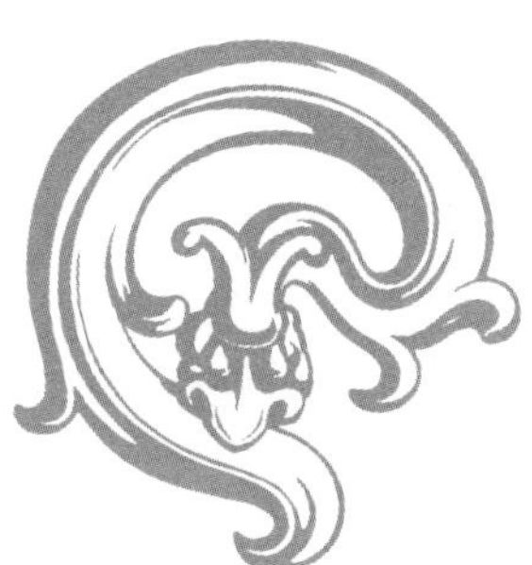

Benefactors
Mrs. Carlton H. Beal
Phyllis and John Bowen
Mr. Wing Tat Lee
Mr. and Mrs. Arthur Murray
Mr. and Mrs. Cornelius Vanderstar

Special Contributors
Florence H. Becker
Dr. and Mrs. Gene W. Doo
Alberta Gillette Dyson
Mr. and Mrs. David W. Eyre
Mrs. L. A. R. Gaspar
Mr. and Mrs. Alan F. Hunt
Mr. and Mrs. Sheridan Ing
Mrs. Cecily F. Johnston
Dr. Ernest K. H. Lee
Mrs. B. L. Sahney
Mr. Paul Trousdale
Dr. and Mrs. William W. T. Won

CONTENTS

Foreword

If it had not been for Betty Zeng Yuhe Ecke and Howard
Link, there would never have been a show entitled *Asian
Orientations: Treasures from Honolulu's Oriental Art Society,* and it is
doubtful if there would even be an Oriental Art Society in
Honolulu if they had not been here. Their initiative and
leadership in countless ways have been all-encompassing, and
we are deeply grateful to them. With Phyllis Bowen, David and
Cynthia Eyre, William Won and Benji Nerio, they have been
moving spirits in the Society since its inception, and they have
been prime movers of this show.

The late Mrs. John M. Allison and the late Robert P. Griffing,
Jr., were also founders of the Society, and they were leaders
whose enthusiasm and close personal involvement in Asian art
have not been forgotten.

The Society owes its largest debt of gratitude for this show to
Mr. Wing Tat Lee whose generosity has provided the catalogue
as well as other support. Other major benefactors are Mrs.
Carlton H. Beal, Phyllis and John Bowen, Mr. and Mrs. Arthur
Murray and Mr. and Mrs. Cornelius Vanderstar. The Society
wishes to acknowledge special contributions from Florence H.
Becker, Dr. and Mrs. Gene W. Doo, Alberta Gillette Dyson, Mr.
and Mrs. David W. Eyre, Mrs. L. A.R. Gaspar, Mr. and Mrs.
Alan F. Hunt, Mr. and Mrs. Sheridan Ing, Mrs. Cecily F.
Johnston, Dr. Ernest K. H. Lee, Mrs. B. L. Sahney, Mr. Paul
Trousdale and Dr. and Mrs. William W. T. Won.

Taking their cue from the Director of the Honolulu Academy
of Arts, the entire staff of the Academy has been the epitome of
helpful and concerned cooperation during the planning and
execution of this show. The Society is indebted to George Ellis
and the Academy personnel, and this collaboration on a labor of
mutual interest and community benefit has been a happy one.

Special Thanks to China Airline and the Halekulani Hotel.

Windsor Gregory Hackler
President, Oriental Art Society of Hawaii

Hawaii's more recent history has been closely linked with Asia through ancestry, commerce and culture, the latter being the particular province of the Honolulu Academy of Arts since its founding in 1927, and the special interest of the Oriental Art Society of Hawaii since its inception a decade ago. It is no small coincidence then that the two organizations should join forces to present the exhibition "Asian Orientations: Treasures from Honolulu's Oriental Art Society," to help celebrate the beginning of the Society's second decade of activity.

The exhibition profiles the Society's broad range of collecting interests as documented in members' private holdings. The selection includes a number of fine examples: sumptuous Japanese paintings and lacquerware to ravish the eye; ink paintings of both China and Japan to provide insights into the creative personality of two distinct but related cultures; the ceramic arts of China, Korea, Japan and Southeast Asia to increase appreciation and document the spread of this art form throughout Asia; and, finally, Buddhist sculpture of India, China and Japan to recount in part the story of the spread of Buddhism throughout Asia. The assemblage is also rich in specialized collections of Chinese jade, Korean Yi Dynasty water droppers, Japanese *netsukes* (toggles), Chinese snuff bottles, Chinese prints and Japanese prints, including not only the classic ukiyo-e, but Nagasaki prints and contemporary prints as well.

The exhibition also helps to celebrate the centennial year of the first arrival of Japanese immigrants in the islands. What better way to mark the occasion than to show the arts of Japan as collected by Hawaii residents, harmoniously juxtaposed with the arts of China, Korea, Southeast Asia and India! The exhibition is truly a reflection of Hawaii's Asian heritage and at the same time an in-depth look at Hawaii's broad collecting interests.

Our debt to the participating collectors of the Oriental Art Society is great, for they have disrupted their own homes in order to share generously their treasures with us. The Society's officers and members also have our sincere appreciation for the interest and critical assistance given in working out many organizational details. In particular we wish to thank Windsor G.

Hackler, President of the Society, for his kind cooperation in planning the exhibition and related activities with our staff. Collectors David W. Eyre and Peter Morse contributed fine essays for the catalogue, while Drs. Willa Tanabe, Charles Weber and Mr. L. B. Nerio helped the curatorial staff to research and write individual entries on given art objects. To all those who contributed their time, energy and expertise, may I extend my heartfelt thanks.

Support for the exhibition and catalogue required an all-out effort on the part of the Society also. Along with the benefactors to the exhibition listed at the opening of this catalogue, generous grants were received from Duty Free Shoppers and China Airlines. A special thanks is due Mr. Wing Tat Lee of Hong Kong and Hawaii for a very generous grant which made possible the printing of this catalogue. Without this kind of support, exhibitions such as this would not be financially feasible.

Primary responsibility for the concept and realization of the project rests with the Academy's Senior Curator of Asian Art, Dr. Howard A. Link, and Adjunct Curator for Chinese Art, Dr. Zeng Yuhe Ecke, both senior members of the Oriental Art Society as well. As author and editor for the catalogue, Dr. Link, in addition to his own research and writing, has successfully integrated the various contributions of a number of other scholars and collectors in the Society to produce a document of considerable distinction. Dr. Ecke has been responsible in large part for authoring the Chinese portion of the catalogue, for the initial selection of some eight hundred art objects that led to the outstanding loans included here, and for coordinating much of this effort. The contributions of both Curators is acknowledged with gratitude.

Of the Academy staff members who helped in the undertaking, grateful recognition must go to Mr. Joseph Feher, the Academy's Senior Curator, for his skillful design of the catalogue; Mr. James Furstenberg, Curator of Program Development, for his outstanding slide tape on the exhibition; Mr. Fujio Kaneko, Exhibition Designer, for his superb installation of the show, and Mrs. Marion Campbell, Asian Art Department Secretary, for her expert typing of a most difficult manuscript.

The dedication of time, energy and expertise on the part of the Academy staff and the members of the Oriental Art Society has resulted in a memorable exhibition and catalogue for the community and for art lovers the world over. We invite your attention.

George Ellis
Director, Honolulu Academy of Arts

The Oriental Art Society of Hawaii

The Oriental Art Society of Hawaii is composed of approximately sixty members whose common interest is a love of Asian art and a passion for collecting it.

While the Society has serious purposes, it prefers the relaxed setting of a private home for the presentation of art objects, papers and symposia, to the more formal atmosphere of an academic institution. At the first meeting on November 4, 1974, a half dozen founding members expressed their solemn intention "to increase our knowledge of Oriental art." But the same minutes stressed that this erudition was to come in a casual contexture. "Robert's Rules of Order, by-laws and the like are to be de-emphasized," the secretary recorded.

And thus was born a relaxed, sit-on-the-floor Society, meeting mostly in the homes of members, often to see and handle the objects of a private collection, learn how it was assembled and the history of the subject, be it Chinese porcelains, jade or cricket cages.

Frequently the Society hosts a guest speaker at a collector's home, and occasionally meetings are held at the Honolulu Academy of Arts or at the University of Hawaii Art Gallery (in conjunction with an Asian exhibition) or wherever appropriate to the month's program.

Membership includes professionals in the field of Asian art, persons well informed through self-study, and hesitant tyros who confess they hardly know a Ming from a Tang art object, but are eager to learn. All are collectors of Asian art, whether their judgments be solely intuitive or based on considerable study.

It cannot be over-emphasized that the strength of the Society is due to the professional members who have given so generously of their time in sharing their knowledge with the general membership and in planning programs that would stimulate and instruct the Society's members.

Fine friendships based on the common bond of collecting have resulted from the monthly get-togethers. Hosts have proffered wine and cheese at the close of a particularly lengthy meeting as a refreshing capstone. In this way, the "casual contexture" mentioned previously is maintained in an ambience of Asian culture and friendship.

Nothing is predictable: the attendance, the slide projector, the wine's vintage—and sometimes the program. Yet a review of the some 100 programs presented in the past decade shows an impressive diversity and a quality often of high order.

Some examples: Mrs. John Allison, the Society's first president, discussed and displayed "Export Blue and White Porcelain of China" as the initial program. Members have seen and heard presentations on modern Japanese prints, Chinese snuff bottles, Korean folk art, Chinese bronzes, art restoration, a Zen Buddhist approach to ink painting, how to develop a sense for authenticity, calligraphy, Indonesian daggers, Philippine ceramics, ukiyo-e from the James A. Michener Collection, Chinese furniture, costumes and carpets . . . and, on occasion, members have simply enjoyed a lively conversation with the likes of Isamu Noguchi, the noted Japanese-American sculptor.

The Society has even had two presentations on the seldom-studied art of erotica, one dealing with late Chinese ivory carvings in a member's collection and another on the history of Japanese erotica from the Neolithic to the 20th century. "Show and Tell" programs have been a regular occurrence when members bring dubious "treasures" from their collections to have an evaluation from other members with specific expertise. "My dear, you have a beautiful NOTHING," former Academy Director and ceramic authority Robert P. Griffing, Jr., told a solemn-faced collector who had tendered her favorite "Korean celadon" vase. She held back her disappointment.

Three years ago the Society decided that Honolulu should share the beauty of the members' collections in a public exhibition, thus creating an awareness of the variety of collecting interests in Oriental art that exists in the community. It is the first time the Society has put aside its low profile.

Zeng Yuhe Ecke, Hawaii's well-known artist and art connoisseur, was a founding member of the Oriental Art Society of Hawaii. After 10 years, how does she measure its accomplishments?

"First of all, we are collectors," says Dr. Ecke. "We are few in number but are extremely congenial and have successfully inspired one another. We have kept our group small in order to keep our learning on an intimate basis. It has helped our members to become better connoisseurs.

"Aesthetic curiosity is best when it begins in the home where one can learn from the actual art object and exchange experiences with persons who have the same interests. It is very different from the impersonal studies of classrooms and museums.

"Now selections from our collections are being shown in 'Asian Orientations.' The art objects included in this exhibition represent only one-tenth of what was available. They do, truthfully, represent our membership as we are."

David W. Eyre

The Collector Who Shares Facts

As collectors, we all take enormous pleasure in collecting
beautiful objects. We all make sacrifices and also commit
horrendous blunders. And, hopefully, we all learn something
about both art and life in our pursuit of beauty. What we learn,
however, is all too often kept locked within our own minds or
shared only with a few close friends. Some cultures, indeed,
consider that the private possession of knowledge confers
prestige upon the holder. If you know something that no else
knows, it's believed, your stature is greater. Such an attitude is
contrary to everything I value. "He who collects that he may
have the best collection, or better than his friend's, is little more
than a miser," wrote Robert Chapman. The same might be said
of the one who keeps knowledge to himself.

I am a collector of prints—Western prints as well as Japanese
prints. Why *prints* specifically? Well, there was a perfectly
mundane reason at the beginning: I could afford them. The price
of prints when I was young was well within the range of a
college student's means. Since that time, alas, prints in general
have risen out of a beginner's reach—but that is another story.

There is a further reason for collecting prints, one which is
compelling to me. Since prints exist in multiple originals, the
collector is able to share his love of a given print with others;
that is, collectors are able to enjoy the *same* work in *other*
impressions. Of course, there is the reverse of the coin—that
you can possess and enjoy for yourself the same work that
hangs in the world's great museums. The collector who could
never think of owning a painting by Hokusai can have one of
the artist's masterpieces in color woodcut for his own. Either
way you look at it, the collecting of prints is an act of sharing in
a way that is unique to the medium.

While no one would deny this premise, it is equally true that
collecting, no matter what the field may be, offers similar joys of
sharing for the collector, albeit with less inherent convenience,
first with other connoisseurs and finally through an exhibition
and publication such as this.

It is my opinion that *knowledge* should be shared in the same
fashion as art objects. Information about a work of art is an
inseparable part of the work itself. The essence of knowledge is

not in the facts themselves, however. It is the organization and ultimately the dissemination of those facts that gives them value. Perhaps some personal experiences will help illustrate the point.

In 1972 Roger Keyes and I published an article about the fakes of Hokusai's eight "Waterfall" prints. There is an extremely deceptive set of copies, made in the early Meiji era, that had fooled connoisseurs for a century. True, an expert of good taste and good judgment could tell the genuine from the false. He would be right 95% of the time. This did not prevent fakes from appearing in reputable books, auction catalogues and in the greatest museum collections. There is even a case of a twentieth-century copy made from one of the Meiji copies. I had become aware of the problem in my own collecting and study of Hokusai's prints. Over the years I made notes of precise points of distinction, so I would not inadvertently buy a fake. Dr. Keyes and I undertook to describe and illustrate, in minute detail, the differences between the two sets. Since that article appeared in *Oriental Art,* there has no longer been any serious question about the "Waterfall" prints. Information that began as a collector's private notes helped to clear up a major area of doubt in the work of a great artist. As a bonus, it also showed how the Meiji copyist had worked from a trimmed set of originals.

In 1974 I collaborated with Howard A. Link, Curator of Asian Art at the Academy and Keeper of the Ukiyo-e Center, where the James A. Michener Collection of ukiyo-e is maintained and exhibited. The collaboration resulted in a show of alternate states from Hokusai's most famous series of prints, "Thirty-Six Views of Mount Fuji." In my own collection I noted that some of my earliest impressions from this noble series were monochromatic blue, and I began to make notes wherever I encountered a variant.

Working with Dr. Link and the Michener Collection made it possible to compare a still larger number of variant prints of different editions than I had available in my own collection. We organized prints from both collections according to signature, seal, impression and color. From this organization it was possible to conclude that the earliest prints (identifiable by the cleanness of the impression) were probably monochromatic blue (aizuri-e) and that slightly later impressions had added to them a second color, usually yellow.

Moreover, when ten additional prints utilizing a black key block line were added to the original set of thirty-six (all originally published using a blue key block line), the entire set was reprinted in black outline with additional color variants. This was confirmed by the fact that, save for the additional ten prints, all other black line prints were late, weak impressions. That my curiosity about my own monochromatic blue prints should ultimately lead to this reconstruction of the publishing history of Hokusai's most famous series of prints, involved a number of acts of sharing: first, the wedding of two collections that contained alternate states of the same subject, and, second, the wedding of knowledge and method possessed by two different collectors. The results have subsequently been published in summary form and detailed in exhibition. Some of the prints used in this work from my own collection are included here.

To be sure, my own on-the-job experience as Curator of Graphic Arts at the Smithsonian Institute provided important training for this kind of scholarly fact-collecting. Most people, however, are too modest when it comes to publishing scholarly articles. How do I write it down? What do I say? Who will publish it? Who cares? First of all, you, as a collector, are already an "expert." You probably know more about your field than all but a handful of scholars. Though you may not know it, you have knowledge that will be new and revealing to others with the same interests.

In my opinion, you should write the same way you speak, clearly and simply. Much "scholarly" writing is afflicted with complicated sentences and jargon in the belief that this will impress other scholars. It is quite unnecessary. Clarity and short sentences will get the message across. Write something and then ask a fellow collector to read it. If he understands it without trouble, then it probably will reach the audience for whom you are writing.

What you say depends on what you know. Think of a unique piece in your collection. Think of the last time someone told you: "Oh, I didn't know that!" Above all, stick to *facts*. Collect facts;

organize them; look for gaps and fill them. Record where the facts come from and put that information in your footnotes. A scholarly article needs an "audit trail" as much as any corporate report. Even the dimensions of a work of art may play an important role in attributions. Don't be sidetracked into rhapsodies about the "beauty" or "inner meaning" of a work of art. This is the province of only the greatest—and the least—of writers on art. A statement of newly-discovered facts or a new organization of known facts is plenty. I've seldom tried to go beyond this in my twenty years of research.

Publication is a lot easier than you imagine. Particularly in Oriental art, there are plenty of magazines looking for concise factual articles. There are netsuke journals, jade journals, porcelain journals and Japanese print journals. If the content is interesting, an article need be no more than two or three pages long. If you are in doubt, take it to the nearest museum curator—Dr. Howard Link here in Hawaii—and ask for advice on publication. A collector-author should probably learn something about close-up photography. An article on art will almost certainly require pictures. If you do not do it yourself, get a professional photographer.

Several of our own members, not including the professional art historian, have gained reputations in their fields by writing about their own collecting interests. George Lazarnick, for instance, has combined his knowledge of photography with his collecting experience to produce several reference works on netsuke. Mitchell Hutchinson is respected for his writings on Chinese paintings of the Ming and Ch'ing Dynasties. Oliver Statler, a world-renowned authority on Japanese culture, wrote a classic book about modern Japanese prints, his personal area of collecting, and is the authority on the important artist Koshiro Onchi (1891-1955).

The point is that every collector possesses special information about his collection that should be recorded. Will anyone care? Certainly. His information may be exactly what another collector or scholar needs to know to complete a larger picture. There is no reward quite like having made a contribution, however small. It is this premise that has encouraged the Society to undertake its first exhibition devoted to Asian art from members' collections. Not only may the record of the image serve a useful purpose to the art historical community, but the facts that have been gathered about each object may have lasting value also. By sharing our facts as well as our art objects we become part of a larger community of connoisseurs. Together with professionals we can increase the total of human knowledge and enhance our common love of Oriental art.

Peter Morse

Note: In the essays and catalogue notes to follow, the Pinyin system is utilized for all Chinese transliterations; the Hepburn system is preferred for all Japanese transliterations; the McCune-Reischauer system is followed for Korean romanizations. Following the example of Dr. Pratapaditya Pal in the recent "Light of Asia" catalogue, we have omitted diacritical marks in Sanscrit and Pali words.

The Exhibition: An Historical Overview

The earliest object in the exhibition is a Chinese jade pendant dated to the 12th or 11th century B.C. from the Shang Dynasty. (No. 114) Shang is the first recorded dynasty (1523-1028 B.C.) to have been completely documented by excavation through the discovery of tombs at the last Shang capital in the Anyang region of northern Henan, and at other sites, some thought to be Shang capitals of still earlier date. The tombs at Anyang yielded large quantities of bronze vessels, jades, and other sacrificial objects. The crescent-shaped pendant in the exhibition with incised lines representing a curved fish is typical of the jade materials uncovered. The succeeding Zhou Dynasty (1027-256 B.C.) was a period of civil wars and multiple political states. The Zhou people adopted many of the rituals and arts of the conquered Shang as demonstrated by the numerous bronze artifacts that survive. Although the superb bronze ritual vessels of the Shang and Zhou Dynasties are not represented here, the exhibition includes a pair of bronze ornamental fittings, possibly for a chariot of Zhou age. (No. 1) These fittings are of interest since they are incised with a zoomorphic motif that may have been derived from the *Taotie* mask (ogre mask) so commonly observed on Shang bronzes. The *Taotie* seems to have disappeared from use during the early Zhou Dynasty. A jade *Bi* and jade *Cong* cylinder are also included in the assemblage, and reflect the quality of craftsmanship possible in jade during the Zhou Dynasty. (Nos. 2a and b) It should be mentioned at this juncture that China was most profoundly influenced by an ethical system introduced by the late Zhou philosopher, Confucius, a practical moralist advocating moderation, modesty and right thinking. Along with Confucianism, Taoism also developed during the Zhou Dynasty, and argued that nature and harmony, the natural forces, are the only true guides to behavior and social balance. These philosophies will play an influential role in the arts of China as will be demonstrated.

While the succeeding Han Dynasty (206 B.C.-A.D. 220) may be characterized as a period when foreign customs and beliefs made their way to China as a result of territorial expansion and active trade, the following Six Dynasties period (220-589 A.D.) was one of political unrest, foreign invasion and foreign occupation. During the so-called Wei Dynasty (386-535 A.D.), northern China fell under foreign domination. The Wei, or Toba Tartars, were to actively promote the Buddhist religion in China, and to adopt Buddhism as the official state religion. A fine Buddha's head of sandstone from the Yungang Cave in Shansi Province in the exhibition documents the northern Wei Dynasty and the introduction of Buddhism to China. A classical example of Buddhist sculpture, the work can be dated to the late 5th century. (No. 3) The style of the head, although ultimately of Indian origin (as transmitted through Buddhist kingdoms of Afghanistan, Khotan and Kucha, the Kizil region), is already very Chinese in feeling. A terra cotta figure of a statesman, also in the exhibition, is in a style and technique that dates the work to the late Sui or early Tang Dynasty (some two centuries later), and is probably an example that originally came from the vicinity of Sian in south China where the Silk Road from central Asia ended. (No. 5)

The succeeding Tang Dynasty (618-906) attained the first fluorescence in all the arts, and this era is often called China's golden age. Art, literature and scholarship flourished. Tomb art retained its importance in the Tang Dynasty, and fine sculpture in the form of ceramic figurines survives, much of it glazed in three colors. The passion and excitement of the Tang spirit was followed by an exclusionist policy during the Song Dynasty (960-1279). The result was isolationism and cultural introspection. Nevertheless, the Song Dynasty produced some of China's greatest art. The expressive wood sculpture of a Lohan in the exhibition is a rare example to survive from the Song Dynasty, and possesses a self-reliant individualism that is typical of Lohan interpretations of the age. (No. 8)

Although painting had been recognized as an aesthetic entity for some centuries, few examples survive today even from the Song Dynasty; no example of painting occurs in this exhibition before the Ming Dynasty (1368-1644). In ceramics, however, the situation is different. The dynamic vessel shapes first introduced during the Tang Dynasty gave way to shapes and glazes of the utmost refinement and elegance of line in the Song Dynasty. The stoneware tea bowl of the Tenmoku family in the exhibition may be dated to the Northern Song Dynasty (960-1126), while the fine Jun incense burner is dated to the Southern Song

Dynasty, the 12th or 13th century. (Nos. 7, 9) Both reveal the beauty of form and glaze that typifies Song ceramics with their clear emphasis on complex curves and countercurves. The celadons of the Song Dynasty are among the most beautiful in the world; we will have occasion to examine China's celadons in a later context. Rarely does one encounter lacquerware of the Northern Song Dynasty in private collections. One example included here, a plate with five lobes in the shape of a plum flower, corresponds to recent finds dated to the Northern Song Dynasty; we have dated the example in the exhibition to this time. (No. 6)

In 1126, at the defeat of Mongol invaders, north China was abandoned, but the southern Song court, newly established at Hongzhou, continued to encourage the flowering of the arts, especially painting and ceramics. In the 13th century the Mongols destroyed the southern Song Dynasty as well, and the period of Mongol rule that followed (the age of Kublai Khan) is known as the Yuan Dynasty (1280-1368). Many leaders in art and government preferred to retire from public life during this time rather than face barbarian rule. One result of this rustication was the emergence of the *wenren* (literati) tradition in painting, steeped in Confucian and Taoist philosophy. In ceramics, celadon continued to be produced as it had been in Song times; one plate of good quality may be dated to the 14th century and is included in the exhibition. (No. 10) Underglaze decorations in cobalt blue and copper red also occurred in porcelain and revolutionized the decoration of porcelain. We will have occasion to examine representative examples of blue and white porcelain of the Ming and Qing Dynasties in due course; the wellspring for its technical development, however, occurred in the Yuan Dynasty.

With the restoration of native rule under the Ming emperors (1368-1644), a new interest in China's past emerged. The grand style of the Tang Dynasty was soon reinstated at court (now moved to Beijing) and workshops were actively seeking to recapture past glories, particularly in the decorative arts. Jingdezhen, a center of ceramic production since the early Song Dynasty, developed into the porcelain capital of China with an ever-increasing number of kilns employing thousands of potters. This center supplied porcelains to the imperial court, the domestic market and the export market as well.

In general, the celadons and monochromes which dominated the Song Dynasty continued to appear. For example, the celadon incense burner of the 16th century (No. 12) and the early Blanc de Chine figurine (No. 13) are representative of the fine quality that was possible in the area of monochrome ceramics; the covered jar of the late 16th century, with combination underglaze and overglaze enamels in five colors, is typical of late Ming ware. (No. 14) A number of blue and white examples have been included in the exhibition. A late 15th century blue and white *Guan* deserves particular mention not only as the earliest blue and white in the exhibition, but because of its outstanding painting of ladies in a gardenscape. (No. 11) Special mention also should be made of an early 17th century blue and white porcelain plate. (No. 15) Clearly, the manufacture of traditional wares was an important duty of the kilns.

Led by such artists as Chen Zhou and Wen Zhengming, literati painting had come into its own, despite the quasi-official painting style of the academy. One artist working in the Wen style, represented in the current exhibition, is Sheng Maoye who was active from 1625 to 1640. (No. 22)

China was once more subjected to foreign rule when the conquering Manchu established the Qing Dynasty (1644-1912). The new rulers, however, strove to maintain fastidiously Chinese native culture. During the rule of Emperor Kangsi (1662-1722), the cultural pattern for the Dynasty was established with an emphasis on painting, ceramics, scholarly research and Confucian etiquette. Painting in the *wenren,* or literati, tradition gained official status when leading artists of the day were recognized by the court. The plethora of fine paintings included in the exhibition documents aspects of the painting tradition as it existed from this time into the 20th century. Particularly fine are the following: a rare landscape by Lo Ping (1733-1799; No. 25) one of the eight Eccentric Masters of Yang Chou; a bird and flower study by Chen Hong-shou (1768-1822; No. 31), a landscape album by Tang Ifen (1778-1853; No. 35), two nature studies by Wang Su (1794-1877; No. 36), illustrations from the novel, "Dreams of the Red Chamber," by Fei Danxu (1802-1850; No. 37), a painting of a peony and rock by the Shanghai master, Wu Zhangshi (1844-1927; No. 43), a painting featuring Sparrow and Corn by the 20th century master, Gao Jienfu (1881-1951; No 49) and finally a landscape by one of the most recognized artists in the People's Republic of China, Fu Baoshi (1904-1965; No. 50).

Calligraphy is an area of collecting that presents a special problem for most Western connoisseurs. The two representative examples shown here, both by recognized masters of the Qing Dynasty, may still be appreciated as pure brush designs without a knowledge of the language. (see No. 44) It should be remembered, however, that the meaning of the calligraphy adds immeasurably to the enjoyment of the art, and the artist's full intentions may never be truly understood without this knowledge, for it involves an inner dimension that is a manifestation of the complete man.

The Chienlong Emperor (1736-1795) amassed a vast collection of antique and contemporary art during his reign. Jade carvers worked their fractious materials into fantasies of unbelievable intricacy. In its impersonal technical perfection and exquisite beauty, the 18th century jade carving expresses, perhaps better than anything else, the exacting standards and aesthetic spirit of Qing period art. Two 19th century Chinese jades meticulously engraved reflect the "rococo" era of Chienlong. Two other examples, featuring lotus root jade, reveal a stylized naturalism. These examples serve to demonstrate the wide range of jade art that existed at this time. (No. 134, a, b, and c)

The literati tradition had a particularly interesting effect on the history of Chinese art. Art was the product of the scholars; it was the manifestation of their culture and their philosophy. Art, for the literati, was confined to poetry, music, calligraphy and painting. Lacquerware, textiles, metalwork and pottery were relegated to a kind of industry—a decorative art to furnish the scholar's home. Certain crafts, however, came to be appreciated by the scholar-artist more than others. Items for a scholar's desk—wonderfully diverse accoutrements of culture and at the same time functional excuses for such indulgences—form a special group of accessories in which the *wenren* took particular pride. Brush pots, brush washers, seal ink boxes, water pots, water droppers, censors and brushes are among the scholar-painter's most valued possessions, with the so-called four treasures of the study (the brush, the ink, the paper and the ink stone) heading the list. To these items are sometimes added bamboo carving, Ixing wares, wood, ivory, bone, rhinoceros horn, jade, soapstone and hard stone carving, textiles, lacquer and metalwork. Even examples of the seal carvers' art are appropriate and prized for their skilled carving. In this exhibition a number of items that might be found on the desk of a literati scholar have been exhibited together. (Nos. 51, 52 and 53 a-l)

Represented also in the exhibition is a selection of Qing snuff bottles meticulously rendered using a variety of mediums including jade, glass, ivory and porcelain. The selection provides superb documentation on this intriguing miniature art. Exquisite examples with elegant painting or intricate workmanship make these snuff bottles prized objects the world over. (Nos. 129-133; 135 a-e; and 136-141)

The Korean peninsula was first inhabited about five thousand years ago by peoples migrating from Siberia. These people were not of Chinese racial stock, but during centuries to follow, China substantially influenced Korean culture, first with the introduction of metal (5th-3rd century B.C.) and later when parts of the northern peninsula were under Chinese control (206 B.C.-A.D. 9). In the exhibition there are fine examples of pottery from the Kimhae and Old Silla Kingdom (Nos. 54 and 55) and stoneware from the succeeding Koryŏ Dynasty (No. 56, dated to the 12th century) that reflect the golden age of celadon in the 11th, 12th and 13th centuries.

Korea was far from being a colorless colony of China clinging to Chinese art and culture, despite ethnocentric Chinese histories to the contrary. Indeed, the Chinese themselves sought out the superb celadons of the Koryŏ Period (918-1392), which often surpassed Chinese counterparts in glaze, color and individual elegance. Even Emperor Yunglo is known to have admired Yi Dynasty white ware which had been presented as official gifts. Included here are representative examples of Koryŏ celadon and a bronze vessel of Koryŏ age, providing documentation on Korea's achievements in bronze casting. (Nos. 57 and 58 a & b)

Confucian orthodoxy in the succeeding Yi Dynasty (1392-
1410) produced a conservative inward attitude, and the "Hermit
Kingdom" produced Korean pottery of such natural charm that
the Japanese Tea Masters of the 16th century were fascinated by
the aesthetic richness. The ingenuity of the Yi potter is given
demonstration in a group of anthropomorphic water droppers of
great charm and wit. (Nos. 155-158) Also documented in this
exhibition is a rare Korean ancestral portrait of fine quality,
dated to the Yi Dynasty. The painting is representative of the
achievements of the Korean artists in this area. (No. 59)

The history of Japan is documented by a broad range of art
objects in the exhibition. Japan was the last barrier between the
Asian mainland and the Pacific Ocean and was the recipient of
cultural and religious influences from the continent. At the same
time, the isolated position of the islands encouraged the
development of a native culture. The prehistoric age is broken
down into a number of eras based upon the pottery found in
these eras.

The first is called the Jōmon Period (ca. 4,500 to 200 B.C.).
The name derives from pottery unearthed from the shell mounds
of the culture decorated with distinctive twisted cord
impressions called *Jōmon*. The Jōmon people migrated from
Siberia to northern Japan and settled throughout the island
chain. A good example of a Jōmon vessel is included in the
exhibition. (No. 60) The configuration suggests a certain delight
on the part of the potter and an artistic freedom that suits the
medium.

A second migration of peoples and technology came to Japan
from the south, from Kyūshū, and spread to the Kantō Plain in
central Honshū. This culture is called Yayoi, (ca. 200 B.C. to
A.D. 250).

The third wave of cultural influence entered from Korea in
the mid-third century and introduced continental techniques
that were considerably more advanced than either the Jōmon or
Yayoi cultures. This period is called the Kōfun, or Tumulous
period (ca. 250-552). The Tumulous period is named after the
massive mound tombs which dominated the age. Clay cylinders,
known as *haniwa*, studded these mounds, apparently in an effort

to retard erosion. Some *haniwa* were surmounted with fanciful figures of humans or animals. The top portion of a *haniwa* in the current exhibition is representative of the fine quality that could be achieved in primitive sculpture. (No. 61)

The Imperial lineage dates at least to the Kōfun Period, and many of the mound-tombs surrounded by *haniwa* are associated with historical Emperors. The Imperial lineage is believed to be descended from the Sun Goddess and is a central tenet of Japan's native Shinto religion. This religion initially combined nature worship with animism but was for a time overshadowed by Buddhism. It was during the mid-sixth century that Buddhism was imported from China and became the favorite religion of the Asuka Court (552-645), receiving official sanction from the Prince Regent, Shōtōku Taishi, who fully embraced the new religion. This was followed by the proliferation of Buddhist temples and religious art at Nara, the capital of the Asuka Court. Seventh century Buddhist sculpture in Japan generally reflected Korean styles derived from China. In addition to adopting the Buddhist religion, the Nara Court followed artistic cultural patterns set by the Tang Dynasty of China.

The Heian Period begins in 794 when the capital was relocated at Heian-kyō (modern Kyōto) in an effort to escape the domination of the Buddhist monasteries at Nara that had grown politically powerful. The monasteries that rose around the new capital, however, also came to threaten the nobility. Japanese priests who had studied in China came back to introduce to Japan esoteric Buddhism, the Tendai Sect and the Shingon sect. These religious variants assumed distinctive Japanese traits and the religion was further naturalized when the nature spirits (Kami) of Shinto were recognized as the avatars of Buddhist deities.

Another new sect from China was the Jōdo, or Pure Land Sect of Buddhism. It was an uncomplicated and direct form of religion, promising eternal life in paradise merely by the recitation of Buddhist names. By the tenth and eleventh century the reassuring tenets of Jōdo Buddhism were eagerly translated into painting and sculpture. The name generally applied to the sculptural style in Buddhism of the early Heian Period is Jōgan, after the era of the same name (859-876). A fine Bodhisattva image of the 10th century or late 9th century in the exhibition represents the sculptural style of this period. (No. 62) The simplified expanse of the torso and legs as well as the full and rounded fleshy face and sense of austere dignity are typical characteristics associated with the Jōgan style. During the Heian Period the use of a solid block of wood (*ichiboku*) for carving the image tended to accentuate the solidity and heaviness of this style, which is usually more sober than encountered here. The sculpture, in fact, seems to presage the lighter, more graceful style of the late Heian Period. The more relaxed posture of body and intimations of movement in space suggest a late ninth or early tenth century date.

Continental influences remained strong well into the ninth century. However, by the end of the century, official contact with China ceased. With the consolidation of power at the new capital, the nobility (led by the Fujiwara family) were active patrons of the arts, and Japanese secular art evolved a characteristic native style known as Yamato-e (literally Japanese picture). Out of Yamato-e grew the Tosa painting school of later times, the Rimpa tradition (which was a kind of Yamato-e revival) and the ukiyo-e genre tradition of the Edo Period. These traditions will be examined in a later context.

With the decline of the Fujiwara family, the Taira and Minamoto clans vied for political control. The Taira clan were defeated in 1185 by the Minamoto family, ushering in the Kamakura Period from 1185 to 1333. This period marks the appearance of a clearly feudal, pyramidal power structure based on the personal loyalty of vassal to lord. During this period Buddhist painting and sculpture reached their culmination in beauty and form.

Some of the loveliest of all Japanese Buddhist sculpture dates to the Kamakura Period, and we are fortunate to be able to exhibit a fine example, a seated Dainichi Nyōrai, bearing the signature Genbei Daibusshi Kōyasan. This esoteric Buddhist deity represents the most profound doctrines of the sect. (No. 65) Dainichi Nyōrai was believed to be the embodiment of the dharma (truth) in addition to his role as the source and incarnation of all forms of existence. He is represented in sculpture as a bodhisattva with jewelry, crown, flowing garments, with his hands forming the mudra meaning non-duality. Stylization of the carving, the intricacy of the crown and the gracefulness of the flowing garment support a Kamakura date for this work.

Central authority of the Kamakura Period was soon eroded by regional despots or daimyo, and the Kamakura lineage of successors was finally ended in 1333 by the revolt of General Ashikaga Takauji, ushering in the Ashikaga or Muromachi Period (1392-1573) the latter named after the district in Kyoto where the Ashikaga ruled. The shoguns of this era preferred to play the role of political manipulators and artistic dilettantes. As a result, some of the richest cultural patrimony was created under the Ashikaga regime. Of particular interest was the renewal of contact with China and interest in Chinese ink painting. Zen priest-painters such as Shūbun and Sesshū established new standards in the presentation of ink painting known as *suiboku,* from which the Kanō School and other schools emerged. Although this exhibition does not include an example of early Muromachi *suiboku* painting, we are fortunate to have an album painted by a Kanō School *suiboku* artist of the mid-Edo Period that faithfully retraces the inspiration of a Muromachi album by Kenko Shōkei that still can be seen today. (No. 67) Three striking ink paintings featuring legendary Zen sages, painted by Kanō Tan'yū in the early 17th century, are also worthy of note. (No. 68)

The Momoyama Period (1573-1615) brought to Japanese art a vigor and bravura that in its grand sweep surpassed even the old conceptions of Kamakura artists. The colorful energy of Momoyama art is best documented in screens and wall paintings featuring landscapes and nature studies in which the bold brush of ink painting is combined with rich color of Yamato-e to produce subtly decorative, yet bold and forceful works of art. The style was created by Kanō Eitoku and his followers and persisted for about 30 years into the Edo Period (1615-1868), but under the Tokugawa rulers new forces, introspective and conservative, were moving to dominate the artistic as well as the political outlook.

The Edo Period was established in 1615 when Tokugawa Ieyasu emerged triumphant over his rivals and made himself Shogun. He established a capital in the remote village of Edo (present-day Tokyo) in order to escape the effete activities of the aristocracy in the former capital of Kyoto. Around this time Yamato-e, first introduced in the Heian Period (897-1185) and kept alive through the Tosa School, was restored to popularity by the remarkable artists, Hon'ami Kōetsu and Tawaraya Sōtatsu. Sōtatsu, in particular, selected themes from Japanese literary classics and subjects from nature, arranged them in bold compositions and painted them in vivid colors unequaled in the art of Yamato-e, creating a new, unprecedented vision of Japanese beauty. Ōgata Korin, a master active in the middle of the Edo Period (1615-1868), took up Sōtatsu's style and infused it with the sumptuousness and love of the decorative that typified the age. (No. 70) Also represented are two later followers of this neo-Yamato-e revival, Nakamura Hōchu (fl. late 18th to early 19th century) and Suzuki Kiitsu (1796-1858). Nos. 79, 80) The painting style exemplified in these works may be regarded as the quintessence of the Japanese taste. Their art has been characterized as an art of subtle defiance against the new regime in Edo headed by members of the samurai class. Indeed, artists of the Edo branch of the Kanō School of painting, who often worked in an austere style of ink painting favored by this warrior class, were appointed the official painters of the Tokugawa government instead of artists of the neo-Yamato-e revival. We have already had occasion to mention the trio of ink paintings by Kanō Tan'yū who was the head of this Edo branch.

Edo Period art also continued to reflect the Momoyama screen style begun by the Kyoto branch of the Kanō School and dominated by colorful bird and flower studies as well as landscape. In this exhibition are two screens which document the Edo Period's love of opulent colors and use of gold leaf. One screen featuring a flower cart can be dated to the early part of the Edo Period, while a second screen featuring kimonos on a rack has been judged a 19th century product. (Nos. 69 and 76) Both paintings were probably done by *machi-eshi,* or town artists, who were not connected to the official Kanō or Tosa

Schools that dominated the art of the Edo Period.

A new school of popular art known as ukiyo-e emerged from the *machi-eshi* tradition of genre painting and flourished in the commercial center of Edo. This school was patronized by the wealthy merchants who came to prominence during the long period of peace fostered by the Tokugawa official policy of isolation. The exhibition is particularly rich in ukiyo-e prints and includes early examples by Torii Kiyomasu II (1706-1763), a portrait of a Kabuki dancer by Torii Kiyohiro (perhaps the finest surviving impression of this noble subject), and an actor portrait by the artist Shunsen (fl. 1780's-1790's). (Nos. 213, 214, and 215) Without question, however, the finest assemblage of ukiyo-e prints in the exhibition are the landscapes of Katsushika Hokusai (1760-1849), the greatest ukiyo-e artist of the 19th century. Superb first impression examples from most of the major sets that Hokusai produced during his long lifetime have been chosen from a collection that is noted for its richness and breadth. (Nos. 216-229)

Other developments in painting in the 18th century were the Nanga (southern painting), or Bunjin School. Bunjin (literati painting) found its immediate inspiration in the Chinese *wenren* style popularized through paintings and illustrated woodblock print books coming through the port of Nagasaki. The books are represented in the exhibition with pages from one of the more celebrated woodblock painting manuals to be used by the Nanga School artists, *The Mustard Seed Garden Manual.* (No. 212) This book provides a useful introduction to the battery of Nanga paintings on view, including one of bamboo signed Ike no Taiga (1723-1776). (No. 82) Other artists included in the Nanga grouping are Kagen Kyōu, Kyōson and Tachihara Kyōsho. (Nos. 83, 84, 85 and 86)

The appearance of Admiral Perry's black ships off the coast of Japan in 1853 marked the end of Tokugawa isolationism and also heralded the close of the feudal age. In 1868 the Shogunate collapsed, and Emperor Meiji was restored to the throne, catapulting the country headlong into the modern age. The traditional arts were among the first casualties in the rush to Westernize. However, literature and painting adapted to the new age with more success than most arts. Reflecting this metamorphosis is the art of Shibata Zeshin (1807-1891), an outstanding traditional master who made the leap into modern life. Included in the exhibition is a fine lacquer box and a painting of the Rashomon witch by this versatile master. (Nos. 87 and 88) A number of prints and paintings featuring westerners and Japanese in western garb illustrate life in the port of Nagasaki, where Dutch trade had once flourished. These fine paintings and prints serve as a reminder of the East-West encounter of two centuries ago. (Nos. 73, 74, and 231-242)

As a capstone we also include an extremely fine selection of netsuke (the Japanese toggle) featuring a variety of sculptural forms of inherent beauty. The selection includes the earliest surviving netsuke to carry an inscribed date and examples that are regarded by experts as among the best in the world. (Nos. 168-211)

"Art moves in cycles. There must be continuous interchange. The new must become old and die. The old must come back . . ." This note of optimism quoted from the writings of James A. Michener describes the rebirth of prints today—the sōsaku hanga movement—and is the motivating statement for Oliver Statler's book on the subject, *Modern Japanese Prints: An Art Reborn*. A selection of sixteen different artists representing the sosaku hanga movement from two major collections (including the Statler Collection) concludes the Japanese assemblage, and a finer conclusion would be difficult to find. (Nos. 243-258)

There are fewer collectors of Southeast Asian and Indian art works in the islands, so there are fewer objects in this exhibition from these areas. Nevertheless there are good pieces worthy of comment; it also is important that they be placed within an historical context.

Indian civilization began in the Indus Valley circa 3000-1500 B.C. The surviving art of the period already shows the propensity of the Indian artist for fine sculpture, and the earliest examples exhibit characteristics that were to remain a basic quality of Indian sculptural forms. The provocative posture of the 15th century Siva in bronze from the Chola Kingdom (No. 94) is essentially no different in sensuous appeal than the copper dancing girl from Mohenjo-daro, made thousands of years earlier. Indeed, sensuous feminity has been a persistent theme in Indian art. The carved 19th century Ajanta-style wooden relief of voluptuous women clearly documents the profound impact of the sensuous style on Indian sculptural art throughout its long history. (No. 95)

With respect to the development of art throughout Asia and the role of India, the greatest impact was made by Buddhism. We are fortunate to be able to exhibit two early Buddhist sculptures of the Gandhara School, a Buddha dated to the 2nd century A.D. (No. 92) and a rare head of Buddha dated between the 3rd and 5th centuries A.D. (No. 91)

Anthropomorphic representations of Buddha first appeared during the Kushan Dynasty (ca. A.D. 50-300) and are linked to the rise of new Buddhist sects whose devotional exercise required a representation in human form rather than symbols. Under the aegis of the Kushans, numerous Buddhist stupas (relic mounds) and monasteries were built in the ancient province of Gandhara. Buddhist iconography was codified along with the story of Buddha's life and miracles, the latter to be repeated on countless stone reliefs. The Gandhara School waxed and waned in the period from the first to the fifth century and blended Indian sculptural form with Greco-Roman features in the image of Buddha and bodhisattva. These Hellenistic influences were brought to Northwest India by journeying craftsmen from the eastern outposts of the Roman Empire. The two sculptural images chosen for exhibition here clearly demonstrate the hybrid nature of Gandhara art.

Cambodia, Siam (modern Thailand) and Burma received Buddhism and Hinduism from India and Sri Lanka (Ceylon) in waves of consecutive influence. Evidence of this influence in the exhibition is the fine 12th century stone Standing Female Figure of the Khmer School (Cambodia; No. 103); two volumes of Buddhist regulations rendered on lacquered wood of the 19th century (Burma; No. 107); a pair of Jakata paintings of the 18th century (Thailand; No. 109); and a sandstone standing Vishnu figure of the 12th century (Cambodia; No. 106). Each work reveals native qualities and distinctive period-styles of great aesthetic and art historical interest.

China was an important cultural force throughout Southeast

Asia as the fine blue and white Anamese (Viet Nam; No. 112) ceramics and Siamese ceramics (both Sukhothai and Sawankhalok) testify (Nos. 96-102). With the ceramic tradition of India essentially undeveloped, the Southeast Asian potter turned to the highly refined ceramics of China for inspiration. Again, the results reveal native qualities that make the various ceramic traditions found in Southeast Asia easily differentiated. Each has a provincial charm of its own and in some cases considerable sophistication. As a footnote to the ceramic history of this area, we include two representative pieces of Ban Chiang ware (Thailand), the prototypes of which, when first excavated, created a stir in the archeological world. These ceramic pieces along with other relics provide documentation for further research on the prehistory of this region. (No. 110)

How do the best examples of Asian art compare in technical excellence and aesthetic worth with the best examples of western art? An entire book might be written on this question. More often than not, however, such questions are proffered and argued by the wrong people for the wrong reasons. Nevertheless, the following highly compressed judgment will probably not be reversed once that book is finally written. A conclusion which is as generous as it is correct is that the Asian artists did superbly well in their specialized areas and western artists did equally well in what interested them. That they never both concentrated on the same thing at the same time merely means that the world is now richer than it otherwise would have been. As any serious art collector will agree, the harvest is infinitely better this way.

Howard A. Link

Selected Catalogue

The 258 catalogue entries to follow document aspects of Asia's long and complex history, and make reference to nearly 350 works of art included in the exhibition. Of these works of art, 179 are reproduced here and may be distinguished by the use of the symbols (*) for items in black and white and (†) for those reproduced in color. As in the exhibition, the material, which is drawn from the collections of nearly half of the members of the Oriental Art Society, is divided into three broad categories: Classical Arts, Miniature Arts and Prints. Within each category, the art objects are ordered according to country and chronology, allowing for greater ease in reference and in explaining the various aspects of artistic development.

Exact dates are given only when an inscribed one occurs on the work of art. Speculative dating is considered in the commentary and is based on style, inference and technical matters. Dates follow the old lunar calendar except for art dated to this century. Technical information on medium and format is provided, and measurements are given in both inches and centimeters, with height preceding width for painting and prints; dimensions are clearly marked for three dimensional objects including the miniature arts.

In the case of works bearing a signature and/or seal, transliterations have been rendered. The text of each entry describes the subject, suggests its aesthetic quality or art historical worth and relates the piece to other works of art where appropriate. Differing points of view and justifications of a tentative date or attribution are also given where necessary. Most, but not all, inscriptions or poems have been loosely translated.

The notes that follow were prepared by three members of the Oriental Art Society and reviewed by me as editor. Each writer's contribution is indicated by the inclusion of his or her initials in parenthesis following the entry. Along with the undersigned, who wrote entries on Japan, Korea, Southeast Asia and India (H.A.L.), Drs. Zeng Yuhe (China, Southeast Asia and India; Z.Y.H.) and Willa Tanabe (Japan and Korea; W.T.) made substantial contributions in their areas of specialization. In addition, Dr. Charles Weber and Mr. L. B. Nerio served as general advisors and offered their expertise and editorial skills where appropriate. It should also be noted that the collectors themselves often provided valuable information for the writing of an entry. Collectors who have contributed substantial research include Mr. George Lazarnick (netsuke), Mrs. Patricia Miller (snuff bottles and jade), Mr. Yung-Fu Yang (snuff bottles and jade), Dr. William Won (Chinese ceramics), Mrs. Cecelia Doo (Chinese ceramics), Mr. Windsor G. Hackler (contemporary Japanese prints) and Mr. Peter Morse (ukiyo-e prints). Miss Lilette A. Yamamoto, a graduate student in Art History at the University of Hawaii, contributed her knowledge to the identifications of Southeast Asian painting and sculpture. (L.A.Y.)

In certain instances, authorities from outside the membership were sought to confirm an opinion. These include Dr. Prithwish Neogy of the University of Hawaii, Dr. Pratapaditya Pal of the Los Angeles County Museum and Dr. Tōru Shimbo of Tsukuba University, Japan. To all who have made contributions, my best thanks.

Howard A. Link
Senior Curator of Asian Art, Honolulu Academy of Arts

CLASSICAL ARTS

1.
A PAIR OF BRONZE FITTINGS(*)
China, Middle Zhou, circa 8th century B.C.
Cast bronze, each measuring
H. 4¾" × 5" (12.1 × 12.7 cm.)
Private collection

This pair of bronze ornaments is
anthropomorphically designed and could be
chariot fittings. Their broad band stylization is
typically Middle-Zhou and may have been
derived from the Taotie mask. (Z.Y.H.)

2a.
BI-DISC(*)
China, Middle Zhou, circa 9th-8th century B.C.
Jade
Diam. 7", Thickness ⁵/₁₆" (17.8, .7 cm.)
Private collection

This Bi-Disc is of dark green nephrite with areas
of light calcification. It shows saw lines but has no
design. Judging from its size and the proportions
of the orifice, it may have been a funeral piece.
(Z.Y.H.)

2b.
CONG-CYLINDER,(*)
China, Late Zhou-Early Han, 3rd-2nd century
B.C.
Jade
H. 1³/₁₀", Diam. 2¹/₁₀" (3.3, 5.3 cm.)
Private collection

The nephrite Cong-cylinder, a symbol of the
earth, was known as far back as the Neolithic
period. It was used at ceremonial and funeral
rites. This custom ceased by the Han period, but
the form remained as decorative design. (Z.Y.H.)

3.
BUDDHA'S HEAD
Yungong cave, Shansi
China, Northern Wei dynasty, late 5th century
A.D.
Granite
H. 12" × 7" × 7" (30.5 × 17.8 × 17.8 cm.)
Private collection

This Buddha's head, with some sharpened lines of
a later age, has all the features of the early phase
of Yungong, a classic example of Buddhist
serenity. (Z.Y.H.)

4.
SEATED BUDDHA
China, Sui dynasty, dated 590 A.D.
Stone stele
H. 12½" (31.5 cm.)
The Patricia Miller Collection

On top of the seated Amitabha Buddha is a small
seated Buddha and four flying devas. The Buddha
is flanked by a bodhisattva on each side. Below
the lotus seat are two kneeling devotees and a
flaming pearl. Inscribed words on two sides of the
stele read:
*"Engraved on the fifteenth day, ninth lunar month, in
the year 590 of the Great Sui dynasty. Under his
Majesty's blessing, all living creatures have its
revelation."* (Z.Y.H.)

5.
A STATESMAN(*)
China, Sui-Tang, early 7th century
Terra-cotta
H. 36" × 9" (91.4 × 22.9 cm.)
Private collection

This imposing tomb figure at one time was
painted; now only traces of lime remain.
Compared with the recent finds in China, this is
probably from the vicinity of the capital, Zhangan
(Sian). The style and workmanship are close to
examples dated to the Sui or early Tang period.
(Z.Y.H.)

6.
PLATE(*)
China, Northern Song, 960-1125
Lacquer
Diam. 7" (17.8 cm.)
Private collection

This plate is coffee-brown in color and is encircled
by a copper rim. The five lobes are in the shape of
a plum flower. In streamlined terseness, it has a
simplicity corresponding to recent finds in
mainland China that have been dated to the
Northern Song. (Z.Y.H.)

7.
TEA BOWL
China, Northern Song, 960-1126
Stoneware
Diam. 4¾" (12.1 cm.)
The Cecilia and Gene Doo Collection

Within the Tenmoku family of dark-glazed
stoneware there is the Jizhou (or Jian) production,
located in Kiangsi province. Although this kiln
produced many other types of ceramics, this dark-
brown tea bowl, along with the Jian-ware (of
Fujian), became famous through the tea masters.
Different from the Jian ware, Jichou pottery often
has designs applied in various techniques. The
painted designs are free and imbued with a
calligraphic quality, such as the plum blossoms on
this bowl. (Z.Y.H.)

8.
LOHAN(*)
China, Song dynasty, 12th-13th century
Wood
H. 28⅜" (72.1 cm.)
Private collection

This rare example of a priest, represented in
wood, is of the Song period. Originally it was
painted; now only certain traces of colors remain.
The statue is in a good state of preservation. This
indicates that the wood substance is of a precious
nature. The figure stands in a humble manner; he
has the rugged face of a Central Asian, but the
dress is fashioned in Chinese style. Over the
shoulder he has a garment-hook for the cape. The
garment is draped in orderly lines; all the features
recall the painted priest portraits of the Song
period. This type of Lohan interpretation began in
about the 11th century and prevailed in the 12th
and 13th centuries. (Z.Y.H.)

9.
INCENSE BURNER(†)
China, Southern Song dynasty, 12th-13th century
Stoneware
H. 3½", Diam. 4¼" (8.9, 10.9 cm.)
The Cecilia and Gene Doo Collection

Although several kilns in Henan province were
known to have produced this type of rich blue-
glazed ceramics, it is identified mostly with
Junzhou. Variations of color tones are found in the
Jun family, but they all shared in its generous
proportion and wholesome forms. The best period
of Jun wares lasted from Northern Song to the
Yuan period. (Z.Y.H.)

10.
PLATE(†)
China, Yuan-Ming dynasty, 14th century
Celadon stoneware
Diam. 18⅛" (46 cm.)
Private collection

This large Longquan celadon dish, with foliate rim
and deeply grooved pattern surrounding a central
design of flowers and leaves incised to the surface
under the glaze, is in all respects a fine example of
late 14th century celadon from the Longquan kilns
of South China. (Z.Y.H.)

11.
LARGE JAR(*)
China, Ming dynasty, late 15th century
Blue and white porcelain
H. 13½", Diam. 13" (34.2, 33 cm.)
The L.B. Nerio Collection

This large jar once may have had a cover. The
underglazed blue decoration consists of a
continuous gardenscape; above the landscape are
key-fret and floral spray bands, and beneath is a
band of upright leaves. One scene shows a lady
looking at a painting, while others are playing
chess and enjoying music. The depiction affords a
fascinating glimpse of the lifestyle of the period
with examples of furniture then used. (Z.Y.H.)

12.
INCENSE BURNER
China, Ming dynasty, 16th century
Celadon stoneware
H. 7½", Diam. 11" (19, 28 cm.)
Private collection

13.
LIUHAI DEITY(†)
China, late Ming dynasty, 16th century
Dehua porcelain
H. 6″ × 2.6″ × 2.2″ (15.2 × 6.8 × 5.6 cm.)
Private collection

White Dehua porcelain, also known as Blanc-de-Chine, is well-known for its hand-modeled sculpture. More commonly seen are statues of the Goddess of Mercy and Damo of the Buddhist faith. Liuhai is also a popular folk deity who grants wealth. This is a rare interpretation of the Liuhai deity and a superb example of workmanship. (Z.Y.H.)

14.
COVERED JAR
China, Ming dynasty, late 16th century
Porcelain
H. 6¾″, Diam. 6½″ (17, 16.5 cm.)
Private collection

Polychromeware with a combination of underglazed and overglazed enamels, is generally referred to as *wucai* (five colors). On this jar are three panels of mythical beasts, popular motifs in late Ming period. The painting in bold brushwork shows no underglazed blue, and this is probably a provincial piece. (Z.Y.H.)

15.
PLATE(*)
China, Ming dynasty, early 17th century
Blue and white porcelain
Diam. 8″ (20.3 cm.)
The Cecilia and Gene Doo Collection

This fine Jingdecheng underglazed blue piece displays two dragon-shrimps in an unusual design. The white area has a nearly invisible pattern (anhua). An eight-word verse inscribed next to the shrimps reads: "Swimming in waves, in dragon visage." (Z.Y.H.)

16.
PERFUMER(*)
China, Ming-Qing dynasty, 17th century
Bamboo
H. 7⅛″, Diam. 1¾″ (18.2, 4.5 cm.)
Private collection

The design of this perfumer is carved in high relief with openwork and shows a lone lady sitting in a garden under two trees, one a pine. Behind her are some garden rocks, and next to her a giant garden rock, taking up nearly half of the tube space. There is no signature, but the skillful handling of the engraving, the style and composition are similar to the signed bamboo works of Zhu Shouzheng (1573-1620) of the Jiansu school. The type of bamboo perfume holder is also typical of the region and date. (Z.Y.H.)

17.
INCENSE BURNER(*)
China, Ming-Qing dynasty, 17th century
Dehua porcelain
H. 3½″, Diam. 4¼″ (8.9, 10.8 cm.)
The Cecilia and Gene Doo Collection

Dehua kilns of Fujian province produced a superlative fine cream-white porcelain that became famous in the latter part of the Ming dynasty. In the 19th century, collectors in France introduced the name, "Blanc-de-Chine," for this superlative ware. At its best Dehua vessels are plain in form and undecorated. The ware is also well-known for its table-size sculpture. (Z.Y.H.)

18.
INCENSE BURNER
China, early Qing dynasty, late 17th century
Dehua porcelain
H. 4½″, Diam. 11″ (11.4, 28 cm.)
Private collection

19.
INCENSE BURNER
China, Qing dynasty, late 17th century
Blue and white porcelain
H. 5″, Diam. 10¼″ (12.7, 26 cm.)
The Cecilia and Gene Doo Collection

This deep-set bowl could also be used as a narcissus plant container. A typical Kangsi-style landscape motif is painted on the burner in underglaze blue. (Z.Y.H.)

20.
PLATTER
China, 17th century
Porcelain
H. 3½", Diam. 13" (9, 33.1 cm.)
Prof. and Mrs. Robert Desowitz Collection

This platter is typical of Swatow ware, with
underglaze blue floral decoration in the interior.

21.
LANDSCAPE
Wang Jian, 1598-1677
China, Qing dynasty, dated 1666
Painting, ink on gold paper, hanging scroll
H. 79" × 33½" (200.7 × 84.8 cm.)
Private collection

Wang Jian, known also as Yuanzao and Xiangbi,
was from Taizhang of Jiangsu. Active during the
transition from the Ming to the Qing dynasty, he
was included in the Nine Friends of Painting
centered around Dung Cizhang in late Ming, and
was also considered as one of the Four Great
Masters of Qing. He was one of the most
influential artists of the Qing period.
   This painting was done on gold paper, a
common practice by Ming and Qing masters, and
a manner known in China since the Tang period.
On the top is written:
*"Early spring of 1666, inspired by the brushwork of
Mei Daoren (Wu Zhen, 1280-1354). Painted for the
birthday of Mr. Iweng. Wang Jian."*
   Two artists' seals follow below. (Z.Y.H.)

22.
SNOW ON MOUNT OMEI
Sheng Maoye, active 1625-1640
China, Ming dynasty
Painting, ink and very slight color on silk,
hanging scroll
H. 80" × 40⅜" (203.2 × 102.6 cm.)
Private collection

Maoye also known as Yenan, was from Suzhou,
Jiangsu. He painted landscapes primarily but
occasionally did floral subjects. His style closely
followed the Wen family, especially that of Wen
Poren (1502-1575).
   The artist inscribed on the painting:
*"Snow on Mt. Omei, 1631, 15th day of the 9th lunar
month. Sheng Maoye of Wu."*
   Two of his seals are impressed below. On the
lower left corner are two collectors' seals. (Z.Y.H.)

23.
AFTER THE SONG MASTERS
Liu Yung, 1719-1804
China, Qing dynasty
Calligraphy, ink on paper, handscroll
H. 12½" (31.5 cm.)
Private collection

Liu Yung, also known as Shihan, came from
Juchen, Shangtung. He served as the Grand-
secretary and finally Grand-tutor to the Heir-
apparent. He was a connoisseur, author of many
books and a respected calligrapher.
   This work is signed but bears no date. Judging
by the mature style and alert brush movement in
this scroll, it probably was written in his fifties. It
consists of four sections. He stated that it was
copied from Dung Qizhang (1555-1636), who
followed the Four Great Masters of the Song
period. However, neither of these artists copied
older masters slavishly; they preferred to show
their understanding of the old masters in their
own terms. Following his calligraphy there are
three colophons dated to the late 19th century.
(Z.Y.H.)

24.
CIRCULAR JAR
China, Qing dynasty, Yungcheng year mark,
1723-1735
Blue and white porcelain
H. 7" (18 cm.)
The Cecilia and Gene Doo Collection

This fine blue and white Jingdecheng piece has a
wintermelon shape. Seen at a distance, the relief
on the mouth edge could be the stalk and leaves
of fruit, but instead it is made into a dragon and a
bat. There are three well-confined medallions
sketchily painted with foliage in an impressionistic
manner. (Z.Y.H.)

29.
SPRAYS OF FLOWERS
Qian Weicheng, 1720-1772
China, Qing dynasty
Painting, colors on silk, in frame
H. 42" × 23" (106.7 × 58.4 cm.)
The Henry Piltz Kramer Collection

The artist signed on the left:
"Qian Weicheng of Wuchin, Jiansu (province)."
   Qian Weicheng was also known as Jiaxuan. At

the age of 25 he won top honors on the national graduation list (titled Zhuang-yuan); after that he served in several high posts in the court. His grandmother, Cheng Shu (1660-1736), was a well-known and accomplished lady-artist, from whom Weicheng inherited his talent and interest in art. His floral subjects were painted under the influence of Yun Shouping (1633-1690) which accounts for the boneless manner in this painting. In later years he was more devoted to landscape painting. (Z.Y.H.)

25.
Lo Ping, 1733-1799
China, Qing dynasty
Painting, ink on paper, hanging scroll
H. 13⅜" × 9⅞" (33.5 × 24.9 cm.)
Private collection

Lo Ping was known also as Liangfeng, Tanfu, and Huazhisiseng, and came from Shexian, Anhui. A free-lance artist and a strong individualist, he lived and was active mostly in Yangzhou, Jiangsu. He was a follower of Chan Buddhism and a student of Jin Nung (1687-1764). He and his teacher, with six other painters, were known collectively as the "Eight Eccentric Masters of Yangzhou."

He painted many subjects and was especially known for his Buddhist painting. This is a rare landscape. He signed it on the left, with a short inscription which reads:
"Lo Ping painted (this) in the Studio of Brooding Mist and Fragrant Tea."

One of his seals is below the inscription, and another is impressed at the lower right corner. (Z.Y.H.)

26.
POMEGRANATE VASE
China, Qing dynasty, Qienlong mark, 1736-1795
Porcelain
H. 4¹/₁₆", Diam. 3¾" (10, 9.3 cm.)
Private collection

Among the monochrome glazes of the Qing period, the most beloved was the even, light blue which the Chinese named "moonlight." Made in Jingdecheng, its even hue is derived from cobalt-oxide. In the 19th century it acquired the international name, Clair-de-Lune. This is a perfect example which shows a gentle shade of color and a fineness in potting. On the base is the imperial mark of Qienlong. (Z.Y.H.)

27b.
RUI SCEPTER(*)
China, Qing dynasty, 19th century
Boxwood
L. 18⅝" (47.2 cm.)
Private collection

Rui, meaning "as you wish," sometimes is translated as "lappets." This stylized form was thought of as a stalk of lotus flower in Buddhism, or the sacred fungus, lingzhi, in Taoism. The latter symbolizes longevity. It is a motif most frequently seen in the applied art of China. As an independent object to be held in the hand, it generally indicates certain religious and civil authority, and it became a wish-granting token. By the time of early Qing, larger scepters carved out of precious materials began to appear more often. It is a welcome and luxurious table ornament.

This Rui, carved out of boxwood, has on it the character shou (longevity), written one hundred times in different styles. There are 66 characters on the top and 34 on the side. The workmanship is exquisite and uniquely Chinese. (Z.Y.H.)

27c.
RUI SCEPTER(*)
China, Qing dynasty, 18th century
Sandalwood
L. 18⅝" (47.2 cm.)
Private collection

Engraved here are the Eight Immortals of popular Taoism, in lacy openwork with floral vines winding around the figures. Consistent with its delicate details, the scepter is rendered with soft edges and a gentle sway in the stalk. The exquisite workmanship makes it a beautiful ornament for the table. (Z.Y.H.)

27d.
RUI SCEPTER(*)
China, Qing dynasty, late 18th century
Ice jade
L. 17½" (44.5 cm.)
The Cecilia and Gene Doo Collection

This jade scepter is carved with a design of entwined soft fungus clinging around the handle and a more stylized fungus forming the bent head. This semi-translucent white jade has a cream tone, the sign of good quality ice jade *(dungyu).* Generous in size, it makes a luxurious table decoration. (Z.Y.H.)

27a.
RUI SCEPTER(*)
China, Qing dynasty, late 18th century
Iron
L. 17¼" (43.5 cm.)
Private collection

This iron scepter has a silver inlaid lozenge
pattern with a pointed, bent head of a perfect
lappet form. On the back are eight inlaid words in
seal script, which translate:
*"Lasting prosperity and longevity, good fortune as you
wish."*
    The first use of iron in art occurred in the Song
period and remained as a low cost material for
other uses. This scepter is simple, weighty and
easily handled. It could have been made for a
military person or for a country home; in a
moment of need it could be used as a defensive
weapon. (Z.Y.H.)

28.
RUI SCEPTER(*)
China, Qing dynasty, 18th century
Coral
L. 14" (35.6 cm.)
Private collection

Carved design of Buddha's-hand citron,
pomegranate and peach. In China these fruits
symbolize the "three plentifuls" (good fortune,
many sons and long life). (Z.Y.H.)

30.
WILD GEESE
Pien Shouming, active 1741-1750
China, Qing dynasty
Painting, ink and slight colors on paper, hanging
scroll, now mounted on board
H. 58" × 40" (147.3 × 101.6 cm.)
Private collection

Pien is also known as Weizi, Ikung, Moxien and
Jianseng, and came from Huaian of Jiangsu. He is
well-known for his paintings of reeds and wild
geese and was also known for his poetry and
calligraphy. He lived on the waterfront with reeds
surrounding his house. This is reflected in his
own paintings. (Z.Y.H.)

31.
LOTUS AND BIRD(*)
Chen Hongshou, 1768-1822
China, Qing dynasty
Painting, ink on paper, hanging scroll, now
mounted on board
H. 100" × 38" (254 × 96.5 cm.)
The Mrs. L.A.R. Gaspar Collection

Signed by the artist on the left: *"In the spirit of
Xinlo shanren (Hua Yen, 1682-1765). (Painted by)
Elm-studio host, Chen Hongshou."* Below this are
two seals of the artist.
    Chen, also known as Mansheng, was from
Qiantang, Hangzhou of Zhejiang. He was gifted
in poetry, painting, calligraphy, and also was
outstanding in seal-engraving. He was one of the
literary scholars who designed and supervised
pottery at Ixing, a type made in unglazed earth-
colored stoneware (see No. 32). (Z.Y.H.)

32.
TEA POT(*)
Potter: Yang Pengnien, active early 19th century
China, Qing dynasty, circa 1811-1817
Ixing stoneware, in rust-brown color
H. 3", Diam. 4¾" (7.6 × 12 cm.)
Private collection

This pot is unglazed in a rust-brown color. A seal
impressed inside the small cover reads,
"Pengnien." Under the pot another seal reads
"Amanto shi" (Chamber of Amanda) which is the
studio name of Chen Hongshou. Inscribed on the
belly of the teapot is a short verse, which may be
rendered as:
*"In the shade of (my) straw hat (I) sipping tea for
thirstiness,
Is it one or two (happenings)? Buddha made no
comment. Mansheng."*
    Mansheng is the pen name of painter Chen
Hongshou (see No. 31). When he served as a
magistrate of Ixing, between 1811 and 1817, he
designed teapots with the collaboration of the
potter, Yang Pengnien, during his leisure hours.
Yang revived the hand modeling method of Ixing
wares, and the two frequently joined in
production. Examples were referred to as
"Mansheng pots." (Z.Y.H.)

33.
TWO DEITIES(*)
China, Qing dynasty
Wood
Private collection

A. Goddess, 17th century
H. 8¾" × 4¼" (22.3 × 11 cm.)
According to an inscription on the back, this
goddess probably belonged to the cult of "Three
Dames" (Sannai jiao). Although a small statue, it
has the distinct regional sculptural style of Fujian.

B. A Female Fairy, 19th century
H. 5¾" × 1¾" (14.6 × 4.3 cm.)
This figure may be one of a lady's attendants, a
side-figure of a Taoist set. (Z.Y.H.)

34.
PERFUMER
China, Qing dynasty, 18th century
Green jade
H. 3½", Diam. 6½" (8.9 × 16.6 cm.)
Private collection

This perfumer is of mottled cabbage-green jade
with flecks of calcification. The entire piece is
carved in an open reticulated floral pattern. The
cover is a lace-like engraving with bat and gourd
motifs, and the base is an orchid design. This type
of elaborately carved green jade appeared in
quantities in the mid-Qing period but varied in
the quality of individual pieces. This perfume
container is an excellent example of its type.
(Z.Y.H.)

35.
LANDSCAPE ALBUM(†)
Tang Ifen, 1778-1853
China, Qing dynasty, dated 1849
Painting, ink and colors on paper, ten album
leaves, each measuring
H. 11¾" × 13⅜" (29.8 × 34 cm.)
Private collection

Tang Ifen, also known as Joi and Yusheng, was
from Wujin, Jiangsu. He inherited an official title
from his family but preferred to be an artist. He
was also interested in astronomy, geography and
music. The album consists of ten pages of
landscape paintings. On an additional page after
his work is a colophon by Liu Lingsheng. Two of
the landscapes are done in ink only and eight
with slight color. Tang signed and sealed each

page. The last page bears the date 1849, when he
was 72 years old.

Leaf four, "Rock, Bamboo and old Tree."   On
the right is a poem by the artist which reads:
*"Rain sweeping the yellow wooded temple, wind
stirring waves on River Xiang.*
*On the pier of departure, there is a mossy rock leaning
against an old tree. Ifeng."*
    Below his name is his seal. (Z.Y.H.)

36a, b.
TWO NATURE STUDIES(*)
Wang Su, 1794-1877
China, Qing dynasty
Painting, ink on paper, album leaves, each
measuring
H. 15" × 19½" (38 × 49.6 cm.)
Private collection

Wang Su, also known as Xiaomei and Xunzhi,
was from Yangzhou, Jiangsu. He was best known
for his figure paintings, but he also frequently
painted flower subjects. In addition, he was a
seal-engraver. These two loose pages belonged to
an album.
A. Plum blossom, signed on the top: Wang Su,
   and followed by his seal.
B. Still life of vegetable and fruits, his seal
   impressed on the right. (Z.Y.H.)

37.
TWO EPISODES FROM DREAMS OF THE RED
CHAMBER(*)
Fei Danxu, 1802-1850
China, Qing dynasty
Painting, ink and colors on paper, album leaves,
each measuring
H. 14¼" × 18" (36.3 × 45.7 cm.)
Private collection

Also known as Xiaolou and by a few other pen
names, he was from Wuxin, Zhejiang, but active
most of his life in Shanghai. He painted many
subjects and was known especially for his dainty
ladies. He painted several versions of subjects in
the novel, "Dreams of the Red Chamber," which
were highly admired for their appropriate style.
These are two loose pages from the set. He could
be regarded as a Chinese "ukiyo-e" type of
painter; he went even further in illustrating the
frailty of womanhood.
A. Baozai catching Butterflies (reproduced here)
B. Xianyun contesting flowers. (Z.Y.H.)

41

38.
FAN
China, Qing dynasty, 19th century
Blue and white porcelain
L. 15" × 7½" (38.1 × 19 cm.)
Private collection

A typical Taoistic temple fan, this work is made of fine porcelain and is painted in underglazed blue with a design of the Eight Immortals in the midst of the clouds. (Z.Y.H.)

39.
COUPLET
Yang Isun, 1813-1881
China, Qing dynasty, dated 1881
Calligraphy, ink on paper, a pair of hanging scrolls, each measuring
H. 98½" × 12" (250 × 30.4 cm.)
Private collection

A couplet is two matched verses on twin scrolls. A literary style that began in the fifteenth century, it became popular as a wall-hanging in China.

Yang Isun, also known as Yungzhung, was from Zhangsu, Jiangsu. He was an outstanding calligrapher and seal-engraver, and this work shows his specialty in small-seal script. The words may be translated as:
"All day long (I am) a man of leisure, who prefers to cultivate willow plants, silkworms and the concerns of firewood.
(I am) deeply in the classics where words are (precious) like pearls and jade, and that is expressed in (my) calligraphy." (Z.Y.H.)

40.
PORTRAIT OF A ZHUANGYUAN
Ren Xiong, 1820-after 1857
China, Qing dynasty
Painting, ink and color on paper, hanging scroll
H. 79" × 23½" (200.7 × 59.7 cm.)
Private collection

Ren Xiong's family came from Xiaoshan, Zhejiang. Four brothers were known for their painting and were active mostly in Shanghai. Ren Xiong was famous for his figure painting. Zhuangyuan is a title given to someone who is awarded the top honor at the national imperial examination. Such a person is portrayed in this painting by Ren Xiong. Legend has it that for a candidate who wins this award, the literary deity, Kuixing, would appear

in his dream. The painting here shows the scholar in a red gown sleeping on his desk, a green-colored literary deity in the clouds; the scene is set in a huge landscape. (Z.Y.H.)

41.
TWO LARGE FISHBOWLS
China, Qing dynasty, 19th century
Porcelain
H. 24½", Diam. 28" (62.2 × 71 cm.)
Private collection

This pair of famille-rose large basins are decorated with flowering plants and butterflies. Painted with polychrome enamels and gold that cover the exterior, a complete composition is inside the bowl. All is done in an exceptionally fine painterly technique and is reminiscent of the type of meticulous butterflies done by the lady painter Ma Quan, who was active in the late 18th century. (Z.Y.H.)

42.
FANS
Xiang Jinghe, active late 19th century
China, 19th century, dated 1886
Painting, ink and colors on paper, four panels mounted in frames, each panel measuring
H. 41" × 11½" (104.1 × 29.2 cm.)
Private collection

The two miniature fan paintings come from a set of four panels and total twenty-four paintings: eight landscape paintings, eleven flower and still life subjects, and five calligraphy. They are all done by one artist. Beside her given-name, Jinghe, four other pen names appear on different fans, which include: Shuangging, Ifang, Zhaolan and Erhru jushi. Three of the fans give the date 1886, while other inscriptions identify her as a woman from Siling of Hangzhou. (Z.Y.H.)

43.
PEONY AND ROCK(†)
Wu Zhangshi, 1844-1927
China, Qing dynasty, dated 1895
Painting, ink and slight color on paper, hanging scroll
H. 87" × 25¾" (221 × 65.3 cm.)
Private collection

Wu Zhangshi, originally named Junqing, also was known as Foulu and had a few other pen names.

He was from Anci, Zhejiang, and was active most of his life in Shanghai. Beside his bold painting, he was known also as a calligrapher and a seal-engraver. He painted this work at the age of 51. It does not have his usual bold color but is rendered in a soft, wet brush with pale tones that are most attractive. It represents a rare side of him which is not well known. (Z.Y.H.)

44.
RIDING ON THE CLOUDS(*)
Kang Yuwei, 1856-1927
China, Qing dynasty-Republic
Calligraphy, ink on paper, hanging scroll
H. 83″ × 29½″ (210.7 × 74.9 cm.)
Private collection

Kang also was known as Quangxia and Gengsheng, and came from Nanhai, Guangdung. He was a leading advocate for modernization of China at the turn of the century but was unable to influence the Manchu imperial court. An intellectual with wide interests in the arts, he was the author of many books and was well known for his individualistic style of calligraphy. This is a fine example of his work. The writing was dedicated to a friend named Tianru. A phrase of twelve words translates:
"With a noble course, intelligent supervision and a wonderful program, (you are) riding on the clouds."
(Z.Y.H.)

45.
VASE(†)
China, Hongxien, 1915-16
Porcelain
H. 13″, Diam. 6¼″ (33 × 16 cm.)
Private collection

This lemon-yellow glazed vase includes three medallions; inside the medallions are enamel paintings of flowers and birds. On the yellow ground there are lightly incised fine-line designs and, over it, sprays of painted flowers. On the base is the mark of Juren tang, a workshop which made the same wares for Yuan Shikai. (Z.Y.H.)

46.
SMALL JAR(†)
China, Hongxien year mark, 1915-16
Porcelain
H. 3⅝″, Diam. 3¼″ (9.1 × 8.3 cm.)
Private collection

Under a slightly curved lip, the globular body of this small jar is covered with a lemon yellow glaze on which are lightly incised chrysanthemum designs and nearly invisible thin-line reliefs. There are two round medallions with delicate enamel paintings as well. The flower subjects are done in the courtly tradition of the 18th century. On the base a square seal reads, "Imperial ware of Hongxien," the reign name of Yuan Shikai (1859-1916). This imperial ware was produced at Jingdecheng in the year Yuan crowned himself emperor of China. His reign lasted less than one year, but the ware was supervised by an able manager, Quo Shiwu. The excellent workmanship is rated the finest since the 18th century. (Z.Y.H.)

47.
LOTUS
Qi Huang, 1863-1957
China, Republic
Painting, ink on paper, hanging scroll
H. 26½″ × 14½″ (67.3 × 36.8 cm.)
The Cecilia and Gene Doo Collection

Qi Huang is also known by a number of other pen names and is, in fact, better known as Qi Baishi. He came from Xiangtan, Hunan, and was well traveled. He settled first in Shanghai, and then in Beijing for the remainder of his life. He painted a variety of subjects and also was a master in the art of seal-engraving. He developed his personal style firmly and consistently and is the most widely known Chinese painter of the 20th century.

In this work he signed on the left, *"Old-man Jiping, Qi Baishi, painted this at the age of eighty-eight."* Thus the painting can be dated 1951. One artist's seal is impressed below. (Z.Y.H.)

48.
SETTING MOON
Wang Zhen, 1866-1938
China, Republic, dated 1938
Painting, ink on paper, hanging scroll
H. 95″ × 45″ (241.3 × 114.3 cm.)
Private collection

Wang Zhen is known also as Iting and Bailung shanren. From Wuxing, Zhejiang, he was a successful businessman in Shanghai. After thirty years of age, he took up painting seriously under the influence of Wu Zhangshi (1844-1927). He was best known for his figure painting. This is the

simplest of all his works, dated in the year of his
death, at age seventy-two. The painting illustrates
a phrase of a Tang poem:
"Setting moon, crying crows and a sky full of frost."
    Seven flying birds follow the writing, as if the
calligraphy is moving with the birds. (Z.Y.H.)

49.
SPARROW AND CORN(*)
Gao Jienfu, 1881-1951
China, Republic, dated 1948
Painting, ink and color on paper, hanging scroll
H. 83" × 23⅜" (210.8 × 59.2 cm.)
Private collection

Originally named Lun, from Guangzhou,
Guangdong, Gao studied in Japan at the Tokyo
Academy. Returning home, he taught art at
several universities and was among the
forerunners of the "new" Chinese painting
movement in the early twenties. With his
leadership, the group of artists active in
Guangdung are classified as the Lingnan School.
This painting was dedicated to Yuntang. The artist
signed it and impressed one of his seals. Another
seal at the lower right corner belongs to the
former collector, Deng Zhangwu (20th century).
(Z.Y.H.)

50.
LANDSCAPE(*)
Fu Baoshi, 1904-1965
China, Republic, dated 1964
Painting, ink on paper, with a touch of red,
framed
H. 37½" × 25½" (95.3 × 64.8 cm.)
Private collection

Fu was born in Xinyu, Jiangsi, and studied in
Japan at the Imperial Art College in his late
twenties. He also visited the United States.
Returning home, he worked with a group of
artists under the leadership of Xu Beihong.
Author of many books, he generally painted
figures and landscape. He is among the most
widely recognized artists in the People's Republic
of China.
    The artist signed this work with one of his
seals. Another seal belongs to the former 20th
century collector, Deng Zhangwu. (Z.Y.H.)

SCHOLAR'S DESK

51.
BRUSH HOLDER(*)
China, Qing dynasty, Daoguang year mark, 1821-
1850
Blue and white porcelain
H. 5½", Diam. 2¾" (14 × 7 cm.)
Private collection

The kilns of Jingdecheng made imperial pieces,
using a rich cobalt blue. (Z.Y.H.)

52.
SEAL(*)
China, Qing dynasty, 18th century
Black and white jade
H. 1¼" × 1¼" square (3.3 cm.)
Private collection

Making use of the natural color division of the
jade, the engraver has utilized the white part of
the stone as the stamping seal, while the black
portion (the top) is carved with a dragon design.
(Z.Y.H.)

53a.
BRUSHES(*)
1. Japan, Momoyama period, 17th century
A pair with lacquer caps and stalks, each one
measuring L. 11" (27.9 cm.)
The thick and short tuft is a type of brush used in
the Tang period in China, generally referred to as
the "sutra writing" brush (Xiejing bi).
2. China, 18th century
Ivory stalk with cap, engraved designs.
L. 9⅞" (25 cm.)
3. China, 19th century
Blue and white porcelain, no cap.
L. 9" (22.9 cm.)
Private collection (Z.Y.H.)

53b.
BRUSH HOLDER(*)
China, Qing dynasty, 19th century
White jade
H. 3⅞", Diam. 2⅛" (9.7 × 5.6 cm.)
Private collection

53c.
BRUSH and BRUSH REST(*)
China, Qing dynasty, 19th century
White jade
Brush, L. 5⅞" (14.7 cm.)
Brush rest, H. 1⅝" × 4¼" (4.1 × 10.8 cm.)
Private collection

53d.
BRUSH RESTS(*)
Ceramic
1. Five Sacred Mountains, blue glaze,
China, 19th century
H. 3" × 4" (7.6 × 10.1 cm.)
2. Five Peaks, Yingqing-type glaze
China, 19th century
H. 1½" × 3" (3.8 × 7.6 cm.)
Private collection

53e.
INKSTONE(*)
China, Qing dynasty, dated 1831
Stone
H. 4⅛" × 2¾" (10.7 × 7 cm.)
Private collection

The stone of this inkstone came from the quarry
of Duanxi, Guangdung. On one end is a carved
dragon chasing a pearl; on the side is an engraved
inscription giving the date, "Summer in the
second year of Daoguang 1831." (Z.Y.H.)

53f.
TWO INKSTONES(*)
China (see below)
Jade
1. Qing dynasty, 19th century
White nephrite
L. 3" × 2⅛" (7.6 × 5.5 cm.)
2. 20th century
White jadeite
L. 10" × 8" × 2" (25.4 × 20.3 × 5 cm.)
Private collection

53g.
ARMREST(*)
China, Qing dynasty, 18th century
Bamboo
L. 9¾" × 2¼" (24.7 × 5.7 cm.)
Private collection

The engraving on this armrest is done in the
manner of the handwriting of the artist, Huang
Shen (1687-1768), and translates:
"With this to write out my heart." (Z.Y.H.)

53h.
WATER DROPPERS(*)
China, Qing dynasty, 18th century
White porcelain
1. Pot with cover
H. 2" × 3¼" × 2" (5 × 8.4 × 5 cm.)
2. Vase with a dragon
H 1½" × 2" × 2" (3.8 × 5 × 5 cm.)
Private collection

53i.
SEAL-INK CONTAINER(*)
China, Qing dynasty, Qianlong year mark,
1736-1795
Porcelain
H. 2⅛", Diam. 2¾" (5.5 × 6.9 cm.)
Private collection

This covered container is a standard box for a red
inkpad used in stamping seal impressions. The
cover depicts a gentleman and two ladies engaged
in making seal inkpads. Their garments have
modulated shading, and the interior setting shows
sequences of foreground and background,
indicating a knowledge of western perspective.
On the base, a square seal reads: "Made in
Qianlong of Great Qing."
    This type of Chinese enameled porcelain
acquired the international name of "famille rose"
for its predominant pink color in 19th century
France, through the collector, Jacquemart. Just as
Chinese art was popular in the west, China was
fascinated by western art techniques. (Z.Y.H.)

53j.
SEAL-INK CONTAINER(*)
China, Qing dynasty, 19th century
White jade
H. 1⅛", Diam. 2⅜" (3 × 6 cm.)
Private collection

53k.
STAMPING SEALS(*)
China, (see below)
Stones
Private collection

1. A set of three seals.
The engravings on the button-tops of the stamps
are 17th century; words engraved on the oval
piece belong to the same period.
H. 2″ × 1⅛″ (5 × 2.8 cm.)
The two square seals are carved by Deng Erbi of
the 20th century, a famous seal-engraver and
scholar of Guangzhou.
H. 1¾″ × 1″ (4.6 × 2.6 cm.)
2. A green stone from Qingtien, Zhejiang, the
seal is engraved by Wang Zhuangwei of the 20th
century, a famous seal-engraver and scholar of
Taipei.
H. 1½″ × ¾″ (3.6 × 1.8 cm.)
3. Chicken-blood stone, a type of stone highly
valued in China and Japan.
H. 1⅜″ × ¾″ (3 × 1.8 cm.)

53l.
INK STICKS(*)
China, 18th century
Private collection

Two from a set, each stick is engraved with the
motif of one of the Sixteen Lohans of Guanxui
(10th century).
1. The first Lohan, Pindola
L. 2¾″ × 1½″ (7 × 3.8 cm.)
2. The twelfth Lohan, Nagasena
L. 3¼″ × 1½″ (8.3 × 3.8 cm.)
   Ink stick patterns became works of art in the
16th century. Two famous ink stick factories began
to commission fine artists to design ink sticks at
this time. The wood mold engravers, too, were
selected as outstanding craftsmen. This tradition
continued among painters and calligraphers who
were fastidious about their tools. The luxurious
habit waned after the 18th century. (Z.Y.H.)

54.
BULBOUS POT(*)
Korea, Kimhae, 1st to 4th century
Greyware mat pottery
H. 10⅜″, Diam. at mouth 7¼″ (26.5 × 18.3 cm.)
Private collection

This bulbous jar with constricted neck and out-
turned rim is decorated with 11 concentric
horizontal bands filled with narrow combed
striations. Such ware is typical of excavated
Kimhae examples and has been dated to between
the first and fourth centuries. This example comes
from an extensive collection of early Korean
pottery. (H.A.L.)

55.
MALE AND FEMALE HORSES(*)
Korea, Old Silla (5th to 6th century)
Reddish and buff clay
Each approximately L. 7½″ × H. 5⅛″ (19 × 13 cm.)
Private collection

These extremely rare images of horses, while
admittedly crudely executed, possess a naive
vitality and are of great value in the study of old
Silla culture. One horse, thought to be a female,
includes incised details of triangular eyes and a
suggestion of a bridle. Remnants of a saddle have
been covered over by restoration. The second
horse, a male steed with saddle and incised
indication of a bridle and mane and indentations
for eyes, is of even greater interest
ethnographically. (H.A.L.)

56.
VASE(*)
Korea, Koryŏ dynasty, 12th century
Stoneware
H. 9¼″, Diam. 5½″ (23.5 × 14 cm.)
The L. B. Nerio Collection

Although the celadon wares of the Koryŏ Dynasty
are the best known ceramic products of Korea, the
plain stonewares done at the same time also share
in the creative excellence of that artistically
glorious period. Decorated only with a series of
encircling bands, this *maebyŏng* is notable for its
fine proportions and stately grace. The dating is
arrived at by analogies in shape to known celadon
examples. (H.A.L.)

57.
TWO CELADON BOWLS(*)
Korea, Koryŏ dynasty (918-1392)
(a) 12th century
H. 3″, Diam. 6¼″ (7.6 × 15.9 cm.)
The exterior of this bowl has an incised lotus-peta
decor under an even celadon glaze.

Private collection
(b) 12th-13th century
H. 3", Diam. 7¾" (8 × 19.5 cm.)
The Ferdinand Micklautz Collection

Each of these bowls illustrates one of the main
methods used by the Koryŏ potters to decorate
celadon wares: the lotus design bowl is a fine
example of incising while the chrysanthemum
medallions of the other are rendered in inlay.
Inlay, in its Koryŏ context, involves an underglaze
technique of etching designs into the clay and
then filling them with slip (in this case white slip),
all before firing. Reddish-brown slip was also
often used in inlay-work, turning black (or very
dark brown) upon firing. Developing somewhat
later than the plain or incised celadons, inlaid
celadons can be seen as a major contribution of
the Korean potters to world ceramic art. Although
the technique was not altogether unknown in
China, it reached its heights in terms of craft and
creativity in Korea, particularly in the middle of
the Koryŏ period. The lotus-design bowl at the
same time epitomizes the pervasiveness of
Buddhism and of Chinese culture (of the Song
Dynasty) in Koryŏ life. (H.A.L.)

58.
TWO BOTTLES(*)
Korea, Koryŏ dynasty (918-1392)
(a) Celadon bottle (-vase), 11th-12th century
H. 10¾", Diam. 6½" (27.3 × 16.5 cm.)
Collection of Ferdinand Micklautz
(b) Bronze bottle (for wine?), 12th-13th century
H. 12" (30.5 cm.)
Private collection

These two bottles, one ceramic, the other metal,
illustrate how the Korean craftsmen used forms
derived from China with great assurance. The
celadon example demonstrates a thorough
familiarity with analogous forms produced in the
10th century in China, particularly of Yue-ware.
In addition, the piece in this exhibition is quite
similar to the well known Koryŏ bottle in the
Seattle Art Museum. In terms of form, the bronze
bottle clearly shows the influence of Chinese
ceramics of the Song period. The pleasing shape is
enlivened with decoration consisting only of
encircling lines, and the metal has acquired, over
the centuries, an attractive green patina. The
bronze vessels of the Koryŏ period have not
received much in the way of special research, and
dating is usually arrived at by comparisons with

celadon counterparts, for which a general
chronology can now be constructed. (H.A.L.)

59.
PORTRAIT OF AN OFFICIAL(†)
Korea, 19th century
Hanging scroll, ink and colors on silk
H. 36", W. 19" (91.4 × 48.3 cm.)
The Melvin McGovern Collection

This painting is typical of the work produced by
professional painters of the Bureau of Painting at
the Yi court. The chief task of the artist in
portraits such as this is to convey accurately the
facial features of the subject. It was not unusual
for lesser artists to finish the portrait by quickly
painting the body and costume in a conventional
manner. This is a portrait of a prime minister, or a
minister of the left or right, each of whose rank is
signified by twin cranes embroidered on a panel at
the front of their robes. The figure's hat also
symbolizes a high rank since the wing-like
projections appear to be constructed of a double
layer of gauze which is used only for important
officials. (W.T.)

60.
VESSEL(*)
Japan, late Jōmon ware, circa 2000-1000 B.C.
Earthenware with free-form handles and incised
and applied decoration, from the Tsukuba region
H. 15", Greatest diam. 11" (38.2 × 28 cm.)
The L. B. Nerio Collection

The Jōmon phase of Japan's neolithic period is
named after the cord pattern found on pottery
vessels. The phase endured for a long period of
time, from at least 4,500 B.C. to as late as 200 B.C.
There seems to be a relationship, moreover,
between the style of pottery found in the Jōmon
phase and similar pottery found in the neolithic
phase of Manchuria. Early Jōmon pots follow a
simple corded decoration, but, by the middle of
the third millenium, decoration becomes almost
sculptured, producing rather fantastic effects. This
example is more tightly organized than some of
the more bizarre ornamentation found on middle
Jōmon wares. It still retains, however, something
of the knotted effect so characteristic of the ware
during its prime period. The example has been
dated accordingly to the late Jōmon period.
(H.A.L.)

61.
HANIWA(*)
Japan, ca. fifth century
Low-fired clay
H. 16¾" (42.5 cm.)
The Collection of Charles R. Temple

Haniwa, which literally means "cylinders of clay,"
were placed around the large mounded tombs of
the Kōfun period (250-552 A.D.). The early hollow
cylinders gradually gave way to ones in which
inanimate objects such as houses or quivers and
arrows were molded atop the cylinders. By the
fourth century, the sculpted forms included birds
and animals, and in the fifth century cylinders
topped by human forms became common.

This chronological development from
inanimate to animate representations, based on
haniwa finds at tombs that can be accurately dated,
contradicts the more dramatic legend that the
earliest *haniwa* were those sculpted in human form
and arose as a substitute for the practice of large-
scale live burals of attendants who accompanied
the deceased within the mounded tomb.

This example represents the early type of
human figured *haniwa* which have less detailed
costumes and are smaller in size than the later
ones and, thus, can be dated to the fifth century.
The arms are placed in gesture, one arm out and
the other pressed to the chest, which is also
common in the early figures. The figure wears
earrings, a necklace and a jacket that is tied with
small bows. These features can be found on both
male and female *haniwa,* but the type of hair and
the slight protusions on the upper chest suggest
that this figure is a female. (W.T.)

62.
BODHISATTVA(*)
Japan, ca. ninth-tenth century
Wood, *ichiboku* technique
H. 40" (101.6 cm.)
Private collection

Except for the right arm and left forearm, which
are replacements, this bodhisattva is carved from a
single block of wood. The figure has many of the
characteristics of the style of the early Heian
period: a large head, low forehead, short neck and
protruding abdomen which all create a stocky
figure. In this particular example, however, the
slightly flexed knee, the narrow eyes and well-
shaped lips add considerable grace to produce a

figure that is not so heavy or stolid as those of the
more extreme styles of the early Heian period.

The breakup of government-sponsored
workshops and a period of austerity for the
temples, imposed by the government that had
begun to fear the power of the temples, led the
early Heian sculptors to turn to wood, a more
inexpensive and plentiful medium. Moreover,
they rarely gilded or lacquered their works. This
figure appears at first glance to be a Kannon
Bosatsu, the bodhisattva of compassion. But if the
image in the crown is a *stupa* or pagoda, then the
figure would have to be Miroku, the future
Buddha who can appear either in the guise of a
bodhisattva or a Buddha. At this time, however,
Miroku figures are far rarer than those of Kannon.
(W.T.)

63.
FIVE PRONGED VAJRA(*)
Japan, ca. 13th century
Gilt bronze
H. 9¹/₁₆", Diam. 2¾" (23 × 7 cm.)
Private collection

The *vajra,* an esoteric ritual implement that derives
from the trident, representing a lightning bolt in
Near Eastern and Hindu mythology, also stands
for the hardness and durability of diamonds. It
symbolizes, therefore, the eternality and
absoluteness of the Buddha's teaching. Although
the five-pronged *vajra* or *gokōsho* is the most
common form in Japan, the implement can also
appear with one, two, three, four or nine prongs.
The five prongs can be understood as symbolic of
several more specific ideas: the five elements, the
five Buddhas, the five powers to destroy obstacles
to faith or the five kinds of knowledge. Even the
lotus petals around the central section of the
implement symbolize various teachings. Thus, the
five pronged *vajra,* like the rosary, serves as an
aid in recalling the doctrines which lead to
enlightenment. (W.T.)

64.
SHARITŌ(*)
Japan, ca. 14th-15th century
Bronze, with crystal
H. 10¼" (26 cm.)
Private collection

When the historical Buddha, Sakyamuni, died and
was cremated, his ashes and bones were believed
to have been distributed to his disciples, put into

containers and buried. Over these reliquaries *stupa* mounds were constructed. Although the *stupa* form was transformed into pagodas in the Far East, the Chinese, Koreans and Japanese retained the practice of placing reliquaries beneath the pagodas even though the contents were symbolic rather than actual relics of the Buddha. In the Kamakura period, a reaction against the popularity of Buddhist sects which revered Amida stimulated a revival of earlier schools of Buddhism which stressed Sākyamuni Buddha.

With this revival a large number of reliquaries were made and placed within temples as objects of worship and symbols of the historical Buddha. Although the form of the reliquaries varied, many were constructed in the shape of miniature pagodas, and the term *sharitō*, or reliquary pagodas, became the common term for all of them.

This *sharitō*, a complex example of the flaming jewel type of reliquary in which a crystal jewel contains a symbolic relic (in this case fresh water pearls) is surrounded by bronze flames and is placed atop a lotus dais. The dais is supported by a tortoise, symbol of longevity, which stands atop a rocky outcropping in the midst of waves cast onto the base. These rocks may represent Sumeru, the island mountain that stands at the very center of the universe, according to Buddhist cosmology. The tortoise support was used in several Kamakura and Muromachi *sharitō* such as those at Toshodaiji, a 1411 example at Tōdaiji, and a 1460 piece at Ryukoin. In none of these, however, is the tortoise placed atop rocks. This more naturalistic presentation suggests a time in the Muromachi period when sculptures were often mounted on rock-shaped daises. (W.T.)

65.
DAINICHI(†)
Japan, ca. 14th century
Gilt wood, *yosegi* technique
H. 20¾" (53 cm.) (figure only)
Signature: Genbei Daibusshi, Koyasan
Private collection

Dainichi, or Mahavairocana, was the Supreme Buddha for the Shingon sect of Buddhism, which was established in Japan during the Heian period and continued to thrive in the Kamakura period, despite introduction of new schools of Buddhism. All other Buddhas are considered emanations or transformations of Dainichi, according to Shingon belief.

As the Supreme Buddha, Dainichi is not bound by the iconography that rules other Buddhas, and he can appear, as he does here, with the crown, jewelry and robes that usually signify a bodhisattva. However, his identity is obvious because Dainichi alone can use the mudra of supreme wisdom with one fist clasping the index finger of the other hand. This statue, with its inlaid eyes, elaborate metal crown, full face and neatly carved drapery on the broad flat thighs and legs, is a production of the Kamakura period. The work is signed Genbei and was produced for a temple in the monastery complex of Mt. Koya. It is consistent with the style established by the Kei school. (W.T.)

66.
TEA BOWL(*)
Japan, early Edo period, ca. 1620s
Mino ware, *Ki-seto* type, stoneware, yellow mat glaze with green spot
H. 2¾", Diam. 5¾" (6.3 × 14.6 cm.)
Private collection

During the late Momoyama Period (1568-1615) the Mino kilns underwent changes in materials and firing techniques. Of the ware that resulted, *Ki-seto* (Yellow Seto) differed from the *Ko-seto* precursors and was characterized by a white clay body covered with a buff or yellow glaze. More efficient oxidation in the kiln, moreover, resulted in a mat finish known as *abura-age-de*. This is in sharp contrast to the glossy finish of a second type of *Ki-seto* called *ayamede*. The example here is typical of the *abura-age-de* type (literally "fried bean curd" type) with a yellow-buff mat glaze. The shape and size are also typical of the ware. *Ki-seto* shapes responded to the needs of the tea masters by producing small pieces for the tea ceremony—vases, plates, *kashibachi* (cake dishes) or tea bowls, as here. (H.A.L.)

67.
NIGHT RAIN AT XIAO-XIANG REGION (from Eight Views of Xiao and Xiang Rivers)(*)
Japan, mid-Edo Period, ca. 1700
Ink on paper mounted as a folding album
Each image: H. 13¾", W. 8¾" (35 × 22.5 cm.)
Private collection

This album has been judged by Dr. Tōru Shimbo, formerly with the Agency for Cultural Affairs and a recognized authority on Japanese painting, as a *shikomi-e* (practice painting) of the Edo Period, done after a famous album by the late 15th century-early 16th century master, Kenkō Shōkei. A nearly identical album of the Eight Views of Xiao and Xiang Rivers by Kenkō Shōkei may still be seen at the Hakatsuru Art Museum, Kōbe.

Slightly larger than this example and with the addition of some pale color tints, this early Muromachi album influenced many later painters and was the source of inspiration for a number of fine *suiboku* (ink painting) works, including the example in the exhibition. The source for Shōkei's album in turn is thought to have been a painting by the southern Song Dynasty master, Hsia Guei (1190-1225). Masters of the Kanō and Rimpa Schools often made practice paintings such as this in homage and included the seal of the painter being studied. The work has been judged a Kanō School production of the mid-Edo Period. (H.A.L.)

68.
BUKAN WITH TIGER AND KANZAN AND JITTOKU(*)
Kanō Tan'yū (1602-1674)
Japan, 1636-1638
Three hanging scrolls, ink on silk
Each image: H. 36⅞", W. 13¾" (93.8 × 35 cm.)
Signature: Tan'yū (each scroll)
Seal: Kanō (each scroll)
Private collection

This striking trio of hanging scrolls portrays three legendary Zen sages: Jittoku (Chinese: Shih-te) on the left, Bukan (Chinese: Fengkan) with his companion, a sleeping tiger, in the middle, and Kanzan (Chinese: Han-shan) on the right. In their original Kan'ei Period mounts, the scrolls are in only fair condition. Despite deterioration, the strength of the brushwork is still apparent and is appropriate to the style of Kanō Tan'yū (1602-1674), to whom the scrolls are attributed.

Kanzan, Jittoku and Bukan are legendary figures frequently depicted in Ch'an and Zen paintings. Kanzan is believed to have been a recluse in the T'ien-t'ai region of China and to have written an anthology of poems. He is depicted here reviewing his poetry. Jittoku was said to have been found by Bukan as a child and to have been brought up in a monastery. Since he worked in the kitchen, he is usually depicted holding a broom, as here. Occasionally all three sages and tiger will appear in one painting as the

Four Sleepers. This triptych can be regarded as a variant on this theme and can be dated quite accurately on the basis of style, subject, signature and seal. Kanō Tan'yū was the eldest son of Kanō Takanobu, grandson of the great Kanō Eitoku. In 1614 Tan'yū moved from Kyoto to Edo and was patronized by the Shōgun Hidetada. He founded the Edo branch of the Kanō School and in 1636, on the Shōgun's orders, became a priest, changing his name from Morinobu to Tan'yū. In 1638 he received the title of Hōgen and in 1665 that of Hōin. Since neither honorific occurs in the signature of these paintings, it may be assumed that the paintings date between 1636, the time when he first used the name Tan'yū, and 1638, the time when he received the title Hōgen. These paintings follow the Muromachi *suiboku* manner for which he was justly famous. (H.A.L.)

69.
FLOWER CARTS(†)
Japan, ca. 17th-18th century
One of a pair of six-fold screens, color on paper with gold leaf
H. 69", W. 150" (175.3 × 380 cm.)
Signature: uncertain
Private collection

Hanagurumu, a cart filled with flowering plants, was a favorite theme of screen painters from the seventeenth through nineteenth centuries. The example here is presented in a particularly bold and direct way which suggests an early date. Two carts, one painted to simulate black lacquer with gold fittings and wood grain, and the other in gold dust with a red interior, are laden with tubs that themselves are decorated in various floral patterns.

The season for this screen is indicated by the autumn flowers which are complemented by the spring blossoms of the other screen of the pair. Some parts of the flowers are executed in slight relief by a process called *moriage* in which clam or other sea shells are ground into a fine powder, mixed with glue and molded onto the surface of the screen. The flowers are not arranged in any particular style and are placed in the wooden buckets in a way that suggests their actual appearance in the fields. This display of natural growth on carts, carefully crafted by human hands, produces a still life of considerable charm. The signature of the artist can be read in several ways, and his identity is not yet clear. (W.T.)

70.
OX AND HORSE
Japan, early 18th century
Two-fold screen, ink on paper
Each panel: H. 52½″, W. 22″ (133.3 × 56.2 cm.)
Signature: Kōrin
Seal: Hōshuku (also read Masatoki)
Private collection

71.
PAIR OF SHI SHI DOGS
Japan, late 17th-early 18th century
Wood, traces of red, black and white paint
H. 5″ × W. 5″ × D. 10″ (12.7 × 12.7 × 25.4 cm.)
The Henry Piltz Kramer Collection

72.
JAR(*)
Japan, 18th century
Shigaraki stoneware with natural ash glaze
H. 13″ (33 cm.)
The Henry Piltz Kramer Collection

Active from the Kamakura period onward, the
kilns at Shigaraki, east of Kyoto, produced wares
with a distinctive sense of rugged durability.
Originally the kilns specialized in utilitarian pots
such as this *Tane-Tsubo*, or seed storage jar, but
the aesthetic beauty of these unpretentious wares
attracted the attention of the great tea masters to
such a degree that by the 16th century the kilns
expanded to include tea ceremony wares.

The shape of this jar, formed by the ancient
technique of coiling and smoothing, is slightly
uneven and the surface rough and blemished by
scorch marks *(koge)*. Liquified kiln ash accidentally
ran over part of its surface to create a natural
effect that is particularly lovely. The simple appeal
of Shigaraki ware derives completely from the
nature of the clay, its texture and color and the
trenchant shapes with their accidental
irregularities of form and ash glaze. Although a
mid-Edo period example, this *Tane-Tsubo*
preserves the unpretentious quality of this
traditional ware at its natural best. (H.A.L.)

73.
PORTRAIT OF A DUTCHMAN AND HIS
JAVANESE SERVANT(†)
Japan, late 18th century
Ink and colors on paper
H. 19″, W. 9″ (48.5 × 23.1 cm.)
The Melvin McGovern Collection

Although the subject matter is similar to many
prints, this work is a painting executed in bright
colors. The expressive lines in the costume of the
Javanese servant and his animated face reveal a
more Japanese sense of brushwork than does the
depiction of the Dutchman, who is delineated in
narrow outlines and in a stiff posture. On the
other hand, the figure of the servant also shows a
rudimentary attempt at shading, possibly derived
from western models. The remarkable similarity of
physical type and posture in portraits of
Dutchmen in Nagasaki-e suggests that the artists'
renditions of the foreigner were often based on
other prints or paintings rather than on first hand
observation of the Dutch. (W.T.)

74.
CHINESE WITH SERVANT(*)
Japan, early 19th century
Colors and ink on paper
H. 17⅛″, W. 9″ (43.5 × 23.1 cm.)
The Melvin McGovern Collection

Although the Tokugawa government first treated
the Chinese more liberally than other foreigners in
Japan, eventually, in accordance with the closed
country policy, the Chinese were treated like the
Dutch. In 1688 they were separated from the
Japanese population and forced to live in a walled
Chinese settlement in Nagasaki. It is thought that
the change in their treatment arose from fear that
Chinese Christians might influence the Japanese.
After the government severely restricted access to
them, the Chinese became as exotic as the Dutch.
In this painting of a Chinese gentleman, followed
by a diminutive servant holding a parasol, the
similarity to portraits of the Dutch is apparent.
(W.T.)

75.
SHINTO DEITY(*)
Japan, Edo period, 18th-19th century
Wood
H. 17⅛″ (43.5 cm.)
The Mrs. L. A. R. Gaspar Collection

It was under the influence of Buddhism, where
imagery was calculated to inspire the viewer
directly that Shinto sculpture emerged. Shinto
(the way of the Gods) was the native religion of
Japan, and originally the gods of Shinto were
thought to be of unseen presences. It wasn't until
the Heian Period that Shinto imagery developed.
Sculpture of the time preferred a single block of

wood technique, known as *ichiboku*. While
Buddhist sculpture abandoned this technique after
the Kamakura Period, Shinto sculptors continued
to carve their deities from one block of wood. The
present example, dated to the late 18th or early
19th century, is done in this technique and reveals
an almost folk simplicity in its rough-hewn
rendering. (H.A.L.)

76.
TAGASODE(*)
Japan, 19th century
Colors on paper with gold leaf, six-fold screen
H. 66″, L. 147″ (1 m., 67.7 cm. × 3 m. 73.4 cm.)
The Mrs. L. A. R. Gaspar Collection

The phrase "Tagasode" ("whose sleeve?") appears
in a poem from the earliest imperial anthology of
poetry in Japan, the *Kokinshū*, compiled in the
Heian period. In the poem, the poet wonders
whose sleeve it is that stirs such romantic longings
with its scent and colors. From that time
"tagasode" was used as a euphemism for a
beautiful woman whose very garments could
incite one's imagination.

In the sixteenth and seventeenth centuries the
genre artist increasingly concentrated on the
beauty of a woman clad in gorgeous robes, such
as seen in the ukiyo-e prints, and eventually came
to emphasize the garments themselves. Tagasode
screens, which depicted garments folded and
hung on lacquered racks, thus became a popular
vehicle for this interest in resplendent robes.

The exploitation of the literary connotations
and the decorative possibilities of ordinary objects,
such as *kimono* and *obi*, is typically Japanese.
Moreover, it is not surprising that the interest in
textiles arose precisely at the time when textile
decoration was revolutionaized by new techniques
such as starch resist dyeing *(yuzen-zome)*, intricate
embroidery, impressed gold foil *(surihaku)* and
bind resist methods.

This unsigned screen displays a variety of
these techniques in the robes and *obi* that are
folded across clothes stands. Several of the textiles
simulate *surihaku* designs of lions, rondels and
floral patterns and act as a contrast to the more
subtle robes decorated in a wave pattern of *kanako*
(bind resist dots) or in simple stripes and quiet
colors. Similarly, the neatly folded robes act as a
contrast to the unfolded robe on the floor at the
left. There is slight sense of depth created by the
placement of a *shoji* screen and table behind and
in front of the garments, but, on the whole, the

painting embodies the flat, decorative sense of
beauty found in many screens of the nineteenth
century. (W.T.)

77.
WRITING BOX
Japan, early 19th century
Wood with mokume and pewter, horn and metal
H. 9½″, L. 9⅓″, W. 1¾″ (23.8 × 23.5 × 4.3 cm.)
Signature: Jikan Ganbun (or Mebun) To
The George and Verna Lazarnick Collection

78.
TONKOTSU (Tobacco Container)
Japan, early 19th century
Rotted, worm-infested wood with pewter, snail
shell and metals
H. 3″ × L. 5¼″ × D. 2″ (7.6 × 13.2 × 5 cm.)
Signature: Jikan Ganbun (or Mebun)
The George and Verna Lazarnick Collection

79.
WHITE AND BLUE IRIS(†)
Nakamura Hōchu (fl. late 18th, early 19th century)
Japan, early 19th century
Ink and color with gold dust on paper in fan
shape, mounted as hanging scroll
H. (fan only) 7⅛″, W. at greatest point (fan only)
19⅛″ (18 × 48.5 cm.)
Signature: Hōchu
Seal: Kakō
Private collection

Nakamura Hōchu (flourished late 18th to early
19th century) preferred the *ogi* (radial fan) for his
decorative paintings, drawing upon the wellspring
of fan paintings in the Tawaraya School for
inspiration. Although much influenced by Ogata
Kōrin (1658-1716), he rarely painted in the round
flat fan format used by this famous Rimpa artist.
Born in Kyoto, Hōchu lived most of his life in
Osaka. In the early 1800's, however, he moved to
Edo to prepare a book on Kōrin's paintings called
Kōrin Gafu. It was at this time that he changed the
characters of his name, although the
pronunciation of them remained the same. Since
the fan painting shown here is signed with the
later characters, we may presume that it dates to
the early 19th century.

Hōchu made excellent use of the *tarashi-komi*
technique whereby one color is applied with a wet
brush and another put over it before it has dried.
Unlike the hard-edged art of another Rimpa artist,

Suzuki Kiitsu, Hōchu's line is softened by a technique called *tame-komi* in which the ink of the line is reabsorbed into a dry brush after having been applied to the painting's surface. The charming fan painting shown here demonstrates both painting techniques particularly well and is unique in the use of both a blue and white iris in the same composition. (H.A.L.)

80.
MORNING GLORIES AND EGGPLANT(†)
Suzuki Kiitsu (1796-1858)
Japan, ca. 1850
A pair of hanging scrolls, color on silk
Each image: H. 37½" × W. 12⅜" (95.4 × 31.5 cm.)
Signature: Suzuki Kiitsu (both scrolls)
Seal: Isandō (both scrolls)
Private collection

These Rimpa School paintings by the great master Suzuki Kiitsu (1796-1858) demonstrate his brilliant use of *tarashi-komi* (where pigment is permitted to blur on a still wet surface), as well as his use of clear opaque color and sharp edge configurations. Suzuki Kiitsu was born in Ōmi province and was adopted by Suzuki Reitan, a Samurai attached to the Himeji Daimyō. He became a pupil of Sakai Hōitsu who was in the direct lineage of the Daimyō and continued to work with the Rimpa master until his death in 1828.

Based on recently discovered letters from Hōitsu to Suzuki Kiitsu, it seems certain that many paintings signed Hōitsu were actually painted by his students. Kiitsu's position, therefore, in the history of Edo School Rimpa painting is more important than previously thought. Dating the fine scrolls shown here is based upon the use of the gourd-shaped Isandō seal, signature and use of the late pigments. Since only one dated work by Kiitsu is known, dating is based primarily on the style of signature and seal as well as other technical matters. (H.A.L.)

81.
THREE FISH(*)
Japan, dated 1839
Ink and light color on pager, hanging scroll
H. 74¾" × W. 24¾" (189.6 × 62.8 cm.)
Signature: uncertain
Seals: uncertain
The Mrs. L. A. R. Gaspar Collection

Painted with soft, quick, expressive lines and an

impressive command of tonality, these three fish, caught forever in a curving s-shaped composition, clearly convey their individual characteristics. In this sense, they are realistic and can be readily identified despite the speed of the brush and the absence of a naturalistic setting. The trumpet fish (also called stick fish), noted for its elongated mouth and sharp teeth, rises above a sea bream which, in turn, arches over a broad, flat ray.

The fish are also striking for their animated expressions, ranging from the lackadaisical ray to the worried bream to the excited trumpet fish. The painting is inscribed with a date that corresponds to the spring of 1839. Although the signature and seals can be read "Keiten," the identity of the artist is unclear. The style of the painting suggests a master of the Maruyama Okyo tradition. (W.T.)

82.
BAMBOO(*)
Japan, mid-18th century
Ink on paper, hanging scroll
H. 15¾" × W. 8¼" (40 × 20.8 cm.)
Signature: Kyuka sansho
Seals: Ike no mumei
Private collection

Ike no Taiga, 1723-1776, was the leading literati artist in Japan. Despite a lack of formal education, he began the study of calligraphy at age five, sold fans decorated with his Chinese style paintings at fifteen, and had major commissions by the age of twenty-three. His large corpus of work reveals a versatility not always seen in literati painters. He worked on large screens, handscrolls, album leaves, fans and hanging scrolls; he painted in colors on gold leaf and in ink alone, and his subject matter ranged from Zen themes through complex landscapes to simple stalks of bamboo as seen here.

He was equally respected as a calligrapher, and in this painting, which displays the subtle tonalities of ink in the leaves of the bamboo, there is also a poem that refers to the durable but flexible strength of bamboo, a symbol of virtue for the literati artists. It reads:
"Esteemed for its uprightness,
  which endures the frost,
and the calm void at its heart,
  when it responds to the world.
  (translated by Jonathan Chaves)
  Taiga used more than 113 seals and pen names. Among those most frequently used are those inscribed and impressed upon this painting. (W.T.)

83.
AUTUMN LANDSCAPE(*)
Niwa Kagen (1742-1786)
Japan, Edo period, 18th century
Ink and light colors on silk, mounted as hanging
scroll
H. 38½" × W. 14" (97.9 × 35.6 cm.)
The L. B. Nerio Collection

An intimate friend of the Nanga School giant, Ike
no Taiga, Kagen, a native of the Nagoya area,
painted in the semi-Chinese styles dear to that
artistic circle. In fact, Kagen's inscription on this
painting states that he considered this work to be
in the style of Li Yingqui (Li Cheng), a famous
Northern Chinese master of the 10th century.
These "homage" inscriptions, in both China and
Japan, need not be taken absolutely literally; just a
hint of an old master's style was often sufficient to
evoke a connection in an educated viewer. In
truth, this landscape by Kagen seems to be more
in the style of Lan Ying (active 17th century) than
Li Yingqiu. The inscription also states that the
painting was done in honor of Kagen's father. The
inscription ends: "Written by Fuji Kagen in the
seventh year of An-ei (1778), first month." Two
seals of the artist follow: "Fuji Kagen" and
"Shōho." (H.A.L.)

84.
TWELVE LANDSCAPES(*)
Kyōu (fl. 19th century)
Japan, dated on the 12th leaf to 1840
Ink and color on paper mounted as an album
Each leaf: H. 9¼" × W. 6" (23.5 × 15.3 cm.)
Private collection

Born to a farmer in Bungo Province, the Nanga
artist Kyōu became a pupil of Tanomura Chikuden
in 1824. About 1830 he moved to Osaka and
Kyoto where he studied under Uragami Shunkin.
Upon his return to Kyushu, he became a famous
local Nanga artist. His friends included Keishō,
Gentan, Chikuto, Hanko and many others. His
early paintings are done in the style of Chikuden,
his first teacher, but his later works seem to be
based on the styles of the Yuan and Ming.
  Chinese influence is clearly apparent in the
present album dated by inscription to 1840. The
leaf illustrated here (No. 5) provides an interesting
art historical comparison with the previous
painting. In the mid-19th century Nanga style has
still maintained a freshness and vitality, as
documented by this work. In 1879, Kyōu lost the

sight of one eye which ended his painting career.
Individual leaves of this fine album are inscribed
as follows:
  1) "Suitei hanashi tsuki, Kyōu" (Talking in the
     water pavilion by the moon, Kyōu)
  2) "Fūu Hōhō, Kyōu (Visiting a friend in the
     wind and rain, Kyōu)
  3) Ryokuin goryō, Kyōu" (In the shade of the
     greenery on a cool afternoon, Kyōu)
  4) "Seiun mai roku en" (Buried at the foot of
     distant mountains under clearing clouds)
  5) "Ryokuheki hibaku, Kyōu" (Green walls and
     leaping waterfall, Kyōu)
  6) "Shōrin eijō, Kyōu" (Dragging a staff in the
     pine woods, Kyōu)
  7) "Keizan tantei, Kyōu" (Looking for a pavilion
     in a mountain valley, Kyōu)
  8) "Keikyo kanteki, Kyōu" (A valley dwelling
     suitable for leisure, Kōu)
  9) "Sen—jōhaku, Kyōu Sonshi sha" (Spring
     surrounds the pavilion, painted by Kyōu
     Sonshi)
 10) "Chikuhō chawa, Kyōu" (Tea talk in the
     bamboo pavilion, Kyōu)
 11) "Rinsō Kōjun en" (A distant view of sparse
     woods and moist bays)
 12) "Sekkan dokusho, Saiji Kōshi, Seiwa getsu,
     Kyōu sei" (Reading in the snow: Kyōu
     produced under a clear and peaceful moon in
     the rat year, 1840) (H.A.L.)

85.
AUTUMN LANDSCAPE(*)
Nobusawa Kyōsan (ca. late 19th century)
Japan, dated 1873
Ink and light color on silk, mounted as a hanging
scroll
H. 34" × W. 14½" (86.4 × 36.8 cm.)
Signature: Kyōsan
Seals: Nanko; Shuraku (?); additional seal in lower
right corner: unread
Inscription: "In the Late Spring of Meiji, the Sixth
Year"
The L. B. Nerio Collection

This painting in the free style of the Nanga artist,
Ikeno Taiga (1723-1776), and revealing the
"ropey" brushwork derived from the Chinese
master, Wang Meng (ca. 1304-1385), is a fine
example of Nobusawa Kyōsan's fully-developed
painting style. Active in the late 19th century, the
painter has created a panorama of mountains and
stream, dotted with little houses, bridges and
boats. (H.A.L.)

86.
LANDSCAPE WITH SHADOWS AND DUCKS(*)
Tachihara Kyōsho (1785-1840)
Japan, 1815
Ink and light colors on paper, mounted as a
hanging scroll
H. 44″ × W. 20½″ (111.8 × 52.1 cm.)
Signature: Tachihara Nin
Seals: Tachihara Nin and also Kōan Shōshi
Inscription: "Drawn in the mid-spring of cyclical
date"
The L. B. Nerio Collection

Tachihara Kyōsho (1785-1840) was a Nanga School
painter of considerable note. Originally a pupil of
Tani Bunchō and Tanke Gessen, he also studied
Ming and Ch'ing paintings for training and
inspiration. Working mainly in Edo, he was a
great friend of the Nanga artists Tsubaki Chinzan
and Watanabe Kazan. An early example of
Kyōsho's style is documented in this lyrical
painting of a landscape featuring ducks in a pond.
There is a whimsical quality and a spontaneity in
the brushwork that is immediately inviting. The
painting also demonstrates Kyōsho's
inventiveness, for he has chosen to include
shadows of the trees in the water. Such
observation was unusual for Nanga-trained
artists, much less Japanese artists in general.
(H.A.L.)

87.
RASHOMON WITCH(†)
Shibata Zeshin (1807-1891)
Japan, ca. 1845
Ink and color on silk mounted as a hanging scroll
H. 18½″ × W. 20″ (47 × 50.8 cm.)
Signature: Zeshin
Seal: Shin
The L. B. Nerio Collection

While the lacquer art of Shibata Zeshin (1807-1891)
is highly regarded today (see No. 88), artist
directories of the 1830's listed this talented master
principally as a painter. As late as the second
month of 1840 he achieved great fame in painting
by creating a large wooden votive plaque called
"The Demoness." The Tokyo Sugar Association
was in dispute with the Bakufu government over
its commercial rights and decided to make an
offering of a painting to a shrine; Zeshin was
elected to paint the work, a huge *ema* of a
demoness that was a departure from his earlier
landscape paintings.

The painting deals with one of the most
powerful of Japanese legends: the demoness of
Rashomon is depicted in flight, holding her
severed arm as she attempts to escape the wrath
of Watanabe Tsune. The success of this *ema*
produced a number of studio paintings that
exactly copied the work in miniature. This
painting, however, shows sufficient inventiveness
of its own and a more finished quality to suggest
that it was painted by Zeshin himself. The
rightness of the painting is also confirmed by the
use of the *shin* seal which, according to record,
was only placed on authentic Zeshin paintings of
the highest quality. The painting is dated five
years after the unveiling of the *ema*. This date is in
keeping with the style of the signature and the
use of the *shin* seal which was first used after
1832. (H.A.L.)

88.
CANDY CONTAINER(*)
Shibata Zeshin (1807-1891)
Japan, 19th century
Red-brown lacquer with decorations of *seri* (water
parsley) in black lacquer; leaves rendered in
combed lacquer technique
H. 7⅛″ × 3¼″ × 3½″ (18 × 8.5 × 9 cm.)
Signature: Zeshin (in incised characters)
The George and Verna Lazarnick Collection

This very fine *kashiki* (candy container) was
created by Shibata Zeshin (1807-1891), one of the
great lacquer artists of the 19th century. As a child
he was apprenticed to a lacquer craftsman. He
studied painting under Suzuki Nanrei and
Okamoto Toyohiko. He was trained in the lacquer
techniques of Koma Kansai II, but extended many
of his techniques. The scratch signature of this box
is said to have been done with a sharpened rat's
tooth. The *kashiki* has the added distinction of
coming in its original storage box. An inscription
on the inside of the box offers authentication by
Koma Chikushin, a studio follower. Two
inscriptions on the outside of the store box
translate "candy container" and "water parsley
lacquer design made by old Zeshin." (H.A.L.)

89.
MAKEUP BOX
Japan, 19th century
Burled wood with lacquer on top and sides
H. 10½″ × W. 12½″ × Diam. 9″ (26.8 × 31.8 ×
22.8 cm.)
The Henry Piltz Kramer Collection

90.
LECTERN
Japan, late 19th century
Roiro lacquer decorated with flying cranes, grasses
and moon in colored lacquer and silver
H. 18⅞" × W. 19¾" × D. 13½" (48 × 55 × 34.3
cm.)
The George and Verna Lazarnick Collection

The Japanese writing stand, or *kendai,* was
originally used by the nobility, including members
of the imperial household and priests, to hold
books and Buddhist scriptures. In later centuries,
however, it was used as a stand for written music
or scripts of the Japanese theater. In this case we
have a reading stand that was probably used in
the Japanese puppet theater. These stands,
usually executed in lustrous black lacquer and
decorated in gold *maki-e,* have become somewhat
rare in recent years. The circular crest, or *mon,*
includes a character in *tensho* seal script that may
relate to the chanter who used the lectern.
(H.A.L.)

91.
BUDDHA'S HEAD(*)
India, Gandhara, 3rd-5th century
Black schist
H. 7¼" × W. 4¼" (18.4 × 10.8 cm.)
Private collection

This Buddha's head has a deep set urna between
the eyes, and curly hair, which indicates the
second phase of Gandhara style. The sensitive
mouth and nose dominate distinct Hellenistic
features. The hair style and the black polish schist
suggest that the head may have come from the
Pakistan region of northwest India. (Z.Y.H.)

92.
SEATED BUDDHA(*)
India, Gandhara, 2nd-4th century
Gray schist
H. 15" × W. 21" (38.1 × 53.3 cm.)
The Cobey Black Collection

This Gandharan Buddha has wavy hair, and the
deep cut drapery clings realistically over the body.
All features show an early phase of the Greco-
Indian style. The gray schist indicates that this
was carved in northwest India at the time a
Hellenistic influence prevailed in Buddhist art.

The figure, with its strong yet compassionate
expression, is the work of a master. (Z.Y.H.)

93.
STANDING BUDDHA WITH TWO SMALL
ATTENDANTS(*)
India, 9th century
Grey-black stone
H. 21" " W. 12" " Diam. 7½" (52.5 × 30 × 18.75
cm.)
The Henry Piltz Kramer Collection

The central figure of the Buddha displays Gupta
styling with the diaphanous draped garment
falling to his ankles. The two attendants are
reduced in proportion in keeping with their
position. The flaming aureole and the pearl motif
which encompass the entire scene reflect Bamiyam
(Persian) iconography. An unusual feature of this
particular work is the abundance of inscriptions
found within the aureole and at the base beneath
the attendants' feet. Similar characteristics,
reminiscent of Gupta, including face type and
detailing, can be observed in provincial pieces of
the Pala period. Later examples possess a greater
linearity and accumulation of detail than seen
here. (H.A.L.)

94.
STANDING SHIVA(*)
India, Chola School, late 15th century
Bronze with wooden stand
H. 27"; Stand 4" (68.5 × 10.2 cm.)
Private collection

The Trinity of supreme gods in the Hindu
pantheon consists of Brahma, the Creator; Vishnu,
the Preserver, and Siva, the Destroyer. While
Brahma is seldom encountered in art, Siva and
Vishnu were very popular deities. Among the
more commonly encountered images of Siva are
those in bronze from the southern kingdom of
Chola. This kingdom was relatively untouched by
the Muslim conquests in the north of the medieval
period. With Hindu tradition preserved, the cult
of Siva thrived and the deity's various
manifestations became common with the most
prominent image-type being Siva as Lord of the
Dance. This image captured the deity in the
movements of his cosmic dance and epitomized
the bronze caster's achievements.
    While the artistry of the Chola craftsmen
peaked by the twelfth century, a number of later

bronze examples of the area recall the mastery of
Chola's golden age. The Siva as Teacher of Music
represented here, dated to the 15th century, is a
case in point. While the rhythmic posturing
borrowed from the Indian dance is less
pronounced, the iconography is, nevertheless,
beautifully articulated: the deity's lower right and
left hands, positioned as if playing a lute, are in
sharp contrast with the statically conceived upper
arms which hold an axe and black buck. The
bronze craftsman has created a carefully balanced
sculptural form of great appeal. The basic
characteristics of the Chola figural type are also
maintained, including a large head, full lips,
prominent nose and a smooth plastic surface
covering an attenuated torso. (H.A.L.)

95.
ANAPURNA
India, Ajanta Style, early 19th century
Wood
H. 21¾" × W. 8½" × D. 4¾" (55.3 × 21.6 × 11.9
cm.)
Private collection

96.
THREE CERAMIC BOXES(*)
Thailand, Sawankhalok ware, 14th-15th century
(a) Box (right)
Ceramic decorated in underglaze gray and brown
with floral and other designs arranged in panel
format
H. 4¼" × Diam. 5" (10.8 × 12.7 cm.)
Private collection
(b) Box (middle)
Ceramic decorated in underglaze gray and brown
with floral scrollwork; the lid molded with stylized
fruit motifs
H. 4" × Diam. 5" (10.2 × 12.7 cm.)
Private collection
(c) Box (left)
Ceramic decorated in underglaze gray and brown
with floral scrollwork; the lid molded with four
humps in fruit form
H. 4" × Diam. 5" (10.2 × 12.7 cm.)
The L. B. Nerio Collection

Of the Thai pieces found throughout Southeast
Asia, the ceramic wares produced at the
Satchanalai kilns, near modern Sawankhalok,
account for the greatest number. Some
Sawankhalok objects were exported as far as the
Middle East. These wares were first identified and

published by Thomas Lyle early in this century. In
addition to the painted wares illustrated here,
many other types were exported from the prolific
Sawankhalok factories, including numerous
celadon pieces, two examples of which are in this
present show. (H.A.L.)

97.
LARGE BOX WITH COVER
Thailand, Sawankhalok ware, 14th-15th century
Ceramic decorated in underglaze gray and brown
with scrolling vines and band-decor
H. 6¼" × Diam. 6½" (15.9 × 16.5 cm.)
The L. B. Nerio Collection

98.
CELADON BOWL
Thailand, Sawankhalok ware, 14th-15th century
H. 2¾" × Diam. 5" (7 × 12.5 cm.)
Private collection

99.
CELADON JAR WITH FLUTED SIDES AND
TWO HANDLES
Thailand, Sawankhalok ware, 14th-15th century
H. 3" (7.6 cm.)
Private collection

100.
HEAD OF A PERSON CHEWING BETEL
Thailand, Sawankhalok ware, 14th-15th century
Stoneware
H. 2⅛" (5.5 cm.)
The Ferdinand Micklautz Collection

101.
THREE JARS(*)
Cambodia, Khmer ware, 10th-13th century
(a) Brown-glazed stoneware jar with band-decor
H. 12½" × Diam. 8" (31 × 20 cm.)
The Ferdinand Micklautz Collection
(b) Brown-glazed stoneware jar with band-decor
H. 10" × Diam. 9" (26 × 23 cm.)
The Ferdinand Micklautz Collection
(c) Brown-glazed stoneware jar with band-decor
H. 11½" × Diam. 9¼" (19 × 23.5 cm.)
The Ferdinand Micklautz Collection

102.
FOUR JARS(*)
Cambodia (Khmer), 11th-13th century
(a) Brown-glazed ceramic jar with lid and molded
owl motif
H. 3" × Diam. 4½" (7.6 × 11.5 cm.)
The Cecily Johnston Collection
(b) Brown-glazed ceramic jar with lid
H. 3¾" × Diam. 6¼" (9.6 × 15.9 cm.)
The Cecily Johnston Collection
(c) Brown-glazed ceramic jar with lid
H. 3½" × Diam. 5¼" (9 × 13.4 cm.)
The Cecily Johnston Collection
(d) Brown-glazed ceramic jar with moulded owl
motif
H. 2¾" × Diam. 3¾" (7 × 9.5 cm.)
The Ferdinand Micklautz Collection

The dating and typology of Khmer ceramics are
still provisional. Unlike the attention given to the
architectural monuments of that area, the
archaeological work in ceramics has been
unsystematic and tentative. In fact, some
specialists, such as Dean F. Frasche, have tried to
draw some analogies between existing Khmer
ceramic pieces and depictions of wares in the bas-
reliefs at Angkor and Borobudur (in Java).
Although fascinating and ingenious, the
comparisons have not been accepted in all
quarters. Khmer wares exhibit a range of glazes,
and the dark brown examples included in this
exhibition is quite typical. (H.A.L.)

103.
STANDING FEMALE FIGURE, PROBABLY THE
BODHISATTVA *PRAJNAPARAMITA*(*)
Cambodia, Khmer School, 12th-13th century
Grey sandstone
H. 33¾" (84.3 cm.)
Private collection

This sculpture is a particularly elegant Khmer
figure which stylistically resembles sculptures of
the Lobpuri School (Thai) that occurred
simultaneously. However, what denotes this
image as belonging to the Khmer School is the
striated patterning of the garment and the lack of
floral motifs which abound in the garments of
Lobpuri works. (L.A.Y.)

104.
STANDING BUDDHA
Thailand, Bangkok School, 19th century
Lacquered wood
H. 66" (165 cm.)
Private collection

105.
SEATED BUDDHA
Burma, late 18th-early 19th century
Gilt wood
H. 13½" (33.75 cm.)
Private collection

106.
VISHNU
Cambodia, Siem Reap, 12th-13th century
Sandstone, style of the Bayon
H. 19½" (49.5 cm.)
The Douglas Snelling Collection

107.
TWO VOLUMES OF THE *KAMMAVACHA* OR
BUDDHIST REGULATIONS(*)
Burma, late 19th-early 20th century
Lacquered wood, gilt detailing
L. 23¾" × W. 5¾" (89.4 × 14.3 cm.)
Private collection

There are nine *khandhakas* or extracts from the Pali
Vinaya which are put into the Kammavacha
format. The Burmese term is *Kamawas*, and the
examples here present the Pali text in square
Burmese script. These books are generally
presented to monks on such auspicious occasions
as the investiture of the three robes, a grand
meeting of a particular order, and dedication
ceremonies of halls or monasteries. (L.A.Y.)

108.
PAIR OF JATAKA PAINTINGS
Thailand, 18th-19th century
Gouache on cloth
H. 33" × W. 31" (82.5 × 77.5 cm.)
Private collection

109.
PAIR OF PAINTINGS, PROBABLY FROM EPICS
AND JATAKA TALES(†)
Thailand, 18th-19th century
Color on paper
H. 55½" × W. 27¼" (138.75 × 66.03 cm.)
Private collection

These are individual pages from book formats.
Although they are not mounted in the proper
order, special attention has been given to color
and compositional detailing so that an
aesthetically pleasing montage is the result. One
will note the many types of figures, perhaps
mythical (such as the *Asuras* or *Garuda*), as well as
the lay figures and acolytes. (L.A.Y.)

112.
THREE COVERED BOXES(*)
Annamese, circa 15th century
(a) Painted with floral and other motifs; the lid
has molded floral elements
Ceramic with decoration in underglaze blue
H. 2" × Diam. 3" (5 × 7.6 cm.)
Private collection
(b) Decorated with floral and other motifs
Ceramic with decoration in underglaze blue
H. 2" × Diam. 3" (5 × 7.6 cm.)
Private collection
(c) Decorated with designs of waterfowl, grasses,
and other motifs
Ceramic with decoration in underglaze blue
H. 2½" × Diam. 3¼" (6.5 × 8.5 cm.)
The L. B. Nerio Collection

Annamese ceramic studies are only of late coming
into their own. Such fundamental points as kiln
sites and dating are still only tentatively explored.
Yet, particularly with regard to the blue and white
wares, there exist many pieces which form a
recognizable corpus which we call "Annamese"
because of distinctive decoration and materials.
Annam was an area in present-day Vietnam
which was under the sway of China for a very
long time and, understandably, many Annamese
ceramic wares show their Chinese artistic
derivation. However, the originality and freedom
often seen in the Annamese pieces are sufficient
to set them apart from their Chinese counterparts
and to make a special appeal to ceramic scholars
and collectors. (H.A.L.)

113.
SMALL DISH AND TWO WINECUPS(*)
Vietnam, F'u D'ue year mark, 1847-1883
Blue and white porcelain
Plate, Diam. 5¼" (4.5 cm.)
Cups, H. 1¾" × Diam. 2⅛" (4.5 × 5.4 cm.)
The Mrs. Elizabeth Lee Berger Collection

These three underglazed cobalt blue pieces all
have a silver rim and share the decorative designs
of a coiling dragon. They originally belonged to
the same imperial set. On the base bears the year
mark written in Chinese: "made in the years of
F'u D'ue, in underglazed blue."
    F'u D'ue is the reign-name of King Mink Mang
(b. 1829, r. 1847-1883), the second ruler of the Gili
Long dynasty. These are rare examples of dated
imperial pieces which show the type of blue-and-
white ware produced in Vietnam. These late 19th
century works which have the fine quality of
Jingdechen, are Ming in style. (Z.Y.H.)

110.
TWO POTS(*)
Thailand, Middle Period, ca. 1000 B.C.-400 B.C.
Ban Chiang pottery ware with incised design and
hand coloring
Left: H. 9"; Right: H. 7" (22.9 × 17.8 cm.)
The Cecily Johnston Collection

Archeologists in Thailand working along the
northern Khorat Plateau are discovering
prehistorical sites of an artistically distinctive and
technologically precocious people. Known as the
Ban Chiang culture after its type-site, these
communities of farmers began to settle the region
around 4000 B.C. The most amazing finds from
these early sites were evidences of bronze
metallurgy and some highly sophisticated painted
pottery. Two examples of the pottery have been
selected for viewing here and are similar in form
and incised decor to those excavated from Middle
period sites. (H.A.L.)

111.
BOWL WITH FISH DESIGN DECORATION(*)
Thailand, Sukhothai ware, 13th-14th century
Stoneware with underglaze black design
H. 3¼" × Diam. 10¾" (8.3 × 27.5 cm.)
The L. B. Nerio Collection

More than 50 kilns have been discovered just
north of the old capital of the Sukhothai kingdom,

affording us a chance to confirm the wares that
we now identify with that site. Like many other
pieces of this group, this bowl has a freely
rendered underglaze design over an off-white slip
and was fired in a stacked position in the kiln,
resulting in spur marks. The classic Sukhothai
wares seem to date from no later than the 14th
century, since that kingdom went into a decline
during that century. (H.A.L.)

MINIATURE ARTS

114.
PENDANT
China, Shang, circa 12th-11th century B.C.
Jade
L. 2½" (6.4 cm.)
Private collection

This crescent-shaped nephrite jade pendant
includes incised lines representing a curved fish.
(Z.Y.H.)

115.
PENDANT
China, Late Zhou or earlier, 5th-3rd century B.C.
Opaque yellow and dark brown jade engraved
with tiger design
L. 1⅝" × W. ⅝" (4.2 × 1.6 cm.)
Private collection

116.
PENDANT, OLD MAN WENG CHUNG
China, Han dynasty, 2nd-1st century B.C.
Whitish jade with yellow patination
L. 2" × W. ⅜" (5 × 1 cm.)
Private collection

117.
PENDANT
China, Han dynasty or later, 1st century B.C.-
1st century A.D.
Brown-black jade tube
H. 1¾" × L. ⅝" × W. ⅝" (4.3 × 1.6 × 1.6 cm.)
Private collection

118.
GOOSE-NECK VASE
China, Han dynasty, ca. first century A.D.
Bronze
H. 3¼" (8.4 cm.)
Private collection

119.
BI-DISC(*)
China, Later Han dynasty, 1st-2nd century A.D.
White jade with yellow and brown markings
Diam. 1⅞" (4.6 cm.)
Private collection

120.
CAMEL(*)
China, Six Dynasties, 4th-6th century
Black jade (burnt white jade)
H. 1¾" × L. 2¼" × W. 1" (4.3 × 5.6 × 2.6 cm.)
Private collection

121.
BODHISATTVA
China, Sui dynasty, dated 606
Bronze
H. 5" (12.7 cm.)
Private collection

This crowned bodhisattva is in varamudra.
Although miniature in size, it is a central figure.
Inscriptions are engraved around the base, over
the back and on the sides. The words have
suffered from erosion; the readable section,
however, gives the date of the second year of
Daye, A.D. 606. It was made in honor of a
deceased wife. (Z.Y.H.)

122a.
RECUMBENT HORSE (†)
China, Ming dynasty, 15th century
White jade with yellow-brown skin
H. 1½" × L. 2¾" × W. ¾" (3.8 × 6.8 × 1.8 cm.)
Private collection

122b.
LOTUS-SEEDS (†)
China, early Qing dynasty, 17th century
White jade with some yellow markings
H. 1¼" × L. 3" (3.3 × 7.6 cm.)
Private collection

122c.
ELEPHANT (†)
China, Six Dynasties, 4th-6th century
Yellow jade with dark brown markings
H. 1¼" × L. 2" × W. 1¼" (3.3 × 5 × 3.3 cm.)
Private collection

122d.
SQUATTING QUAIL (†)
China, Ming dynasty, late 16th century
White jade with dark brown markings
H. 1¾" × L. 2" (4.5 × 5 cm.)
Private collection

122e.
MOTHER CAT WITH TWO KITTENS (†)
China, Qing dynasty, 18th century
White jade with yellow skin
H. ¾" × L. 1¾" (1.8 × 4.3 cm.)
Private collection

122f.
PENDANT GOOD LUCK-FU (†)
China, Qing dynasty, 18th century
Sandalwood
H. 2¼" × W. 2" (5.8 × 5 cm.)
Private collection

122g.
DRAGON-TORTOISE (†)
China, Tang or Song, 7th-13th century
Grayish white jade with brown markings
H. ½" × L. 2" × W. 1" (1.3 × 5 × 2.5 cm.)
Private collection

122h.
FOUR SEATED BUDDHAS (†)
China, Qing dynasty, 19th century
Wood
H. 1⅛" × W. ⅝" (3 × 17.6 cm.)
Private collection

This toggle, made of boxwood, is carved in two
parts. The main base consists of four seated
Buddhas on a lotus pedestal. A separate shield
which covers the four images is in the form of a
shrine. It has a roof top and walls framed
octagonally. Facing the Buddhas are four open
windows carved in a coin design. The large

copper coin attached to the cord is actual copper currency of imperial China. This coin was attached by a former owner to add weight and was not originally part of the toggle. (Z.Y.H.)

123.
BI-DISC
China, Song dynasty 960-1279
White jade with rustic brown markings
Diam. 3" (7.7 cm.)
Private collection

On one side is a feline carved in high relief; the other side is covered with rice pattern, a design popular in the Han dynasty (206 B.C.-A.D. 220). (Z.Y.H.)

124.
SMALL VASE
China, Ming dynasty, 15th-16th century
Ceramic with Zizhou-type dark brown glaze
H. 2" (5 cm.)
Private collection

125.
TWO BOYS PLAYING A DRUM (*)
China, Ming dynasty, 16th-17th century
Chickenbone (burnt) jade
H. 1¼" × W. 1¾" (3.3 × 4.3 cm.)
Private collection

126.
HAIR PINS
China, Qing dynasty, 17th-18th century
Four white jade hair pins, three with fungus heads, one with plum-blossom, the longest one inlaid with ruby
L. 6¼" (16 cm.)
L. 5½" (14 cm.)
L. 4½" (11.4 cm.)
L. 3⅞" (9.7 cm.)
Private collection

127a.
PERFUMER (*)
China, Ming dynasty, 15th-16th century
Lychee-white jade
L. 2¼" x W. 1½" (5.8 × 3.8 cm.)
Private collection

These two pieces of carved openwork are rendered in the shape of leaves. Together they form a case for flowers or perfumed-bits with a strong scent. (Z.Y.H.)

127b.
PERFUMERY PENDANT (*)
China, Qing dynasty, 18th century
White jade
L. ⅞" × W. ¾" (2.2 × 4.3 cm.)
Private collection

These two matching pieces of jade form a pouch for housing scented wood, leaves or flowers. (Z.Y.H.)

127c.
PLAQUE (*)
China, Qing dynasty, 18th century
White jade
H. 1¾" × W. 3" (4.3 × 7.6 cm.)
Private collection

This meticulously engraved coiling dragon is framed by stylized cloud scrolls. The back, though damaged, includes an additional relief composition and in total creates the appearance of a three-dimensional object. (Z.Y.H.)

128.
RECLINING DOG (*)
China, Qing dynasty, 18th century
Mutton-fat white jade
H. 1" × W. 1¾" (2.5 × 4.3 cm.)
Private collection

129.
SNUFF BOTTLE
China, Qing dynasty, 18th century
Aquamarine crystal
H. 2½" × 1½" (6.3 × 3.8 cm.)
Private collection

A dragon design occurs on both sides of the snuff bottle, and the top is made of tourmaline. (Z.Y.H.)

130.
SNUFF BOTTLE
China, Qing dynasty, 18th century
Ivory
H. 2¾" × 2" (6.8 × 5 cm.)
Private collection

A light-green jade top provides contrast to the
plain body of this ivory snuff bottle. (Z.Y.H.)

131.
SNUFF BOTTLE
China, Qing dynasty, 18th century
Green jadeite
H. 2½" × 1¾" (6.4 × 4.3 cm.)
Private collection

A carved tiger design in thin line-relief
distinguishes this snuff bottle, and a deep-red
tourmaline top completes the form. (Z.Y.H.)

132.
SNUFF BOTTLE
China, Qing dynasty, 18th century
Reddish-brown agate
H. 2½" × 1¾" (6.3 × 4.3 cm.)
Private collection

On one side occur four engraved characters
meaning "Like the sunrise"; on the other side
there is a moon with a lady in it, done in low-
relief. Three characters next to her translate as
"The Palace Guanghan," a reference to the palace
of the Moon-goddess. (Z.Y.H.)

133.
SNUFF BOTTLE
China, Qing dynasty, 18th century
Coral
H. 2½" × 2" (6.4 × 5 cm.)
Private collection

A design of a lion playing with a ball amidst
flowers occurs on both sides of this bottle; the top
is composed of turquoise, coral and a pearl.

134a.
HAIR PIN (*)
China, Qing dynasty, 17th-18th century
White jade
Pin L. 6⅜" (16 cm.)
Holding-piece L. 2" (5 cm.)
Private collection

Two pieces used as a set that could be worn on
the hair by either a man or a woman before the
Qing period. The holder shows signs of wear,
suggesting that it could have been made earlier
than the pin. (Z.Y.H.)

134b.
PENDANT (*)
China, Qing dynasty, 18th century
White jade
H. 2⅝" × W. 2¾" (6.7 × 6.9 cm.)
Private collection

These two rectangles of jade have a six-legged
spider in the center (although spiders usually have
eight legs). The spider in Chinese is pronounced
"zhu" (synonymous with pearl); its presence is
believed to be a good omen. The spider, carved
free, is movable. (Z.Y.H.)

134c.
TWO LOTUS-ROOTS (*)
China, Qing dynasty, 19th century
White translucent jade
L. 1¾" × W. 3¼", and L. 1¾" × W. 2¼"
(4.3 × 8.3, and 4.3 × 5.8 cm.)
Private collection

135a.
SNUFF BOTTLE (†)
China, Qing dynasty, 18th century
Turquoise
H. 2½" × W. 1½" (6.4 × 3.8 cm.)
Private collection

This melon-shaped snuff bottle has a butterfly
design, and the top is made of coral.

135b.
SNUFF BOTTLE (†)
China, Qing dynasty, Jianlong year mark,
1736-1795
Milk-glass
H. 3" × 1" (7.6 × 2.5 cm.)
Private collection

This milky white snuff bottle has melon grooves
and is encircled by a poem; the characters were
engraved and filled with black paint. The top is
made of brass and coral.

135c.
SNUFF BOTTLE (†)
China, Qing dynasty, imperial Jianlong, 1736-1795
Green jadeite
H. 2½" × 1¾" (6.4 × 4.3 cm.)
Private collection

This green jadeite snuff bottle has a carved tiger
design in thin relief, and a deep red tourmaline
top with a pearl.

135d.
SNUFF BOTTLE (†)
China, Qing dynasty, 18th century
Multi-colored overlay glass
H. 3¾" × 1½" (9.4 × 3.8 cm.)
Private collection

This milk-glass snuff bottle has an overlay design
of lotus flowers and gold fish; the top is composed
of green jade and tourmaline.

135e.
SNUFF BOTTLE (†)
China, Qing dynasty, Jiaqing year mark, 1796-1820
Enameled porcelain
H. 2¾" × 1¼" (6.8 × 3.3 cm.)
Private collection

This famille-rose with painted figures is based on
the story of *The Western Chamber*. The top is of
dyed bone.

136.
SNUFF BOTTLE (*)
China, Qing dynasty, 18th century
Black and white jade
H. 3¼" × 2¼" (8.3 × 5.8 cm.)
Private collection

The black side of this snuff bottle is the carapace
with the horned dragon head; the white side
shows the plastron. The bottle has a jadeite top.

137.
SNUFF BOTTLE (*)
China, Qing dynasty, 18th century
Lavender jadeite
H. 2¾" × 2" (6.8 × 5 cm.)
Private collection

Carved in the design of a willow-twig basket, this
snuff bottle includes a top in the form of a lion.

138.
SNUFF BOTTLE (*)
China, Qing dynasty, 18th century
Hair-crystal
H. 2¾" × 2" (6.9 × 5 cm.)
Private collection

The body of this snuff bottle is undecorated which
amplifies the natural design of the hair-crystal. It
has a green jade top.

139.
SNUFF SAUCER
China, Qing dynasty, dated 1878
Engraver: Huang Jingyuan of Beijing
Ivory
Diam. 1¾" (4.3 cm.)
Private collection

On both sides of this saucer are minutely
engraved inscriptions. The back is identified as a
section of the Heart of Prajna-paramita (or
Wisdom) Sutra. The front side is a prose-poem
entitled "The Enlightenment of Lo Jiezu".
(Z.Y.H.)

140.
SNUFF BOTTLE
China, Qing dynasty, 19th century
Overlay blue and white glass
H. 2½" × 1¾" (6.3 × 4.3 cm.)
Private collection

On one side of this bottle occurs a design of a
scholar watching his wife working over a table; a
boy holds a fishing pole and stands to the front.
On the other side 14 characters forming a circle
are engraved in seal script. They read: "(My) old
campanion (wife) painting a chess-plan on (a
sheet of) paper, (my) young son curls a fishing-
hook from a needle." The bottle has an
aquamarine top. (Z.Y.H.)

141.
SNUFF BOTTLE (*)
China, late Qing, dated 1908
Painter: Ding Erchung, active early 20th century
Glass with inside painting
H. 2" × 1½" (5 × 3.8 cm.)
Private collection

One side of this bottle is a landscape painting and
the other an inscription, both done by the famous
snuff bottle painter, Ding Erchung.

142.
A GROUP OF NUTS, SEEDS, AND SHOOTS
China, 20th century
Ixing ceramics
Life size
Private collection

Ten pieces, realistic imitations of nuts
  1,2. Two hard waterchestnuts
   3. Soft waterchestnut
   4. Young ginger shoot
   5. Chestnut
   6. Walnut
   7. Peanut
   8. Baiguo nut
   9. Watermelon seed
  10. Sunflower seed

143.
ARCHER RING
China, 18th century
Cloisonné
H. 1", Diam. 1¼" (2.6, 3.2 cm.)
The Peter Morse Collection

144.
ARCHER RING
China, 18th century
Burl of bamboo root
H. 1", Diam. 1¼" (2.5, 3.2 cm.)
The Peter Morse Collection

Seven engraved characters encircling the ring
comprise a phrase of a Tang poem which reads:
*"The storied pavilion and terrace on water with upside
down reflections."* (Z.Y.H.)

145.
ARCHER RING
China, 18th century
White jade
H. 1", Diam. 1⅛" (2.5, 2.9 cm.)
The Peter Morse Collection

This ring, carved with openwork, consists of two
hydras (water dragons) among waves.

146.
ARCHER RING
China, 18th century
Grayish white jade
H. 1", Diam. 1¼" (2.5, 3.2 cm.)
The Peter Morse Collection

Eight horses, carved in relief, are brown, which is
the color of the jade skin.

147.
ARCHER RING
China, 19th century
White porcelain; H. ⅞", Diam. 1¼" (2.2, 3.18 cm.)
The Peter Morse Collection

Red enamel characters for "happiness" encircle
the ring, and gold is painted on the two rims.

148.
ARCHER RING
China, early 19th century
Dark brown wood with a case
Ring, H. 1", Diam. 1¼" (2.6, 3.1 cm.)
Case, H. 1¾", Diam. 1¾" (4.3, 4.3 cm.)
The Peter Morse Collection

The ring has 20 seal script characters, inlaid in
silver wire, which translate:
*"The valiant general who is able to pull the string of
the bow, shoot at a hundred paces into the heart of the
target."*
   The case has four inlaid images. They are seal
scripts copied from antique bronzes, coins and
stamping seals of Late Zhou and Han periods.
The ring has inscriptions on both sides. One side
has ten characters which read:
*"Accumulations of wealth, prosperity, good-luck and
eminence. Made on a good-omen day."*
   On the back is a date, which could be 1890 or
1830. (Z.Y.H.)

149.
ARCHER RING
China, 19th century
Clear amber, no design
H. 1", Diam. 1⅜" (2.5, 3.4 cm.)
The Peter Morse Collection

150.
ARCHER RING
China, 19th century
Plain walrus tusk
H. 1", Diam. 1¼" (2.5, 3.2 cm.)
The Peter Morse Collection

151.
ARCHER RING
China, early 20th century
Plain green jadeite
H. 1", Diam. 1¼" (2.5, 3.2 cm.)
The Peter Morse Collection

152.
ARCHER RING
China, early 20th century
Plain black jadeite
H. 1", Diam. 1¼" (2.5, 3.2 cm.)
The Peter Morse Collection

153.
ARCHER RING
China, early 20th century
Plain lapis lazuli
H. 1", Diam. 1⅛" (2.5, 2.9 cm.)
The Peter Morse Collection

154.
RING
China, 19th century
White jade with facet showing reddish brown skin
H. 0.7", Diam. 1⅛" (2.3, 2.9 cm.)
The Peter Morse Collection

155.
CURVED FISH WATER DROPPER (*)
Korea, Yi dynasty (1392-1910), 17th century
Porcelain with blue and white glaze
H. 2¾" × L. 6" (7 × 15.25 cm.)
Private collection

156.
TORTOISE WITH DRAGON HEAD WATER
DROPPER (*)
Korea, Yi dynasty (1392-1910), late 17th-early 18th
century
Porcelain with celadon glaze
H. 3¾" × L. 7¼" (9.5 × 18.5 cm.)
Private collection

157.
POMEGRANATE WATER DROPPER (*)
Korea, Yi dynasty (1392-1910), late 17th-early 18th
century
Porcelain with purple-red glaze
H. 3½", Diam. 3½" (8.9, 8.9 cm.)
Private collection

158.
MELON WATER DROPPER (*)
Korea, Yi dynasty (1392-1910), late 17th-early 18th
century
Porcelain with pale greenish glaze and underglaze
copper spots at top.
H. 3⅜", Diam. 4½" (8.6, 11.5 cm.)
Private collection

Among the more interesting accessories of the
scholar's desk is the water dropper from which a
few drops of water are used to wet the inkstone
when rubbing a *sumi* ink stick to produce liquid
ink for the brush. The water dropper began in
China as a small vessel on legs with a lid but later
developed into a closed container with one or two
holes from which water could be dripped onto the
inkstone. The tradition of the scholar's desk was
assimilated into Korean art, and the Korean water
dropper of the Yi Dynasty (1392-1910) is today
collected for its special charm and playful
inventiveness.

Shown here are four porcelain examples
molded into animal, fish and fruit forms. The
glazes reflect the Yi potters' delight in free
decoration and underline the natural vitality of the
Yi potter at his best. Along with porcelain
examples, the Koreans also fashioned water
droppers in metal and pottery. (H.A.L.)

159.
WATER DROPPER
Korea, Yi dynasty (1392-1910), 16th century
Porcelaneous stoneware with celadon glaze
H. 3", Diam. 4½" (7.6, 11.4 cm.)
Private collection

160.
WATER DROPPER
Korea, Yi dynasty (1392-1910), 17th century
Porcelain
H. 2" (5.1 cm.)
Private collection

161.
WATER DROPPER
Korea, Yi dynasty (1392-1910), 17th century
Porcelain, blue grey and white glaze
H. 2¾" × L. 6" (7 × 15.25 cm.)
Private collection

162.
WATER DROPPER
Korea, Yi dynasty (1392-1910), 17th century
Porcelain, pale green transparent celadon glaze
H. 3¾" × L. 7¼" (9.5 × 18.5 cm.)
Private collection

163.
WATER DROPPER
Korea, Yi dynasty (1392-1910), 17th-18th century
Porcelain, purple-red glaze
H. 3½", Diam. 3½" (8.9, 8.9 cm.)
Private collection

164.
WATER DROPPER
Korea, Yi dynasty (1392-1910), 17th-18th century
Porcelain, pale transparent greenish glaze with
underglaze copper spot on the top
H. 3⅜", Diam. 4½" (8.6, 11.5 cm.)
Private collection

165.
WATER DROPPER
Korea, Yi dynasty, 17th-18th century
Porcelain
H. 1⁵⁄₁₆", Diam. 4" (3.4, 10.2 cm.)
Private collection

166.
WATER DROPPER
Korea, Yi dynasty (1392-1910)
Porcelain
H. 3¾" × L. 7¼" (9.5 × 18.5 cm.)
Private collection

167.
WATER DROPPER
Korea, Yi dynasty (1392-1910), 17th-18th century
Porcelain
H. 1½", Diam. 4½" (3.8, 10.8 cm.)
Private collection

168.
TWO MYTHOLOGICAL ANIMAL GHOSTS
(NETSUKE) (†)
Japan, 18th century
Ivory, H. 1⅔" (4 cm.)
Wood, H. 1⅞" (4.8 cm.)
Signatures: ivory: unsigned; wood: Hidemasu
The George and Verna Lazarnick Collection

Netsuke are miniature carvings in wood, lacquer,
ivory, metal or porcelain which serve as toggles
for money purses, cases or bags containing such
necessities as flint and steel for striking a fire,
tobacco, seals or medicines. These toggles were
part of Japanese attire from early in the Edo
Period, circa 1600, until the 20th century. Their
use has traditionally been restricted to men, but
women occasionally used the accessory.
Craftsmen who carved these netsuke were not
under the patronage of a daimyo nor did they
belong to any officially organized school as did
other traditional Japanese artists.

The mythological animal ghost Baku was the
proverbial eater of dreams. The ivory example
shown here is of particularly fine quality and
early, and offers an interesting contrast to the
wood examply by Hidemasu I. The provenance of
the ivory Baku can be traced to Eskenazi, while
the wood example was once in the collection of
Anne Hull Grundy. Mr. George Lazarnick has
made a particular study of the Grundy Collection
which was fully documented on cards by the
netsuke authority, Frederick Meinertzhagen. The
unpublished catalogue is housed at the British
Museum. The result of this research is a new
thousand-page book edited by Mr. Lazarnick
bringing the scholarship of the pioneer authority
and the quality of the Grundy Collection to the
attention of the art community. (H.A.L.)

169.
INRO OF FOUR CASES IN THE FORM OF A
CHIPPED INKCAKE
Japan, early 18th century
Black lacquer
H. 3½" (8.7 cm.)
Signature: Ritsuo
Seal: Kan
The George and Verna Lazarnick Collection

170.
THREE REISHI FUNGUS WITH FROGS, ANTS
AND EGGS (NETSUKE) (*)
Japan, dated 1723
An actual three-part fungus encrusted with three
lacquered frogs (two of wood and one of metal)
and eight metal ants and ant eggs
H. 2½" (6.5 cm.)
Signature: Ichiryu, Kyōhō Hachi U Gōgatsu
(carved by Ichiryu in the eighth year of the Kyōhō
era, the fifth month, i.e., May 1723)
Additional signatures: upper right: Ryusa; lower
left: Kirokusai (with Kahihan); the embossed *nue*
on the back cover is signed Tametaka.
The George and Verna Lazarnick Collection

Occasionally netsuke artists would make use of
actual plant material that had been carefully dried
and combine it with such materials as lacquer and
metal. Such is the case in this extraordinarily fine
netsuke by the artist Tametaka. The inscribed date
corresponding to 1723, the year of the rabbit,
makes this netsuke the earliest surviving example
so far recorded. (H.A.L.)

171.
HAKO (NETSUKE)
Japan, early 18th century, dated 1739
Ceramic
Diam. 3⅛" (8.2 cm.)
Signature: Shutoho, an artist's *go* of Ritsuo
The George and Verna Lazarnick Collection

172.
STANDING FOREIGNER WITH HIS
MATCHLOCK OVER HIS SHOULDER FROM
WHICH HANGS A DEAD DOG (NETSUKE)
Japan, 18th century
Inlaid ivory coat buttons; boxwood with ebony
shoes
H. 3¾" (9.5 cm.)
Unsigned
The George and Verna Lazarnick Collection

173.
TWO NIO (TEMPLE GUARDIANS) ARM
WRESTLING (NETSUKE)
Japan, 18th century
Wood
L. 3⅛" (8 cm.)
Signature: Higo Daijo Saku
The George and Verna Lazarnick Collection

174.
STANDING MYTHICAL ANIMAL WITH
HORNS, A BALL IN ITS MOUTH AND A TAMA
(?) ON ITS HEAD (NETSUKE)
Japan, 18th century
Hinoki (Japanese Cypress) gessoed and painted,
mostly dark gray with traces of blue and red; very
worn.
H. 4" (10.3 cm.)
Unsigned
The George and Verna Lazarnick Collection

175.
GOAT (NETSUKE)
Japan, 18th century
Ivory with inlaid pupils
L. 1¾" (4.3 cm.)
Signature: Okatomo
The George and Verna Lazarnick Collection

176.
FROG ON A MOKUME CARVED BASE
(NETSUKE)
Japan, 18th century
Black wood
L. 2¼" (5.8 cm.)
Unsigned
The George and Verna Lazarnick Collection

177.
CENTIPEDE ON A MOKUME EFFECT BASE
(NETSUKE)
Japan, 18th century
Black wood
L. 2½" (6.6 cm.)
Signature: (included in ukibori inscription)
Hayashi Gendo
The George and Verna Lazarnick Collection

178.
CRAB ON A MOKUME BASE (NETSUKE)
Japan, 18th century
Kurogaki wood
L. 3½" (8.7 cm.)
Signature (included in inscription): Seiyodo
Tomiharu
The George and Verna Lazarnick Collection

179.
SNAIL (NETSUKE)
Japan, 18th century
Wood
L. 4½" (11.3 cm.)
Signature: Tominaru
The George and Verna Lazarnick Collection

180.
CRAB ON A MOKUME BASE (NETSUKE) (*)
Japan, 18th century
Black persimmon wood
L. 3⅔" (9.1 cm.)
Signature inscription: Cho Koku Juchiho Ka
Seiyodo Sekiyo Hako (carved by Seiyodo at the
foot of Juchiho Mountain at Sekiyo, the Hako
area)
The George and Verna Lazarnick Collection

The first half of the 19th century is considered the
golden age of netsuke, and the amazing perfection
of detail observed in this "Crab on a Mokume
Base" is typical of these exquisite miniature works
of art. This netsuke was made by the great Iwami
artist, Seiyodo Tomiharu (family name Shimizu,
1733-1810), and has the added distinction of
including an inscription of some art historical
importance (see above). In only one other instance
has Tomiharu indicated on an object that he lived
at the foot of Juchiho. In only four other instances
has he named the area Hako. In no other case has
he referred to both places on one work of art. A
provenance for the netsuke traces the piece to the
Hayashi Collection in Paris at the turn of the
century. (H.A.L.)

181.
NUE (a mythological animal) (NETSUKE) (*)
Japan, 18th century
Wood with eyes inlaid in horn and snake tail eyes
inlaid in brass
H. 2" (5.1 cm.)
Signature: Tametaka
The George and Verna Lazarnick Collection

Legends, ghost stories, animals (real and
imaginary), genre scenes are just some of the
innumerable themes depicted in Netsuke. In this
case Tametaka, a master of the Nagoya region,
has chosen to depict a mythological Nue. The
distinguished historian, T. Volker, in his book *The
Animal in Far Eastern Art*, aptly describes the

legend surrounding this animal:
*"In the fourth month of 1153 there appeared on the
roof of the imperial palace a strange 'bird' that was
heard to sing there every night and that was thought to
be responsible for the illness the young emperor Konoye
was suffering from. One night (Minamoto No)
Yorimasa with his retainer Ii No Hayata hid themselves
in the palace garden. As the Minamoto heard the sound
of the animal on the roof he shot at it and the arrow
took it down. As it crashed to the ground Hayata,
nothing daunted, sprang at it and dispatched it with
his sword. It was the strangest beast ever seen. It had
the head of a monkey, the back of a badger and the feet
of a tiger. Its tail was a snake with head complete."*
(H.A.L.)

182.
ANTLERED DRAGON FISH (NETSUKE) (*)
Japan, 18th century
Wood with inlaid eyes
L. 4" (10.3 cm.)
Unsigned
The George and Verna Lazarnick Collection
Ex. W.W. Winkworth Collection

The subject matter of netsuke was virtually free
from all restrictions, as this superb unsigned
example demonstrates. An antlered dragon fish of
such arresting detail and expressiveness is, itself,
quite extraordinary, but as the noted netsuke
collector and specialist, W.W. Winkworth, points
out, this particular netsuke is the only dragon fish
so far encountered that includes a second fish
clutched in its mouth. (H.A.L.)

183.
DOG (NETSUKE) (*)
Japan, 18th century
Boxwood
H. 2¼" (6.8 cm.)
Unsigned
The George and Verna Lazarnick Collection

Often, unsigned netsuke were the work of
individual artists who imparted a unique
personality and charm to their work. This is
particularly true in the present example of a
seated dog wearing a broad collar with a
suspended bell attached. Attributed to the 18th
century netsuke master, Tomotada, and formerly
in the famed collection of Henri Vever, the form
of the dog recalls Chinese T'ang Dynasty silver
sculptures of the same subject. Its surface is

particularly smooth with no appendages that
might break off or tear a kimono sleeve. There is a
serenity in the work that sets it apart from many
more detailed examples. (H.A.L.)

184.
KAGAMIBUTA (NETSUKE)
Japan, late 18th century
Ivory with gold
L. 2″ (5.1 cm.)
Signature: Nintosai Masahide
The George and Verna Lazarnick Collection

185.
NETSUKE BOX
Japan, late 18th century
Lacquer
H. 1½″ × W. 1¼″ (3.7 × 3.3 cm.)
Signature: Chikanao and *kakihan* of artist.
The George and Verna Lazarnick Collection

186.
SEATED STAG (NETSUKE)
Japan, late 18th century
Wood with inlaid eyes
H. 1¾″ (4.5 cm.)
Signature: Okatomo
The George and Verna Lazarnick Collection

187.
FROG ON TURTLE (NETSUKE)
Japan, late 18th, early 19th century
Boxwood with inlay
L. 1¾″ (4.5 cm.)
Signature: Goho
The George and Verna Lazarnick Collection

188.
SHOKI ASTRIDE A SHISHI (NETSUKE)
Japan, late 18th century
Wood with double inlaid eyes on both figures and
mother-of-pearl and ivory
L. 1¾″ (4.5 cm.)
Signature: Toyomasa
The George and Verna Lazarnick Collection

189.
PRAWN ON ABALONE (NETSUKE)
Japan, late 18th, early 19th century
Black wood
L. 2″ (5.3 cm.)
Signature: Bokugyuken (Toshinaru)
The George and Verna Lazarnick Collection

190.
CONTORTIONIST KIRIN (NETSUKE)
Japan, 18th to early 19th century
Black wood
H. 2″ (5 cm.)
Signature: Masatoyo Tomita Ju (Masatoyo, a
resident of Tomita)
The George and Verna Lazarnick Collection

191.
BOAR (NETSUKE) (*)
Japan, late 18th-early 19th century
Wood with inlaid eye pupils
L. ½″ (1.5 cm.)
Unsigned
The George and Verna Lazarnick Collection

Along with imaginary animals, real animals were
often depicted in netsuke. The perfection of detail
exhibited in this example is noteworthy and
reflects the material from which it was made.
(H.A.L.)

192.
CICADA ON A MOKUME BASE (NETSUKE) (*)
Japan, late 18th-early 19th century
Wood
L. 2¾″ (6.9 cm.)
Signature: (First two characters unread) Tomita ju
nin Seisendo Masatoyo Saku (made by Seisendo
Masatoyo, a resident of Tomita . . .)
The George and Verna Lazarnick Collection

This is one of the very few surviving examples so
far recorded of netsuke made by the Iwami carver
Seisendo Masatoyo. The large cicada is beautifully
executed on a carved simulated piece of
driftwood. The inscription is extremely worn,
making two of the characters unreadable. (H.A.L.)

193.
MONKEY WITH ITS BABY (NETSUKE) (*)
Japan, late 18th-early 19th century
Shakudo, shibuichi (Japanese metal alloys, mostly
copper content) and gold
H. 1½" (4 cm.)
Signature: (Hamano) Noriyuki
The George and Verna Lazarnick Collection

Noriyuki was a member of the celebrated Hamano
family who for generations produced outstanding
metal craftsmen. There were two members of this
family who used the name Noriyuki, and it is
uncertain which of the craftsmen made this
superb netsuke. In any event, the sensitivity of
the work suggests a great master, and many critics
regard this netsuke as one of the finest examples
in metal to survive. (H.A.L.)

194.
SEATED KIRIN (NETSUKE) (*)
Japan, early 19th century
Black wood with inlaid eyes
H. 1⅝" (4.2 cm.)
Signature: Ikkei Sanjin To (carved by Ikkei, retired
scholar)
The George and Verna Lazarnick Collection

Kirin is the mythological Chinese monster with
the body of a deer, the legs and hooves of a horse
and the tail of an ox or lion. It is usually depicted
with one horn on its head. While some
representations endow it with scales, it is more
usually hairy, as here. It is a paragon of virtue
and filial piety and is most often encountered in
netsuke in its squatting position. The present
example, of particularly fine quality, was once in
the Henri Vever Collection noted earlier. (H.A.L.)

195.
TOAD AND HOLY MAN (NETSUKE)
Japan, early 19th century
Boxwood
H. 2⅛" (5.5 cm.)
Signature in ukibori: Made by Goho Tani
Kimimichi in the beginning of spring, the first
year of the Rat (1804)
The George and Verna Lazarnick Collection

196.
SNAIL ON LEAF (NETSUKE)
Japan, early 19th century
Boxwood
L. 2½" (6.5 cm.)
Signature: Unkoku
The George and Verna Lazarnick Collection

197.
FROG ON LEAF (NETSUKE)
Japan, early 19th century
Boxwood with amber
L. 1¾" (4.2 cm.)
Signature: Sadakazu
The George and Verna Lazarnick Collection

198.
LAO TSU SEATED ON A BULLOCK (NETSUKE)
Japan, early 19th century
Ivory
H. 2¾" (7 cm.)
Unsigned
The George and Verna Lazarnick Collection

199.
BIRD IN A CAGE WITH A MOVABLE SLIDING
DOOR AND SETTING ON FLOWERING PLUM
BRANCHES (NETSUKE)
Japan, early 19th century
Ivory
H. 1¼" (3.2 cm.)
Signature: Kagetoshi
The George and Verna Lazarnick Collection

200.
TWO ANTS AND A CENTIPEDE (NETSUKE)
Japan, early 19th century
Umaregi (jet)
L. 1⅞" (4.9 cm.)
Signature: Shoman Saku
The George and Verna Lazarnick Collection

201.
SNAKE COILED AROUND A FROG (NETSUKE)
Japan, early 19th century
Black persimmon wood
L. 1¾" (4.5 cm.)
Signature, included in inscription: Goho
The George and Verna Lazarnick Collection

202.
ARCHER WITH BOW AND QUIVER STROKING
HIS BEARD (NETSUKE)
Japan, early 19th century
Wood
H. 3⅞" (10 cm.)
Unsigned
The George and Verna Lazarnick Collection

203.
COILED DRAGON (NETSUKE) (*)
Japan, early 19th century
Ivory
Diam. 2¼" (5.8 cm.)
Signature: Koyosai (with unread seal)
The George and Verna Lazarnick Collection

This fine and powerful netsuke of a coiled dragon
bears the signature reading ''Koyosai'' in a vertical
cartouche on the opposite side of the form. As far
as is known, this is the only netsuke to record the
artist Koyosai; the characters do not occur on any
other known example. (H.A.L.)

204.
BAT (NETSUKE) (*)
Japan, 19th century
Rhinoceros horn
L. 2" (5.2 cm.)
Unsigned
The George and Verna Lazarnick Collection

This stylized bat of rhinoceros horn ranks among
the more exquisite netsuke in the world.
Published in the book *Masterpieces of Netsuke Art*
by Bernard Hurtig (p. 220), the piece has long
been praised for its overall quality which has an
almost *art nouveau* aspect to it. (H.A.L.)

205.
SHŌKI WITH THREE ONI (NETSUKE) (*)
Japan, 19th century
Ivory
H. 1¾" (4.6 cm.)
Signature: Jugyoku; *kakihan* (symbolic flourish)
The George and Verna Lazarnick Collection

Shōki (the Chinese demon-queller Chung Kuei)
was a legendary hero of the T'ang Dynasty (618-
906) and the protector of the Emperor Ming
Huang. He was originally a disqualified student
who committed suicide after his failure to pass the
state examination. He was honored with an
official funeral and thereafter his spirit was
resolved to rid the Empire of all types of demons.
Here, with sword drawn, he has successfully
quelled three frightened Oni (devil-demons with
claws, a square head, two horns, sharp teeth and
malignant eyes surmounted by big eyebrows). On
the first of January such demons are expelled from
houses in a special ceremony called *Oni Harai*. The
drama of the scene is brilliantly captured by the
artist in a sculpture of great vitality that conveys a
monumental feeling despite its miniature size.
(H.A.L.)

206.
MYTHOLOGICAL ANIMAL GHOST
(NETSUKE) (*)
Japan, 19th century
Ivory with metal inlaid eyes
H. 2½" (6.5 cm.)
Unsigned
The George and Verna Lazarnick Collection

Illustrated in *Masterpieces of Netsuke Art* by Bernard
Hurtig, this fine ivory netsuke has been identified
as possibly the ghost of Baku, the proverbial eater
of dreams. This identification is based upon the
iconography of the work which shows the strange
creature biting a large ball on which are carved
clouds and the kana characters reading *yume*
(dream) in high relief. It is interesting to note the
presence of long hair hanging over the face of the
monster. Traditionally, long straggly hair is a
popular symbol for a ghost. Often beautiful
women in their ghostly manifestations are
presented in this manner. (H.A.L.)

207.
OIWA (NETSUKE) (*)
Japan, 19th century
Stained ivory with inlaid eyes
L. 1¹⁵⁄₁₆" (4.9 cm.)
Signature: Mitsuhiro
The George and Verna Lazarnick Collection

Mitsuhiro has chosen to reproduce in ivory a
concept first introduced by the ukiyo-e print artist
Katsushika Hokusai (1760-1849). In Hokusai's
famous ghost series there occurs a print featuring
Oiwa, the ghost of an abused housewife, whose
image appears in the form of a paper lantern.
Mitsuhiro's interpretation in ivory combines
meticulous detail with the bold imagery of the
lantern and is appropriate to the ivory medium.

Two inscriptions occur on the netsuke which read
"Namu Amida Butsu," a Buddhist prayer which
translates "Save us, Merciful Buddha;" and
"Zokunyo Iwa Jo," which translates "The Woman
(O)iwa." (H.A.L.)

208.
PEAR AND SALAMANDER (NETSUKE) (*)
Japan, 19th century
Wood, with inlaid eyes
2" (5 cm.)
Signature: Gekka
The George and Verna Lazarnick Collection

This superb netsuke is one of two examples of the
form in the Lazarnick collection. The one exhibited
here was created by the artist Gekka. It shows the
interior of a rotted pear with surface turbacles
formed in the *ukibori* manner, and a salamander
crouching in the interior. The other example in the
illustration but not in the exhibition is by Kogetsu
and features a wasp in the interior of a pear. The
concept is unique and the execution simply
superb. (H.A.L.)

209.
THREE-CASE INRO
Japan, 19th century
Roiro lacquer with shell and inlay
H. 4⅜" × W. 4" (11.2 × 10.5 cm.)
Signature: Zeshin
Seal: Shin
The George and Verna Lazarnick Collection

210.
ROUND RED LACQUER THREE-CASE INRO
WITH NETSUKE
Japan, 19th century
Lacquer with horn; coral netsuke with silver
Diam. 3¾" (8.5 cm.)
Unsigned
The George and Verna Lazarnick Collection

211.
TWO-CASE BLACK LACQUER INRO WITH
NETSUKE
Japan, 19th century
Black lacquer
H. netsuke: 1⅛" (2.9 cm.)
Inro: 2½" (6.4 cm.)
Signature: (both pieces) Zeshin
The George and Verna Lazarnick Collection

PRINTS

212.
MUSTARD-SEED GARDEN (†)
China, Qing dynasty, 18th and 19th century
editions
Woodblock prints, colors on paper, each page
H. 25½" × W. 33¼" (64.7 × 84.5 cm.)
Private collection

A. Ten pages from the third volume of the
Mustard-seed Garden (Jieziyuan huapu). Judging by
the quality, they may have belonged to the third
dated edition, engraved in 1782.

A-1.   Autumn Hollyhock
A-2.   Orchids and Mosses
A-3.   Lupin
A-4.   Passionflower and Cicada
A-5.   Dayflower and Wasp
A-6.   Morning-glory and Bird
A-7.   Daylily
A-8.   Sagitate
A-9.   Water-chestnuts
A-10. Dandelion

B. Two pages of the 19th century edition.

B-1. Autumn Hollyhock
B-2. Narcissus

213.
CARRIAGE STOPPING SEQUENCE (†)
Torii Kiyomasu II (fl. 1720's-1760's)
Japan, ca. early 1740's
Hosoban benizuri-e in green and *beni*
H. 13" × W. 5¾" (33 × 14.5 cm.)
Signature: Torii Kiyomasu *hitsu*
Publisher: Suruga-ya (seal used in the 1740's and
1750's)
Private collection

The actors Ichikawa Ebizo, Ōtani Oniji and Ogino
Bansaburō in the *Karuma-biki* (carriage stopping
sequence) from an unidentified play performed in
the early 1740's. Identified by *mon* (kabuki crest)
and inscription, this superb print reveals Torii
Kiyomasu II's ability at the bombastic style first
created by his namesake, Torii Kiyomasu I, in
1697 for the great Ichikawa Danjūrō and the
aragoto (rough-stuff) acting he created. Torii
Kiyomasu II (fl. 1720's-early 1760's) was the
second titular head of the Torii school and an
artist of considerable talent who also excelled as a
teacher. The print has been dated to the early
1740's on the basis of style, signature, publisher's
mark and technical matters including the known
dates that the actors appeared together in Edo
kabuki. (H.A.L.)

214.
THE ACTOR, NAKAMURA TOMIJŪRŌ I, AS A
SHIRABYŌSHI DANCER (†)
Torii Kiyohiro (fl. 1750's-1760's)
Japan, ca. late 1750's-early 1760's
Large *hosoban, benizuri-e* in pink and green
H. 13" × W. 5¾" (33 × 14.5 cm.)
Signature: Torii Kiyohiro *hitsu*
Publisher: *Honkoku-chō shichichōme,* Sakai-ya
hammoto (this mark was used from 1725-1779)
Private collection

The *onnagata* actor, Nakamura Tomijūrō I (Keishi),
who flourished from 1731 to 1778, wears a high
eboshi (hat) and holds a *chūkei* (a folded fan fixed
with curving stays), a type used for ceremonial
occasions at court and by *shirabyōshi* dancers. The
actor is clearly identified by inscription on the
lower right as well as by *mon,* (kabuki crest on the
costume). The kabuki role is identified as Ono no
Komachi. An unread ode is surrounding the actor
in grass script.

Kiyohiro (fl. 1750's-60's) worked in a figural
style close to Torii Kiyomitsu but was a student of
Torii Kiyomasu II. This composition, however,
reveals a special genius which often surpasses
Kiyomitsu's somewhat prosaic work, and it is
generally agreed that he was a better artist than
Kiyomasu II. Kiyomitsu designed a similar print of
Segawa Kikunojō II as a *shirabyōshi* dancer
commemorating a play presented in 1756.
Nakamura Tomijūrō appeared in the Komachi role
several times in the late 1750's and early 1760's;
we have dated this print accordingly. The work

ranks as a masterpiece of the late Torii style and is
the best surviving impression of the subject.
(H.A.L.)

215.
THE ACTOR, ŌTANI HIROJI III
Katsukawa Shunsen (fl. 1780's-1790's)
Japan, ca. 1796
Hosoban full-color print
H. 13" × W. 5¾" (33 × 14.5 cm.)
Signature: Shunsen *ga*
Publisher: no mark
Private collection

This fine *hosoban* print of the actor Ōtani Hiroji III,
identified by family crest, is probably the central
panel of a triptych. It is dated on stylistic grounds
to around 1796, the time that Hokusai, under the
name Katsukawa Shunrō, was producing actor
prints in the realistic style of his teacher and
founder of the Katsukawa school, Katsukawa
Shunshō (1726-1793). Prints by Katsukawa
Shunsen are exceedingly rare, and it is uncertain
whether the artist identified here by signature was
Shunshō's direct pupil who worked in the 1780's
and 1790's, or Katsukawa Shunei's student who
used the same name and worked in the late 1790's
and 1800's. In any event, it is interesting to
compare this print with the early Hokusai figure
study signed Kako *ga* dated 1796, since both
artists had received similar training in the
Katsukawa School. (H.A.L.)

216.
FIGURE STUDY: Azuma and Yogoro; Date No
Yosuke and Sekiko Koman (*)
Katsushika Hokusai (1760-1849)
Japan, 1796
Undivided *chūban* diptych in full color
H. 11" × W. 16" (28 × 40.6 cm.)
Signature: Kakō *ga* (an early name for Katsushika
Hokusai, 1760-1849)
The Peter Morse Collection

Katsushika Hokusai, with his enormous
imagination and diversity, has sometimes been
hailed as the greatest of all the Japanese print
artists. This opinion, not without considerable
defense, is shared by the local collector, Mr. Peter
Morse, who owns one of the finer private
collections by this master in the west.

Hokusai lived most of his life in an Edo
business district along the Sumida River. At the

age of 18 he became the pupil of Katsukawa Shunshō (that great artist of kabuki who helped to establish a more realistic portrait of the actor), and within one year he was given the name of Shunrō in recognition of his talent. After Shunshō's death in 1792, however, Hokusai left the school and began to experiment in a wide range of different styles. Critics say that he was finally expelled from the Katsukawa School in 1794 because of his experimentation. His names form a vast and confusing study in themselves. He changed his art name nearly 100 times in the 70 years of his active career. We know him today as Hokusai because this particular name appeared on and off during a long period from about 1796 to 1833. Prints signed Kakō, such as this one, are exceedingly rare. The name was used by Hokusai around 1796. It is interesting to add that the work was formerly in the Henri Vever Collection, one of the great Parisian assemblages gathered in the first part of this century. (H.A.L.)

221.
BRUSH DRAWING FOR CLIMBING THE MOUNTAIN
Katsushika Hokusai (1760-1849)
Japan, 1823-1831
Ink on paper; H. 10" × W. 15" (25.5 × 38 cm.)
The Peter Morse Collection

See No. 222, "Climbing the Mountain."

222.
CLIMBING THE MOUNTAIN
Katsushika Hokusai (1760-1849)
Series: Thirty-six Views of Mount Fuji (Fukaku Sanjū Rokkei)
Japan, 1823-1831
Horizontal full-color *ōban* print
H. 10" × W. 15" (25.5 × 38 cm.)
Signature: Zen Hokusai Iitsu *hitsu*
Publisher: Eijudō
The Peter Morse Collection

223.
THE POET ABE NO NAKAMARO LONGING FOR HOME (*)
Katsushika Hokusai (1760-1849)
Series: Shika Shashin-kyō (The Poetry of China and Japan: A Living Mirror)
Japan, early 1830's
Full color *kakemono-e*

H. 28⅞" × W. 9⅛" (73.5 × 23 cm.)
Signature: Zen Hokusai Iitsu *hitsu*
Publisher: Moriya
The Peter Morse Collection

On the balcony of a Chinese pavilion, Abe No Nakamaro gazes at the moon. He was sent to China from Nara when still a youth to study the Chinese calendar. Graciously received by the Emperor himself, it is said that he became drunk at a large imperial feast. The scene depicted in this print probably illustrates the occasion. Abe No Nakamaro, the central figure of the design, is wistfully looking toward the sea and perhaps Japan. The story goes that the Emperor of China kept Abe prisoner and that he was eventually starved to death. In his despair, he bit his thumb, making his finger bleed, and then wrote a poem which has traditionally been associated with this illustration. The poem may be translated:

I gaze up at the field of heaven and wonder is this the same moon that rose over distant Mount Mikasa at my home in Kasuga?

All ten prints from the series are regarded as masterpieces and are extremely rare. There is a sweeping magnificence to the composition that places this print at the very top of all of Hokusai's surviving work. (H.A.L.)

224.
BIRD AND FLOWER STUDY
Katsushika Hokusai (1760-1849)
Japan, ca. 1832
Horizontal full-color *ōban* print
H. 10" × 15" (25.5 × 38 cm.)
Signature: Zen Hokusai Iitsu *hitsu*
Publisher: Eijudō
The Peter Morse Collection

225.
EVENING MOON AT SENKI (*)
Katsushika Hokusai (1760-1849)
Series: Eight Views of the Ryūkyūs (Ryūkyū Hakkei)
Japan, ca. 1832
Horizontal full-color *ōban* print
H . 10" × W. 15" (25.5 × 38 cm.)
Signature: Zen Hokusai Iitsu *hitsu*
Publisher: Mori-ya
The Peter Morse Collection

"Eight Views" are a traditional group of subjects used for depicting various places in Japan. Hokusai, however, may have been the first to apply the formula to the distant and somewhat foreign Ryūkyū Islands. In this print of the "Evening Moon at Senki," the master was apparently drawing a parallel with the traditional subject of "Autumn Moon at Ishiyama," one of the classic "Eight Views of Ōmi." It has recently been discovered that Hokusai, who apparently never visited the Ryūkyū Islands, took his basic composition from an illustrated history book entitled "Ryūkyū Kokushiryaku." Since the only date known so far for this source book is 1831, the series is dated to 1832, one year after the appearance of the book. (H.A.L.)

217.
CHILDREN WITH UMBRELLAS
Katsushika Hokusai (1760-1849)
Japan, ca. 1823
Full color *surimono*, small size
The Peter Morse Collection

218. THUNDERSTORM BELOW THE
MOUNTAIN (*)
Katsushika Hokusai (1760-1849)
Series: Thirty-six Views of Mount Fuji (Fukaku Sanjū Rokkei)
Japan, 1823-1831
Full-color horizontal *ōban* print
H. 15" × W. 10" (38 × 25.5 cm.)
Signature: Hokusai Aratame Iitsu *hitsu*
Publisher: Eijudō (without seal)
The Peter Morse Collection

Between 1823 and 1831 Hokusai's vast talent and long experience crystallized into one single creative effort: "Thirty-six Views of Mount Fuji," regarded by many as his most masterful series of prints. This example has been hailed by many as "the second in the mighty mountain prints and among the rarest and most desirable of the series." The serene summit with white snow and fluffy clouds is in sharp contrast to the dark storm raging below. Based on work undertaken at the Academy's Ukiyo-e Center several years ago, it has been possible to organize the prints of this series according to date, impression and technical matters. The surviving prints can be divided into three groups based upon signature, color and whether the keyblock line is printed in blue or black. This print is easily assigned as a first

edition, group one print and is a splendid impression of this rare subject. (H.A.L.)

219.
TAMAGAWA RIVER IN MUSASHI PROVINCE (*
Katsushika Hokusai (1760-1849)
Series: Thirty-six Views of Mount Fuji (Fukaku Sanjū Rokkei)
Japan, 1823-1831
Monochromatic blue *ōban* print
H. 15" × W. 10" (38 × 25.5 cm.)
Signature: Hokusai Aratame Iitsu *hitsu*
Publisher: Eijudō (without seal)
The Peter Morse Collection

One of a group of ten subjects assigned to the Group One type from the "Thirty-six Views of Mount Fuji," Tamagawa River is shown as a tranquil spot for viewing the moon with silvery rushes bordering the river. Late impressions done with a black keyblock line are known to survive o this particular blue-line print suggesting that, when ten additional prints were added in 1831 (al utilizing a black line), the original set of 36 was reprinted. This accounts for the fuzzy black-line sometimes observed on group one and group two prints. This particular impression is the earliest and finest I have ever encountered in my twenty years of examining Japanese prints. (H.A.L.)

220.
KAJIKAZAWA (†)
Katsushika Hokusai (1760-1849)
Series: Thirty-six Views of Mount Fuji (Fukaku Sanjū Rokkei)
Japan, 1823-1831
Horizontal monochromatic blue *ōban* print
H. 15" × W. 10" (38 × 25.5 cm.)
Signature: Zen Hokusai Iitsu *hitsu*
Seal: Eijudō
The Peter Morse Collection

Group two prints from the series "Thirty-six Views of Mount Fuji" may be distinguished by th signature noted above and the presence of the publisher's seal, which is omitted from group one prints. Generally, sealed prints are thought to be the earliest and are always clear blue-line impressions. The group two blue-line print titled *Kajikazawa*, showing a fisherman standing on a bed of rocks where the River Fuji gathers force and rushes into Suruga Bay and the ocean, is a case in point. The print is a splendid example of an early blue-line impression. From all this we can conclude that the earliest prints in the Fuji series were probably monochromatic blue and that later impressions had added to them a second color, usually yellow. In some cases, such as in this subject, a number of colors were added subsequently. (H.A.L.)

226.
YORO WATERFALL (†)
Katsushiki Hokusai (1760-1849)
Series: Shokoku Taki Neguri (Tour of the Waterfalls of the Various Provinces.)
Japan, ca 1833
Vertical full-color *ōban* print
H. 15" × W. 10" (38 × 25.5 cm.)
Signature: Zen Hokusai Iitsu
Publisher: Eijudō
The Peter Morse Collection

There are eight prints in this series, and all are regarded as the boldest and most original of all of Hokusai's pure landscapes. Peter Morse suggests that "in its unique combination of real and fantastic elements the series may surpass even the Fuji set in its consistently high standard." The broad Yoro waterfall of Mino province dominates this print like no other in the series. Yoro is the subject of many legends, among them that at the spring feeding it has been known to produce sake instead of water. (H.A.L.)

227.
BRIDGE OF BOATS AT SANO (*)
Katsushiki Hokusai (1760-1849)
Series: Rare Views of Bridges in All the Provinces
Japan, ca. 1834
Horizontal full-color *ōban* print
H. 10" × W. 15" (25.5 × 38 cm.)
Signature: Zen Hokusai Iitsu *hitsu*
Publisher: Eijudō
The Peter Morse Collection

All eleven prints from this series depict real places in Japan. This fact, however, does not make them any the less imaginative. The bridge depicted was the Sano in Kōzuke Province. Hokusai has chosen to depict the famous pontoon bridge bent into an arc by the flowing river current in a snow scene, calling to mind the tranquil prints of his competitor, Hiroshige. It seems, however, that this print preceded the snow scenes of the great Tokaidō by Hiroshige and may in fact have served as a source of inspiration for the young landscapist. (H.A.L.)

228.
WINTER LANDSCAPE BY THE SUMIDA RIVER
Katsushika Hokusai (1760-1849)
Series: Snow-Moon and Blossoms
Full-color *ōban* print
H. 9⅞" × W. 15¼" (25.2 × 38.6 cm.)
Unsigned (this impression)
The Peter Morse Collection

229.
SARUMARU DAIYU (†)
Katsushika Hokusai (1760-1849)
Series: Hyakunin Isshu Uba ga Etoki
(One Hundred Poems Told by a Wet Nurse)
Japan, ca. 1835
Horizontal full-color *ōban* print
H. 10" × W. 15" (25.5 × 38 cm.)
Signature: Zen Hokusai Manji
Publisher: Eijudō
The Peter Morse Collection

A party of peasant women, carrying rakes and shouldering baskets, thread their way along a winding path through the mountains. They pause to listen to the far cry of a stag on a distant mountain. The scene was inspired by the verse of the poet, Sarumaru Daiyu, and can be translated: "In the autumn depths among the crimson leaves cries the wandering stag. When I hear the lonely cry, how sad the autumn is." Twenty-eight prints, including one keyblock impression, are known to survive of the series, "One Hundred Poems Told by a Wet Nurse." The prints are uniformly very fine and almost always in mint condition. Critics speak disparagingly of this series as being old-fashioned. I would like to point out how amazingly untouched by fashion was Hokusai in his aesthetic vision. He never mimicked Hiroshige whose romantic reportage had gained such favor. Instead, his works reveal a fusion of humanity and nature. This series represents Hokusai's unflagging commitment to the oneness of man and nature. (H.A.L.)

230.
TRAVELERS AT FUDŌ PASS
Japan, ca. 1830's
Totoya Hokkei (1780-1850)
Series: Famous Views in the Various Provinces
Full-color print; H. 6⅞" × 15" (17.5 × 38.2 cm.)
The Peter Morse Collection

231.
VIEW OF THE DUTCH SETTLEMENT AT
DESHIMA (*)
Japan, 1780
Woodblock print mounted as a hanging scroll
H. 14⅓" × W. 20" (36.4 × 50.6 cm.)
Publisher: Toshimaya Bunjiemon,
Katsuyama-machi
The Melvin McGovern Collection

Dutch merchants arrived in Japan in 1602, some
sixty years after the Portuguese, the first
westerners to come to Japan. The Portuguese
established trade with Japan but more importantly
sent Jesuit missionaries to convert the Japanese.
Their success—they claimed 750,000 believers by
1606—was also their downfall, for the Japanese
government grew apprehensive about the loyalty
of Japanese-Christians and the power of the
Catholic church.

Increasingly in the late sixteenth and early
seventeenth centuries, the government issued
edicts designed to prohibit Christianity. The
denouncement came in 1639 with the expulsion of
all westerners from Japan except for the Dutch
merchants who had shown themselves to be
interested in trade alone. Deshima, a man-made
island in the harbor of Nagasaki, was constructed
originally as living quarters for the Portuguese
from 1636 to their final expulsion in 1639. In 1641
the Dutch were transferred to this small fan-
shaped island whence they conducted all their
business. In this way the Japanese government
insured its policy of keeping the country closed to
foreigners. Permission for Japanese to enter
Deshima or the Dutch to leave the island was only
rarely granted. This small island, then, became the
single center of western learning and the single
conduit for western culture in Japan from 1641
until the middle of the nineteenth century.

This map of Deshima presents a bird's eye
view of the settlement with its vegetable gardens,
houses, and guard houses near the single bridge
that linked the island to Nagasaki. The text notes
the salient points of the history of the Dutch in
Japan. The map was printed by the publishing
house Toshimaya, an important publisher of
Nagasaki-e or pictures of the foreigners in
Nagasaki. The designer, Ohata Bunjiemon, was
also the founder and proprietor of Toshimaya.
This is one of his last prints, for he died shortly
after 1780. (W.T.)

232.
PORTRAIT OF A DUTCHMAN AND HIS
SERVANT FROM BATAVIA (JAVA) (*)
Japan, late 18th century
Woodblock print
H. 17½" × W. 12½" (44.6 × 32 cm.)
Publisher: not listed
The Melvin McGovern Collection

The Japanese government's prohibition of any
casual contact between the Dutch and ordinary
Japanese only succeeded in arousing curiosity
about the "red haired barbarians," as the Dutch
were called. However, the relaxation of the ban or
foreign books in 1720 signaled a modification of
government policy which allowed a limited
dissemination of information about foreigners.

Nagasaki artists and publishers were quick to
take advantage of the interest in foreigners to
produce what is termed "Nagasaki-e," paintings
and prints of foreigners produced in Nagasaki.
Large numbers of quickly and inexpensively
produced prints became famous as souvenirs of
Nagasaki. Through these prints the Japanese
obtained their impression of foreigners. This print
appears to be based on an earlier one published
by the Hariya publishing house, which illustrated
a Dutch man with two servants. This print,
however, has been attributed to the publisher
Tomishimaya by Masanobu Hosono, an expert on
Nagasaki-e, which would suggest that it dates
from the late 1780s.

Here the Dutchman, with clay pipe in hand, is
followed by a single Javanese servant who holds a
parasol over his master's head. His pose and
features—the exaggeratedly long and narrow legs,
curly hair and costume—are found in many other
prints. The diagonal lines in the jacket and legs of
the Dutchman illustrate the Japanese attempt to
imitate western engravings that were reproduced
in the books introduced to Japan at the time.
(W.T.)

233.
DUTCHMAN WITH ELEPHANT
Japan, ca. 1813
Woodblock print
H. 9" × W. 12½" (22.8 × 31.7 cm.)
The Melvin McGovern Collection

An elephant, brought to Japan by the Dutch in
1813, became a popular subject for Nagasaki
prints. Although the Japanese had often depicted
elephants in Buddhist art, few Japanese had ever

seen a real one. Thus many of the illustrations of
elephants included an inscription, such as seen
here, that notes that this elephant came from
Ceylon, was five years old, seven feet tall, seven
feet five inches long, and had a trunk of five feet.
The measurements of its legs and tail are also
given. In this print the size of the elephant is
emphasized by the diminutive servant. But the
impact of its size is lessened, perhaps
unintentionally, by the placement of the
Dutchman on the veranda above the animal.
(W.T.)

234.
DUTCHMEN PREPARING MEDICINE
Japan, ca. 1820's
Woodblock print
H. 12½" × W. 8⅓" (31.4 × 21.3 cm.)
Publisher: not listed
The Melvin McGovern Collection

This print portrays two Dutchmen and their
servant preparing an ointment or medicine within
a house in Deshima. The transition from portraits
of foreigners to themes of their activities occurred
in the early nineteenth century. In this print, the
artist has chosen to imitate western prints by
eschewing color and filling the objects with
parallel lines in order to convey a sense of western
engravings. In addition, he has added the term
"Hollander," in western script above the
illustration, to enhance the exotic flavor. (W.T.)

235.
DUTCH MILITARY PARADE
Japan, early 19th century
Woodblock print
H. 12" × W. 7⅞" (30.8 × 20 cm.)
Publisher: Matsunagaya
The Melvin McGovern Collection

This print, as explained in the inscription, is of a
Dutch procession. Although the soldiers hold
guns, it is not particularly militaristic. The print
combines several types of figures, such as the
drummers or the young man with a dog, that
were frequently used in other prints of military
parades. The publisher, Matsunagaya, began
producing prints in the early nineteenth century
and this print is thought to date from about 1810-
1820. (W.T.)

236.
DUTCH INSPECTION TOUR
Japan, early 19th century
Woodblock print
H. 12½" × W. 7⅞" (31.4 × 20 cm.)
Publisher: Bunkindo
The Melvin McGovern Collection

This print illustrates an inspection tour. The
publishing house, Bunkindo, was founded shortly
before 1800 and established its reputation with
prints of more complex compositions than are
found in earlier Nagasaki prints. A clue to the
dating may be found in the inclusion of depictions
of western women. Western women were not
allowed to enter Japan, but in 1817 a Dutch
merchant brought his wife, child and a nurse to
Japan where they stayed for a few months, and
again in 1829 another wife tried to join her
husband on Deshima. These attempts to defy the
official policy stimulated a renewed interest in
illustrations of western women, a subject that had
been used infrequently in earlier periods. (W.T.)

237.
RUSSIAN SOLIDERS
Japan, early 19th century
Woodblock print
H. 12½" × W. 9" (31.7 × 22.8 cm.)
Publisher: not listed
The Melvin McGovern Collection

The inscription above the five Russian soldiers
informs the viewer that a Russian envoy had
arrived in Japan on the seventh day of the ninth
month of 1804, stayed in Nagasaki and departed
on the nineteenth day of the third month of 1805.
To the left of the Russian flag are the names of the
envoy, Nicolai Rezanov, and the captain of the
ship, Captain Krusenstern.
    The event to which this print refers created a
great deal of consternation within the Japanese
government. The Russian arrival and Ambassador
Rezanov's request for open trade between the two
nations resulted in six months of heated
discussion in the Japanese government. There was
considerable goodwill toward the Russians,
because in 1792 a Russian ship had returned three
shipwrecked Japanese sailors who had spent some
nine years in Russia before they were permitted to
return to Japan. One of the castaways had given
detailed and laudatory descriptions of Russian life.
In the end, however, Japan refused to open their

country, and the Russians, after waiting six
months in Nagasaki, had to return home without
a trade treaty. The print was probably produced
shortly after their departure. (W.T.)

238.
PORTRAIT OF A RUSSIAN SOLDIER
Japan, early 19th century
Woodblock print
H. 14¾″ × W. 6¼″ (37.4 × 15.8 cm.)
Publisher: Yamatoya
The Melvin McGovern Collection

Unlike the Dutch merchants, Russians were
portrayed without servants and often with a quiet
dignity. In this print a Russian soldier stands in
full regalia. His size is emphasized not only by the
long, narrow format but also by the small, distant
ship and hills. (W.T.)

239.
DUTCHMAN WITH SERVANT AND OSTRICH
Japan, early 19th century
Woodblock print
H. 12″ × W. 8¾″ (30.4 × 22.2 cm.)
Publisher: Bunkindo
The Melvin McGovern Collection

This print purports to illustrate a most remarkable
bird, one that eats fire. While the Dutchman gazes
indifferently, his servant offers a flaming piece of
charcoal to an ostrich. In fact the ostrich, which
the Dutch had imported, did peck at pieces of
charcoal, but it was seeking the carbon not the
fire. The mistaken notion that the westerners had
a miraculous fire-eating bird is forever captured
by this print. (W.T.)

240.
CHINESE SCHOLARS AT CALLIGRAPHY
PRACTICE (*)
Japan, early 19th century
Woodblock print
H. 14½″ × W. 10½″ (36.8 × 26.7 cm.)
Publisher: Yamatoya
The Melvin McGovern Collection

The long experience of contact with China allowed
the Japanese to perceive the Chinese in Nagasaki
as less strange and puzzling than the Dutch.
Perhaps because of this perception the Japanese

prints of Chinese tend to have a naturalness that
is lacking in prints of the westerners. Indeed,
depictions of the Chinese often stress the
traditional qualities and activities that the Japanese
had always admired in the Chinese, such as their
reputation as scholars, calligraphers and men of
accomplishment.

In this print two scholars sit at a Chinese table,
surrounded by the bookshelf and books that
characterize them as literary men. While one man
checks a book, the other prepares to inscribe a
fan. In the background is a painting of lotus
flowers. The sophistication of the print is revealed
in details such as the dragons on the back of the
Chinese chairs and the complex treasure pattern
and cloud patterns of the robes. The print can be
dated to the third or fourth decade of the
nineteenth century. (W.T.)

241.
DUTCH SHIP (†)
Japan, early 19th century
Woodblock print
H. 12″ × W. 9″ (30.5 × 22.8 cm.)
Publisher: Bunkindo
The Melvin McGovern Collection

Similar in size and composition to a print of a
Chinese ship also on display, this print depicts a
Dutch ship accompanied by an inscription noting
that the ship is twenty-eight "ken" or almost sixty
meters long, fourteen and one-half meters wide,
with a mast of about fifty-four and one-half
meters, and a crew of about fifty. Distances to
such places as Taiwan, Madagascar, Portugal,
England, Russia and other ports are also noted. In
addition, the inscription mentions that this ship
arrived in Japan in 1641, although the print itself
dates from the early nineteenth century. (W.T.)

242.
CHINESE SHIP
Japan, early 19th century
Woodblock print
H. 13″ × W. 8½″ (33 × 21.6 cm.)
Publisher: Bunkindo
The Melvin McGovern Collection

This print depicts a Chinese ship departing Japan.
The inscription gives the distances to Shanghai,
Nanking, Canton, Peking and other Chinese
ports. In addition, it reveals the length of the ship
to be 25 *ken* or forty-five and one-half meters,

thirteen meters wide, with a mast of about forty-five and one-half meters, and a crew of about one hundred hands. Chinese and Dutch ships were popular subjects for prints and paintings, and, like the portraits of foreigners, the same model was often repeated. (W.T.)

243.
MISTY MORNING (†)
Japan, 1964
Woodblock print in color, artist's proof
H. 19½" × W. 15¾" (50 × 40 cm.)
Signature: Ansei Uchima
The Oliver Statler Collection

This highly sensitive and atmospheric woodblock print is surely one of Uchima's masterworks of the 1960's. Uchima was born and grew up in Los Angeles. After high school came the question of college. He had already decided that he wanted to be an artist, but his father objected on the grounds that art was a precarious way to earn a living. They compromised on architecture, and at nineteen, Ansei went to Japan to study at Waseda University's noted school of architecture. Less than two years later, war erupted in the Pacific; he was cut off from home and thus took advantage of his freedom to leave architecture for art. He studied painting.

In late 1954 Oliver Statler met Uchima and asked him to interpret in a series of interviews with some of Japan's print artists, preparation for a paper on Japan's modern prints that Statler was to present to the Asiatic Society of Japan. Uchima was ideally suited for this work. He was not only bilingual but could talk with other artists as an artist. Uchima continued to assist Statler in more interviews that led to the writing of *Modern Japanese Prints: An Art Reborn*, and helped Statler when he was reviewing art exhibitions for the *Asahi Evening News*. The two formed a lasting friendship. It was largely a result of interviewing print artists with Statler that Uchima turned to prints and especially the woodblock, which he uses in typically Japanese ways.

In 1960 Uchima returned to the United States with his wife and small child and settled in New York. Since then he has achieved a successful career as an artist and as a teacher at Sarah Lawrence College and Columbia University. His prints have been widely shown at galleries and exhibitions. (H.A.L.)

244.
WIND IN THE MAPLE TREE (*)
Japan, 1961
Woodblock print with special embossing
H. 24¼" × W. 18" (61.6 × 45.7 cm.)
Signature: K. Sasajima
Seal: Sasajima
The Hackler Collection

Kihei Sasajima (1906-present) is a student of both Hiratsuka and Munakata, who have specialized in the black and white woodblock medium. Sasajima has usually chosen to work in a similar way, and some critics find him as masterful as his teachers in controlling the interplay of black and white to create a stark, highly expressive effect. Oliver Statler (*Modern Japanese Prints: An Art Reborn*, 1956, p. 167) wrote a particularly apt description: "He uses a line that is longer than Hiratsuka's and closer to the brushstroke. He believes that this has been derived from his study of Munakata, calligraphy and the Nanga painters of both China and Japan, especially Taiga and Tessai."

Ike no taigo is represented in the current exhibition and, particularly in the calligraphy of the painting, one can see a relationship to Sasajima's art. "Wind in the Maple Tree" is a black impression on very thin white paper. The artist has dampened this soft paper thoroughly and has pressed it deep into the surface of the block to create a dappled surface and the three dimensional effect for which he is so famous. Along with the pencilled signature and date is included the fact that this is the 27th impression out of a 50-print edition. (H.A.L.)

245.
POEM—S (*)
Japan, mid 1960's
Woodblock print in black, grey and yellow with embossing
H. 21¼" × W. 14¼" (54 × 36.2 cm.)
Signature: Haku Maki
Seal: Haku
The Hackler Collection

The clean-cut line and embossing in this print are typical of much of the work of Haku Maki (1924-present). He frequently achieves rough texture, as in the three squares here, by working the designs in wet cement. Commenting on a print similar to this, Maki wrote (in free translation): "I have tried to capture the typically Japanese expression of the beauty of space, the sense of reverence for and persistent pursuit of boundless space, while at the same time taking advantage of the boundary provided by the beauty and life of the paper itself. The beauty of sumi, in its monochrome black, penetrates to the back of the paper and forbids decorative exaggeration or irrelevancies. This effect combines with a succinct and straightforward approach to create a space and an expression that, though intentionally compact, still have a quiet and gentle spread."

Maki's international reputation was enhanced by his illustrations, woodblock prints, for *Festive Wine*, a book of ancient Japanese poems, published in 1969. (H.A.L.)

246.
FLUTE PLAYER (*)
Japan, 1970
Woodblock print in blue, white and silver with embossing
H. 14½" × W. 18½" (36.8 × 47 cm.)
Signature: Kōjin Toneyama (in pencil)
The Hackler Collection

Kōjin Toneyama (1921-present) is represented here by a stunning print with a silver horizontal stripe, the flute, embossed to give the design a three dimensional aspect. The specialist, Francis Blakemore (*Who's Who in Japanese Prints*, 1975, p. 215), has written of the artist: "Toneyama has developed a unique talent for reducing a representational motif to the absolute minimum and yet preserving its identifiable qualities—the arms and hands of a flutist executed in one unending brush stroke . . ." (H.A.L.)

247.
WORK-LANDSCAPE
Japan, 1950's
Woodblock print
H. 21½" × W. 17½" (54.6 × 44.5 cm.)
Signature: Ben Itoh
The Hackler Collection

248.
CAT MAKING UP
Japan, 1955
Woodblock print
H. 23" × W. 16⅞" (58.4 × 42.7 cm.)
Signature: T. Inagaki, lower right; Tomo, lower left
The Hackler Collection

249.
DANCE
Japan, 1956
Glass transfer print
H. 13" × W. 21½" (33 × 54.6 cm.)
Signature: A. Uchima
The Hackler Collection

250.
YOUTH
Japan, 1958
Woodblock print
H. 19" × W. 13¾" (48.3 × 34.9 cm.)
Signature: A. Uchima
The Hackler Collection

251.
RIVER
Japan, 1958
Woodblock print
H. 13¾" × W. 12" (34.9 × 30.5 cm.)
Signature: T. Ono
The Hackler Collection

252.
CIRCUS
Japan, 1959
Woodblock print
H. 17" × W. 11" (43.2 × 30 cm.)
Signature: Hideo Hagiwara—59
The Hackler Collection

253.
MOORLAND
Japan, 1959
Woodblock print
H. 16" × W. 22½" (40.6 × 57 cm.)
Signature: Hideo Hagiwara—59
The Hackler Collection

254.
CARRY
Japan, 1959
Woodblock print
H. 15½" × W. 22½" (39.4 × 57.3 cm.)
Signature: Kanji Suzuki
The Hackler Collection

255.
CHANCE ENCOUNTER
Japan, 1960
Woodblock print
H. 20¼" × W. 14" (51.4 × 35.6 cm.)
Signature: Takumi Shinagawa
The Hackler Collection

256.
THUNDER NO. 5
Japan, 1961
Woodblock print
H. 13" × W. 13" (33 × 33 cm.)
Signature: Masaji Yoshida
The Hackler Collection

257.
UNTITLED
Japan, 1965
Woodblock print
H. 17¾" × 12 ¾" (45 × 32.4 cm.)
Signature: Haku Maki
The Hackler Collection

258.
FIGURES
Japan, 1968
Woodblock print
H. 11¾" × W. 17¾" (29.8 × 45.1 cm.)
Signature: Iwata
The Hackler Collection

Classical: *China* and the Scholar's Desk

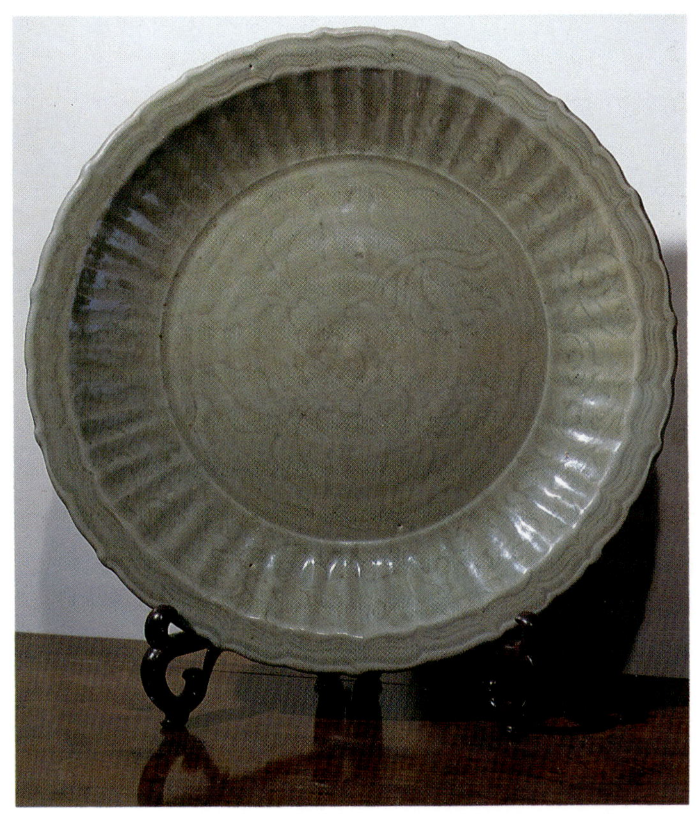

10   PLATE, China, 14th century, celadon stoneware

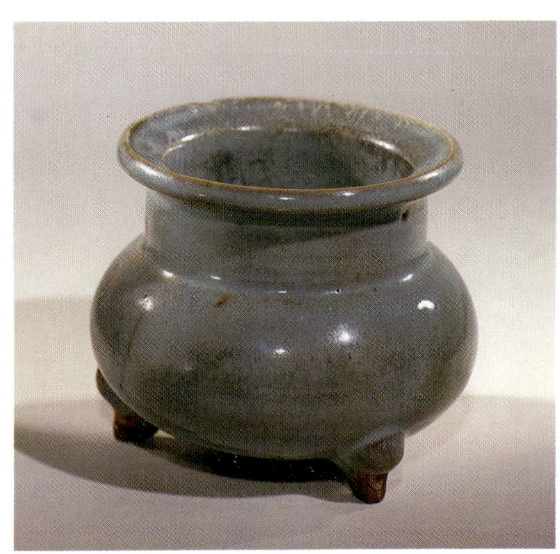

9   INCENSE BURNER, China, 12th-13th century, stoneware

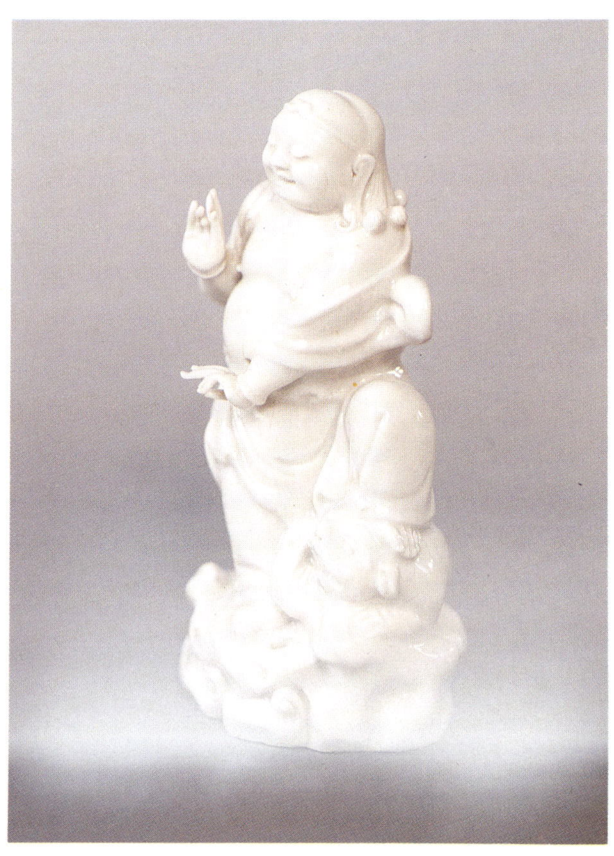

13　LIUHAI DEITY, China, 16th century,
Dehua porcelain

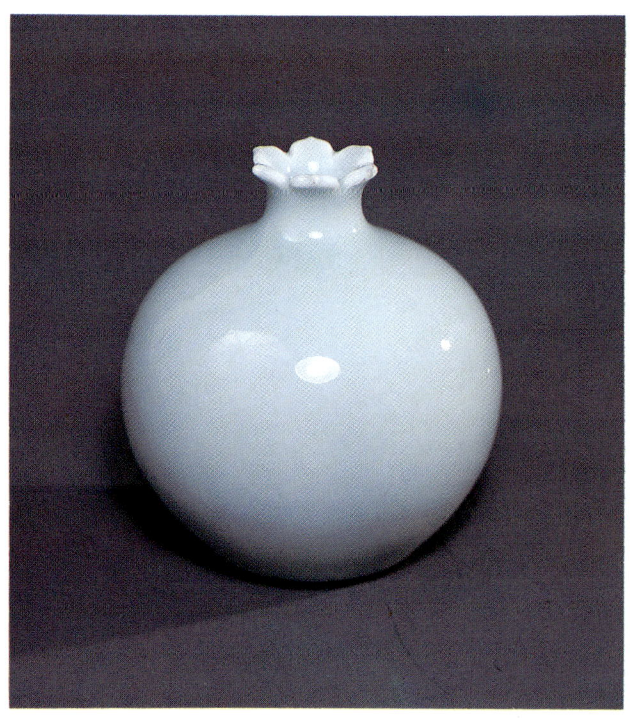

26　POMEGRANATE VASE,
China, 1736-1795, porcelain

43 PEONY AND ROCK, Wu Zhangshi (1844-1927),
China, dated 1895, hanging scroll

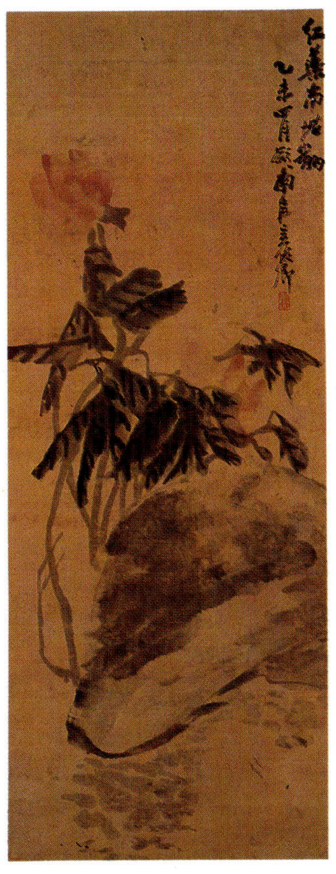

35 LANDSCAPE, Tang Ifen (1778-1853), China,
dated 1849, album leaf

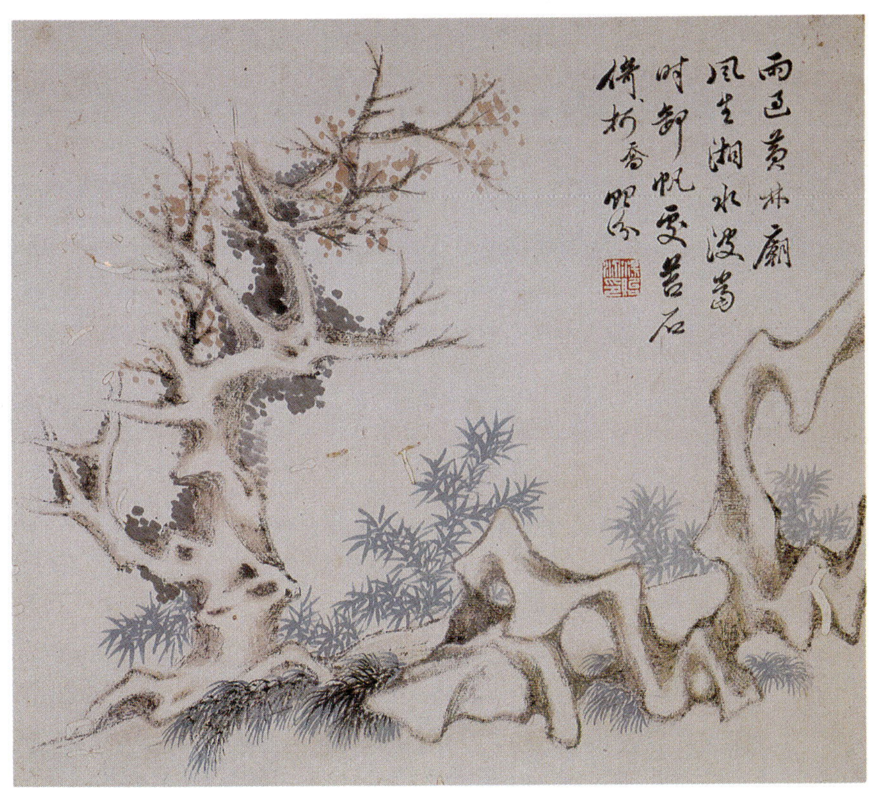

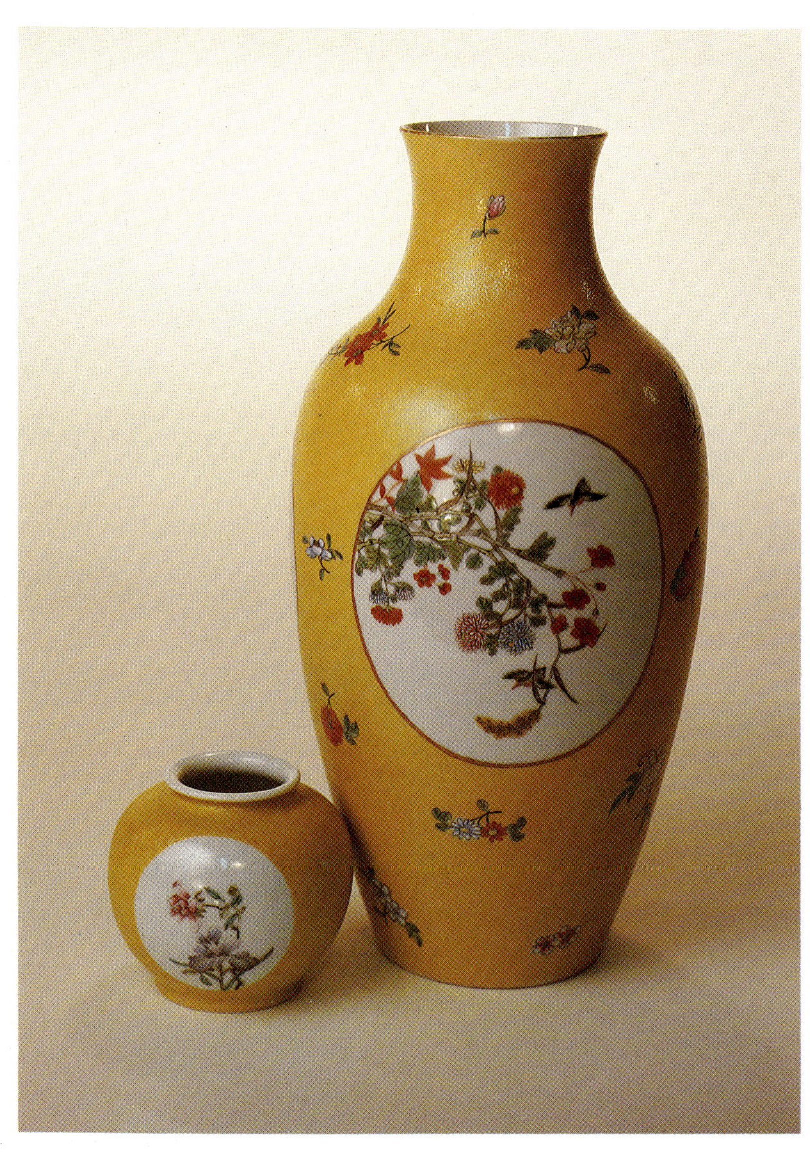

45   JAR AND VASE, China, 1916-17, porcelain

1   PAIR OF BRONZE FITTINGS, China, ca. 8th century B.C.

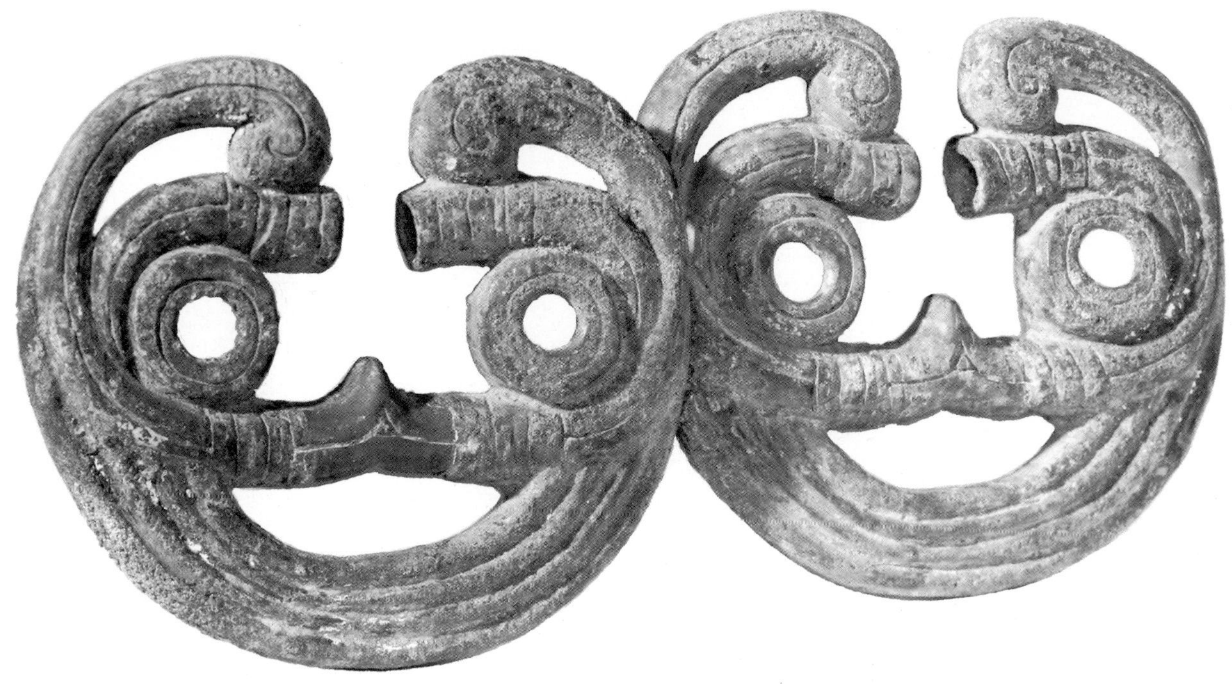

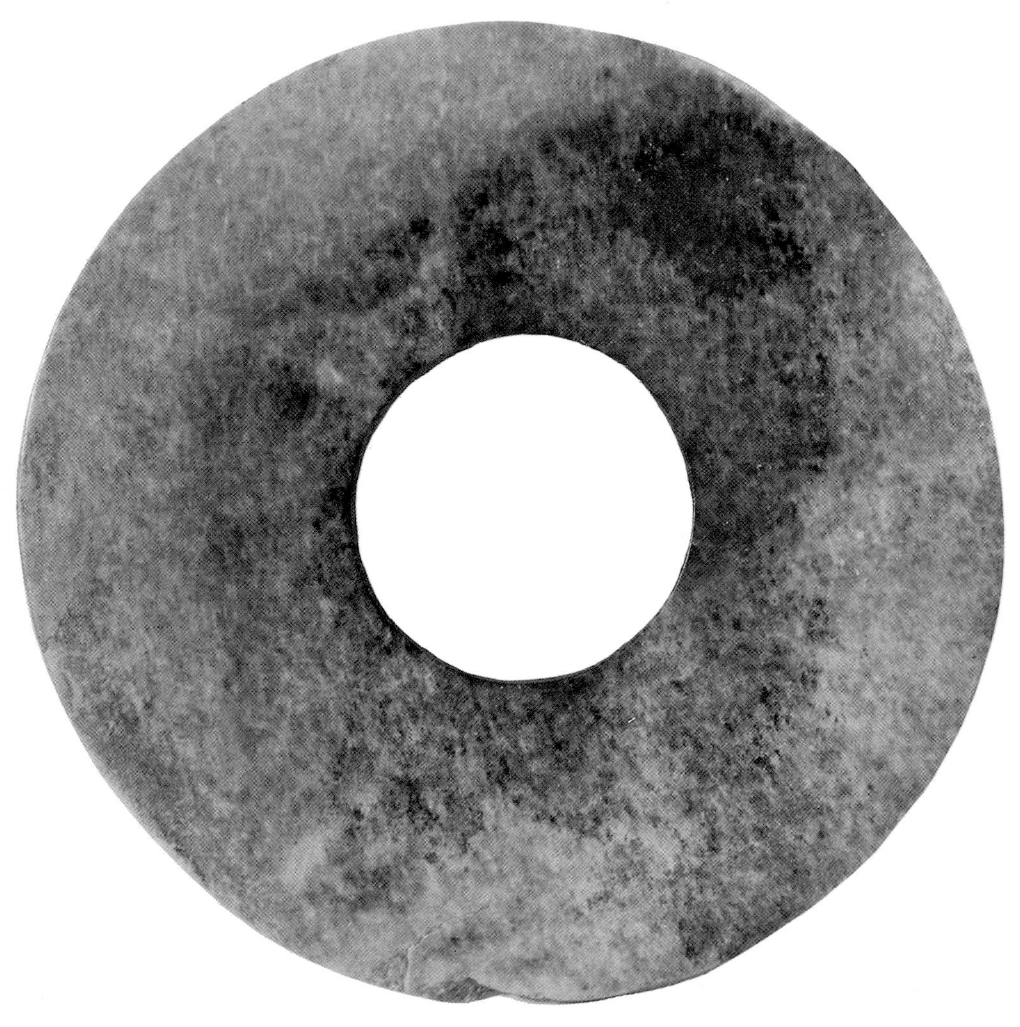
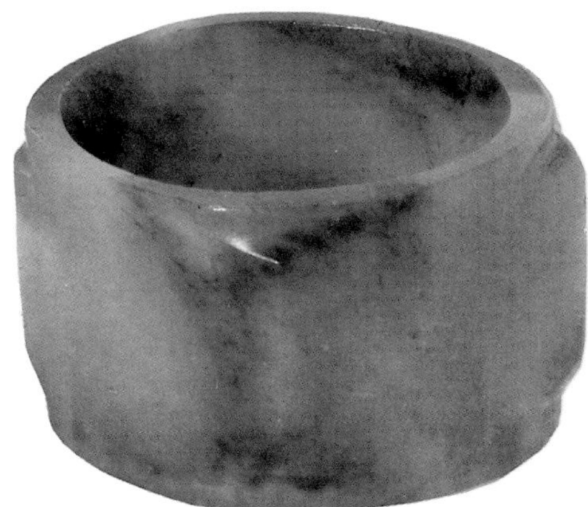

2   (a) BI-DISC (b) CONG CYLINDER (jade), China
     (a) 9th-8th century B.C. (b) 3rd-2nd century B.C.

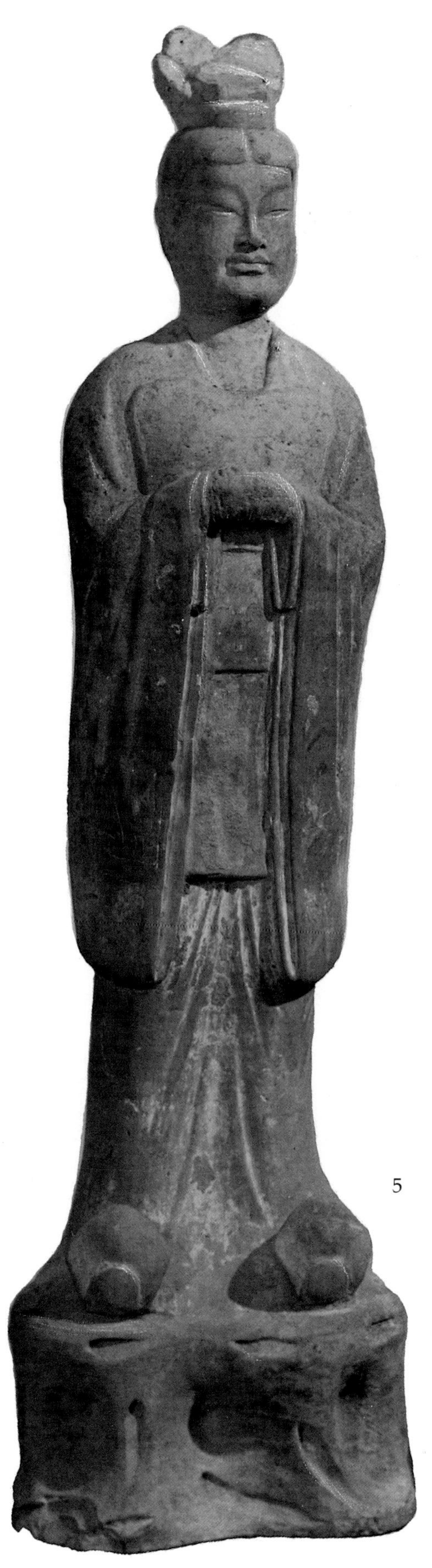

5   STATESMAN, China, early 7th century, terracotta

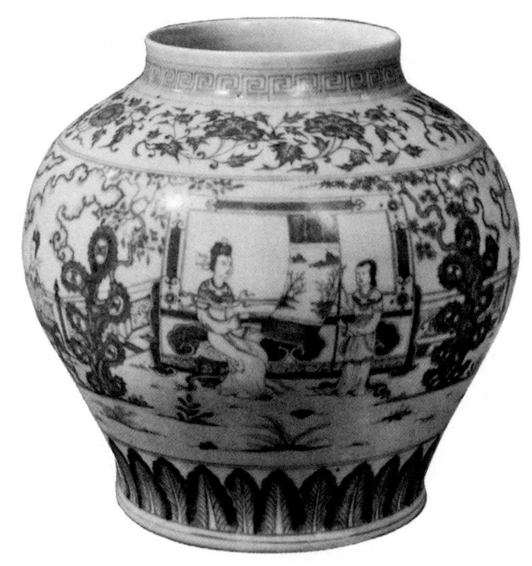

11   LARGE JAR, China, late 15th century, blue and white porcelain

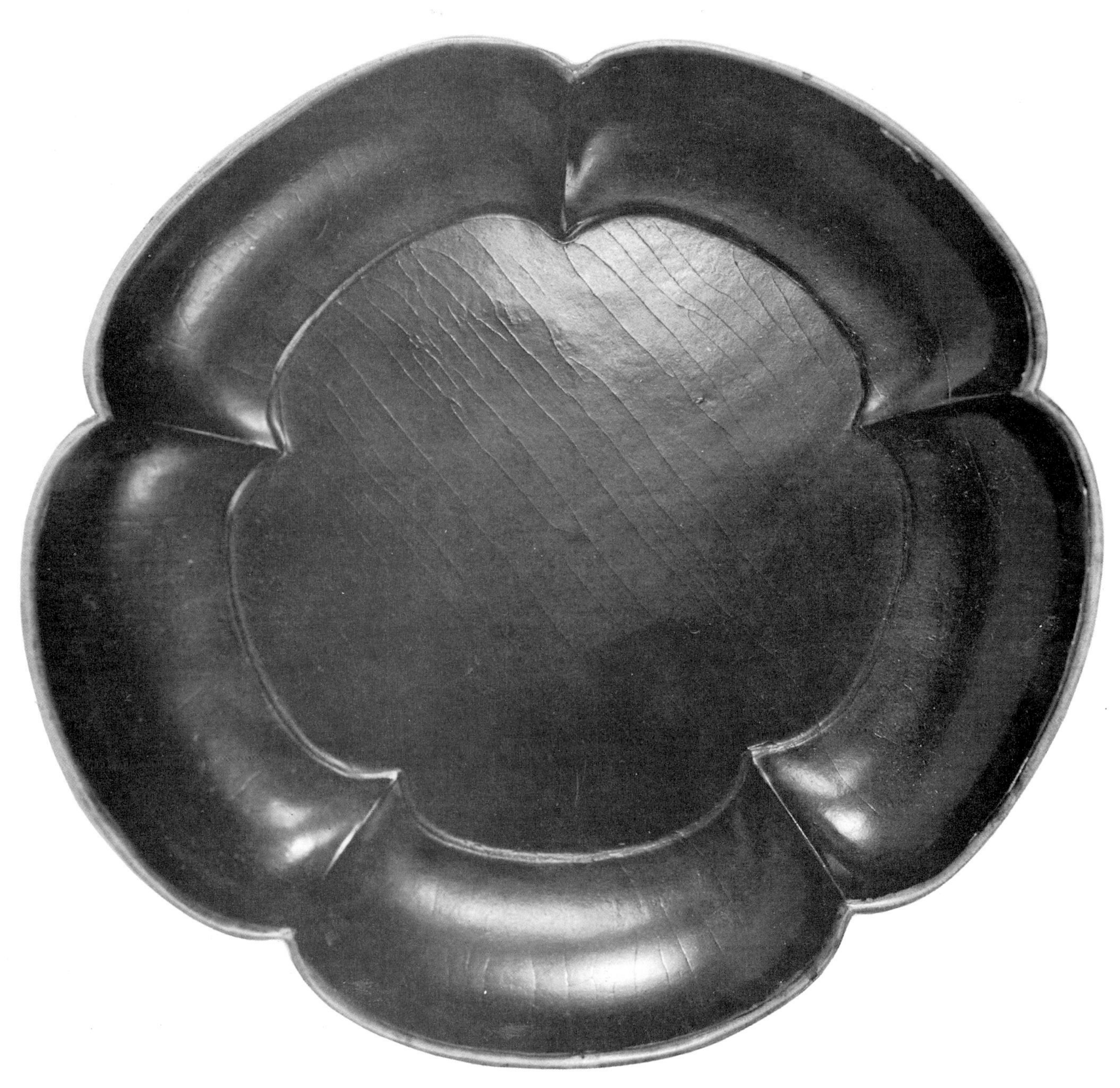

6   PLATE, China, 960-1125, lacquer

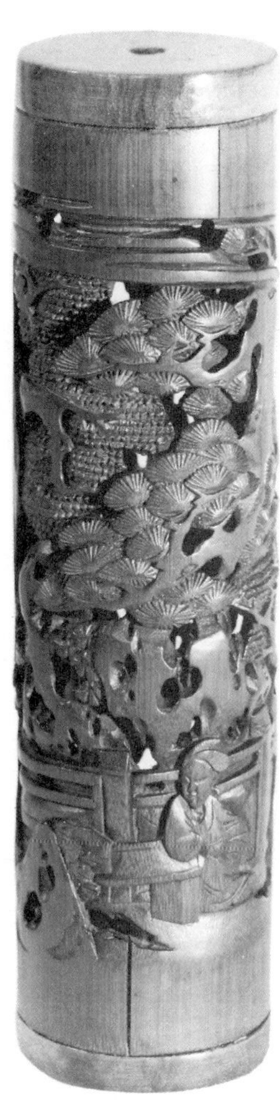

16   PERFUMER, China, 17th century, bamboo

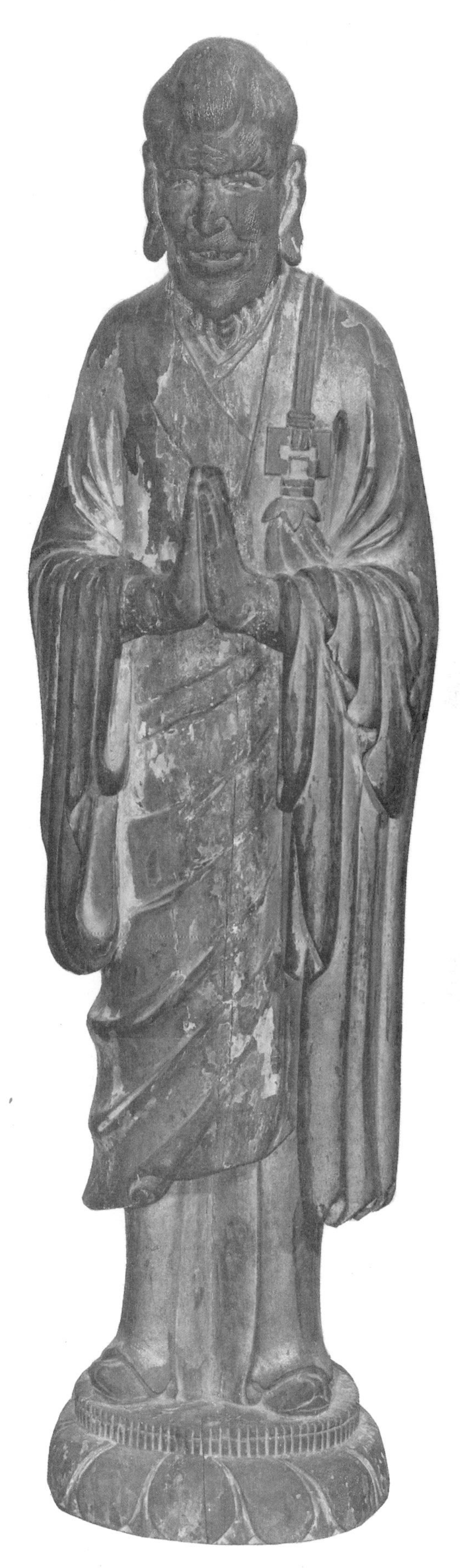

8   LOHAN, China, 12th-13th century, wood

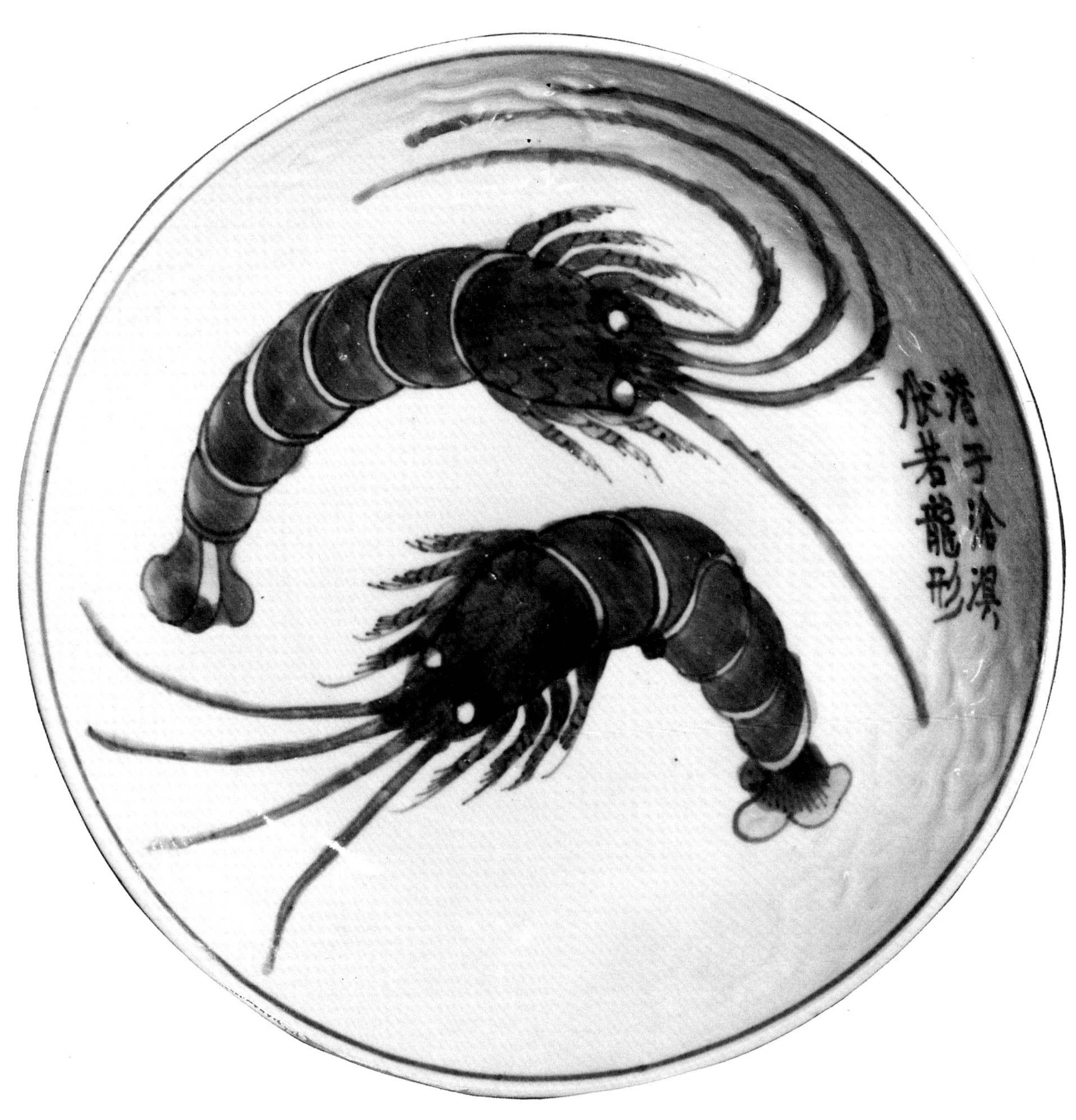

   15   PLATE, China, early 17th century, blue and white porcelain

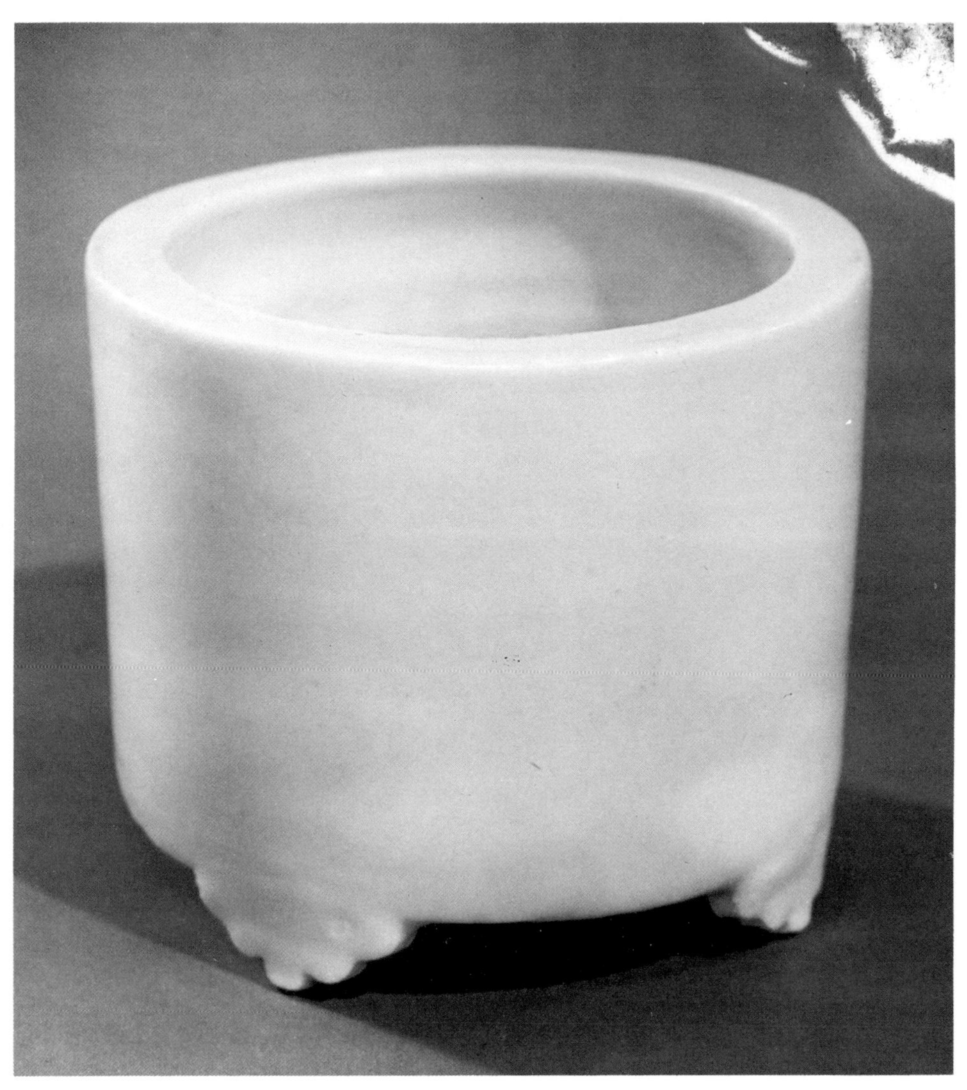

17   INCENSE BURNER, China, 17th century, Dehua porcelain

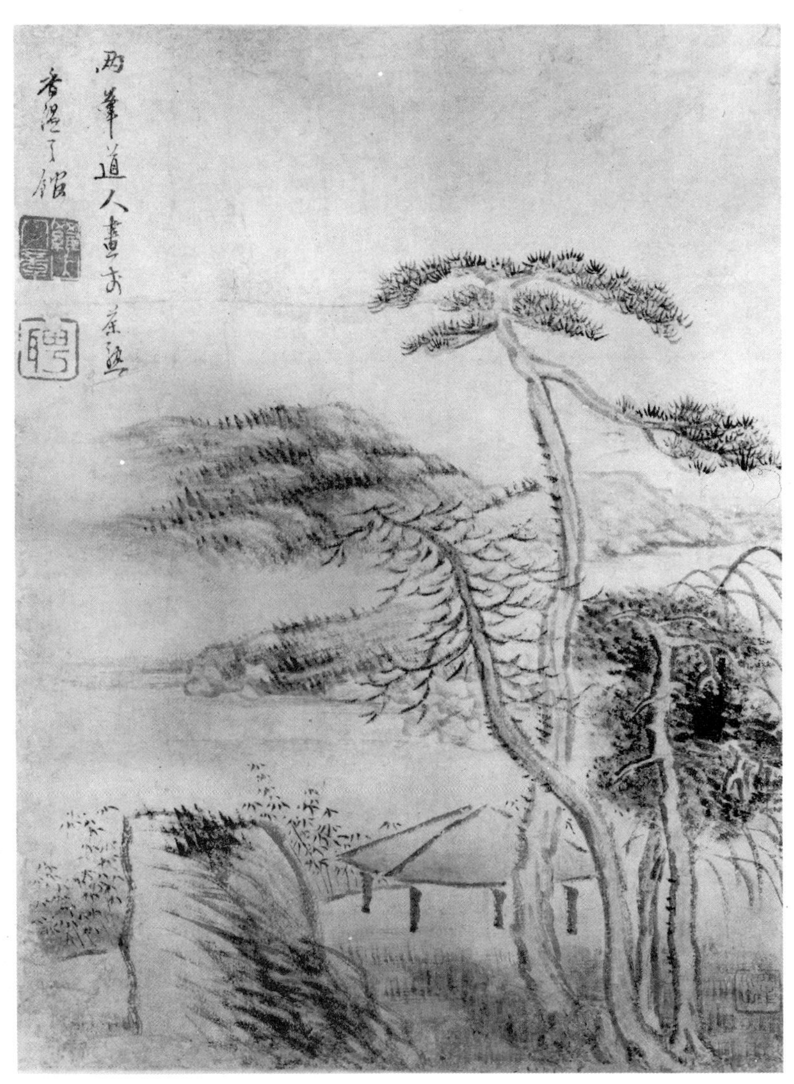

25   LANDSCAPE, Lo Ping, 1733-1799, China, hanging scroll

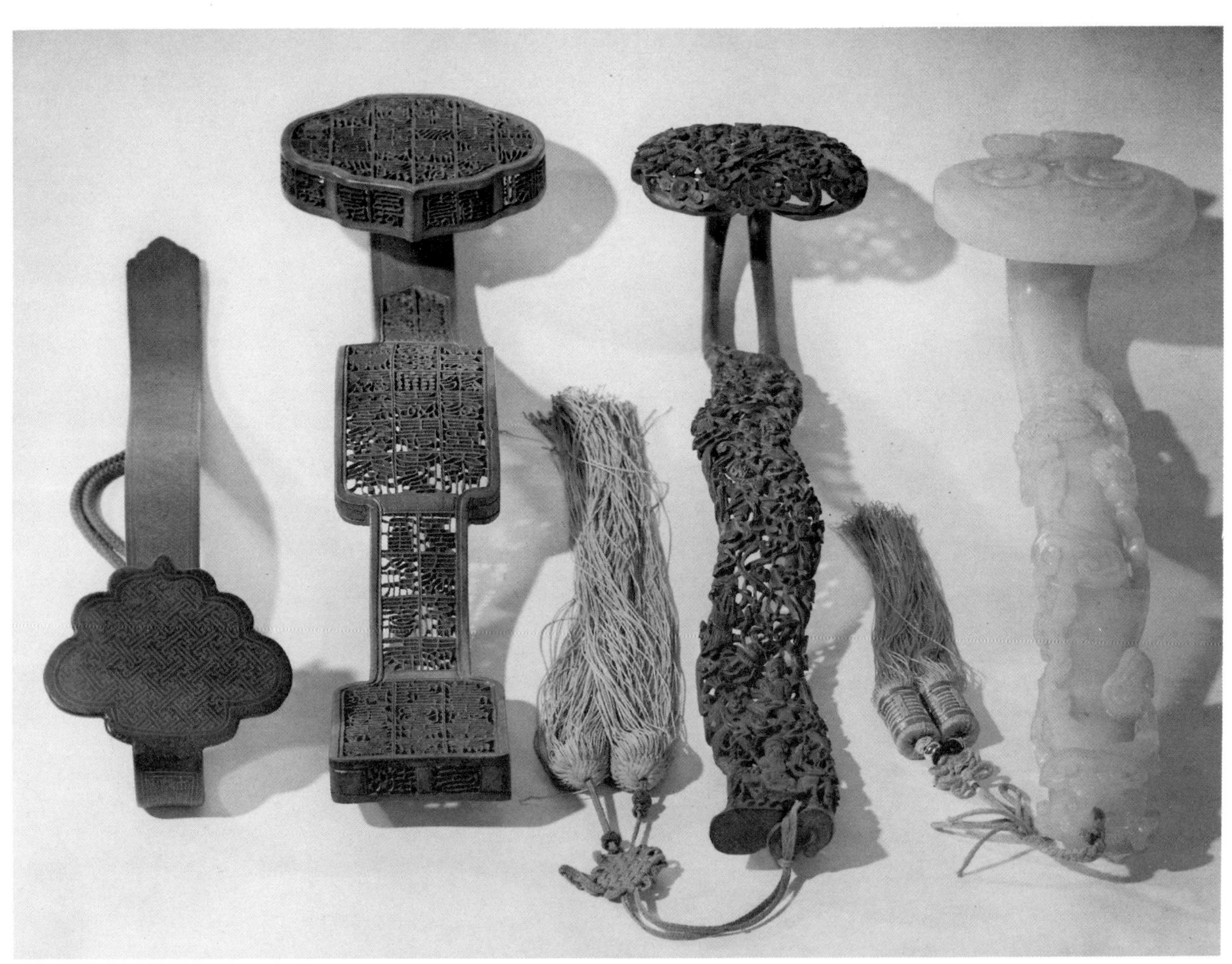

27 (a) RUI SCEPTER, China, late 18th century, iron
(b) RUI SCEPTER, China, 18th century, sandalwood
(c) RUI SCEPTER, China, 19th century, boxwood
(d) RUI SCEPTER, China, late 18th century, ice jade

28   RUI SCEPTER, China, 18th century, coral

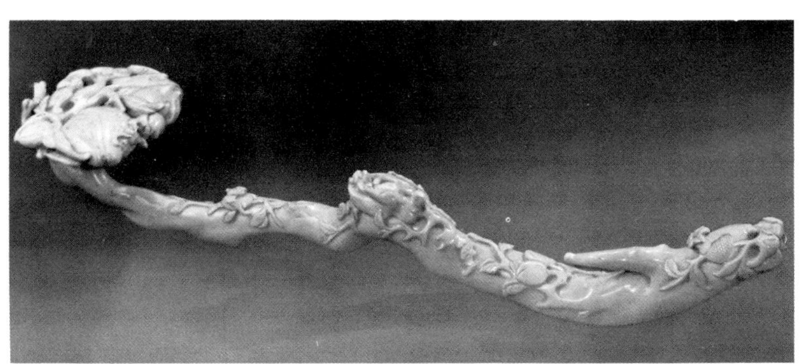

32   TEA POT, China, ca. 1811-1817, Ixing stoneware

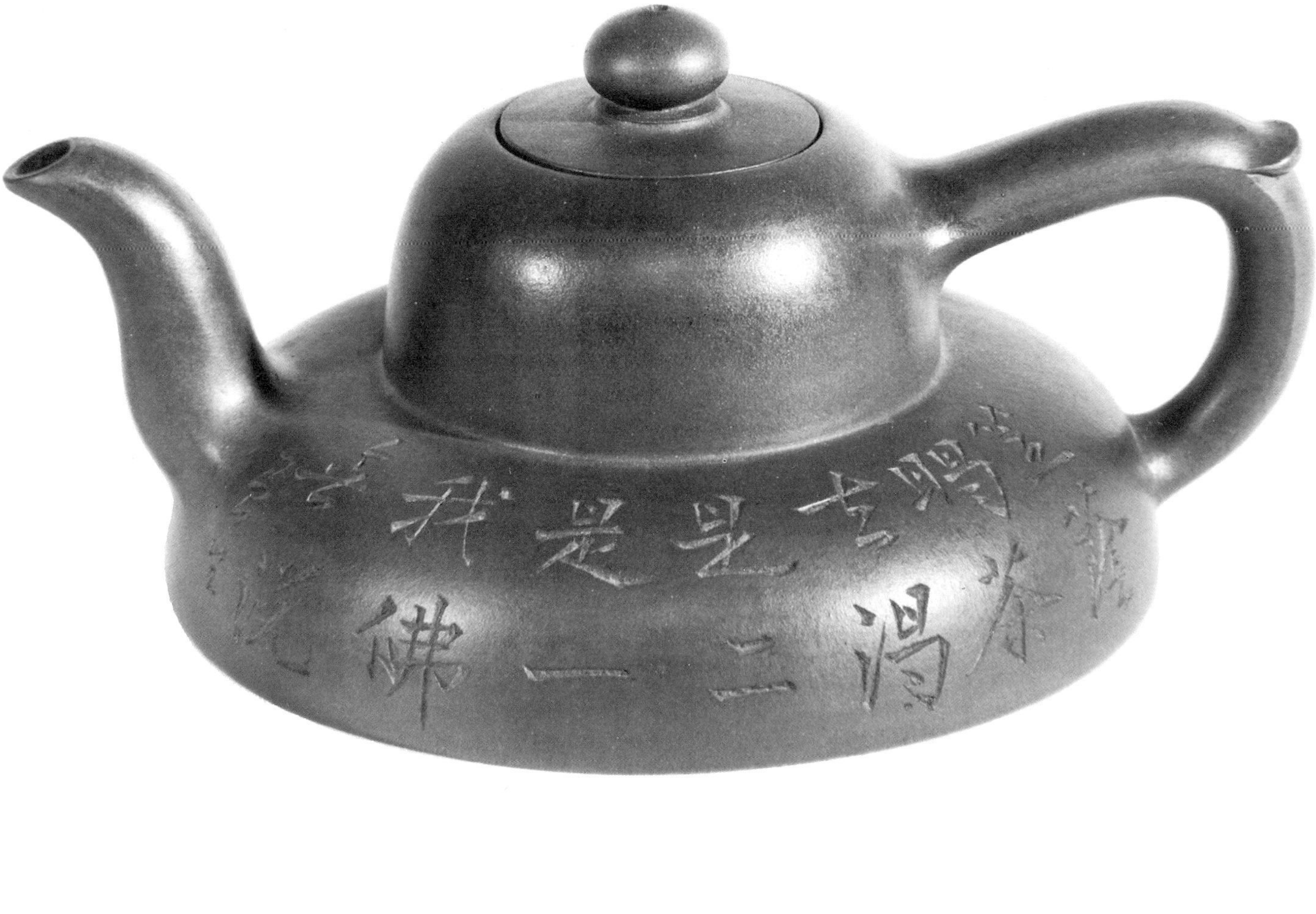

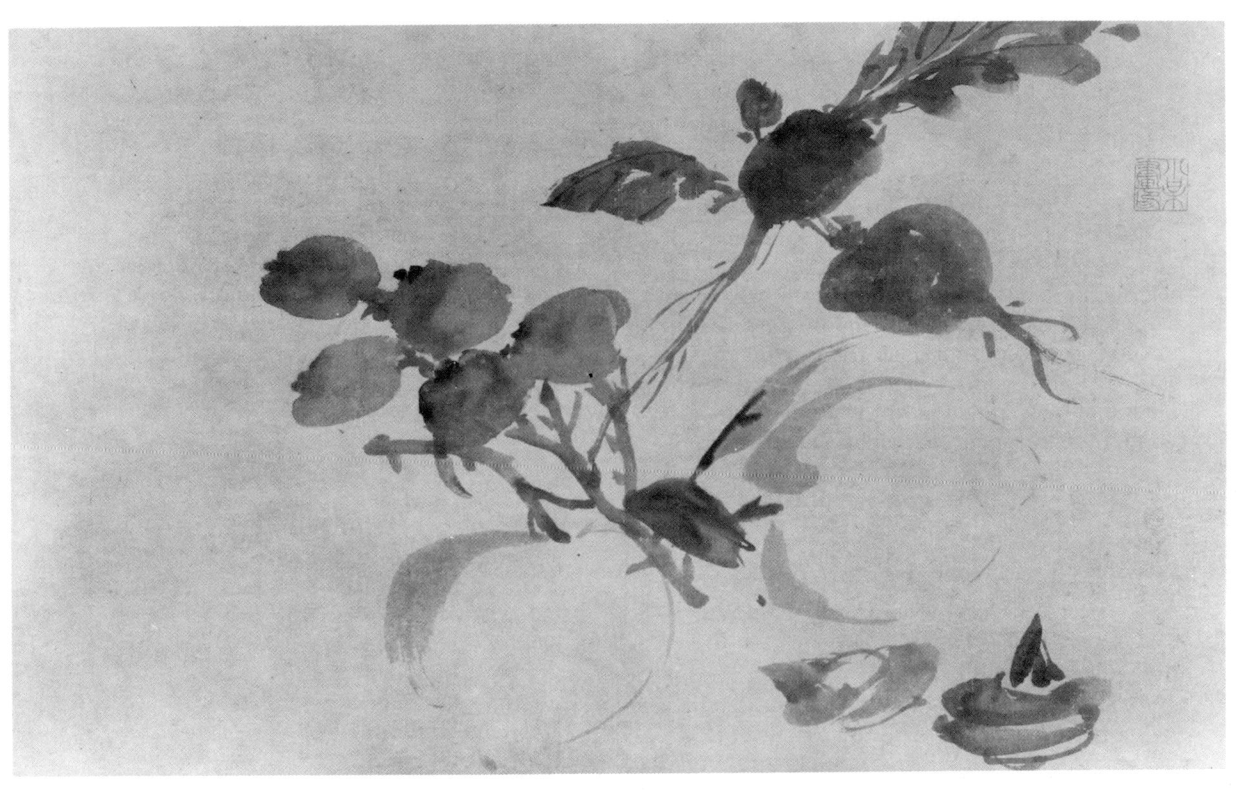

36b VEGETABLE AND FRUITS, Wang Su (1794-1877), China, album
leaf

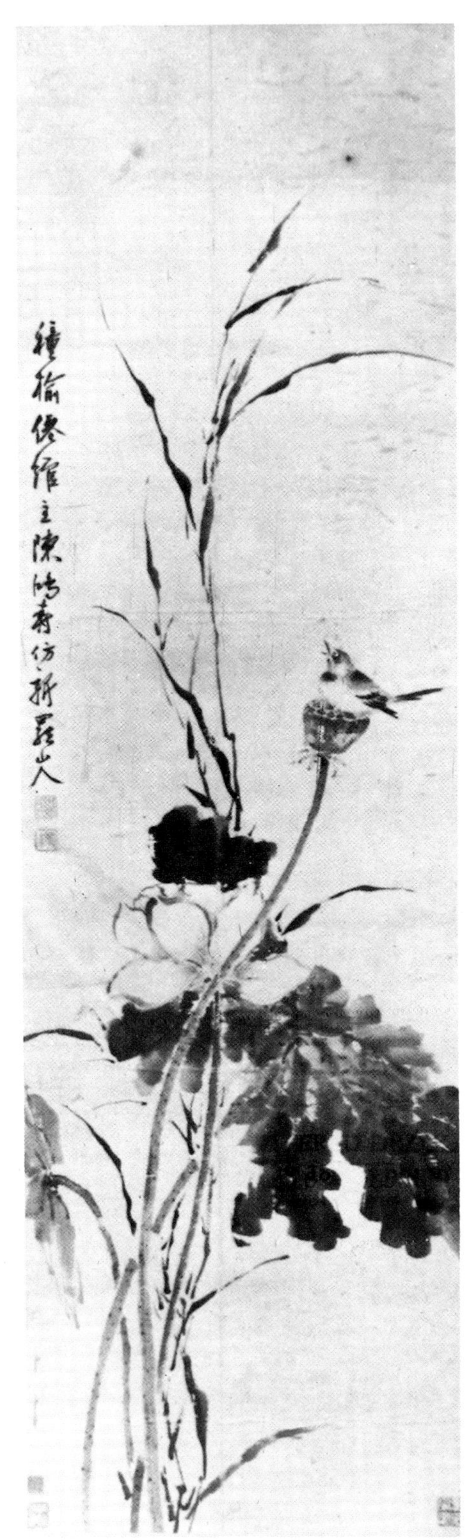

31 LOTUS AND BIRD, Chen Hongshou (1768-1822), China, hanging scroll

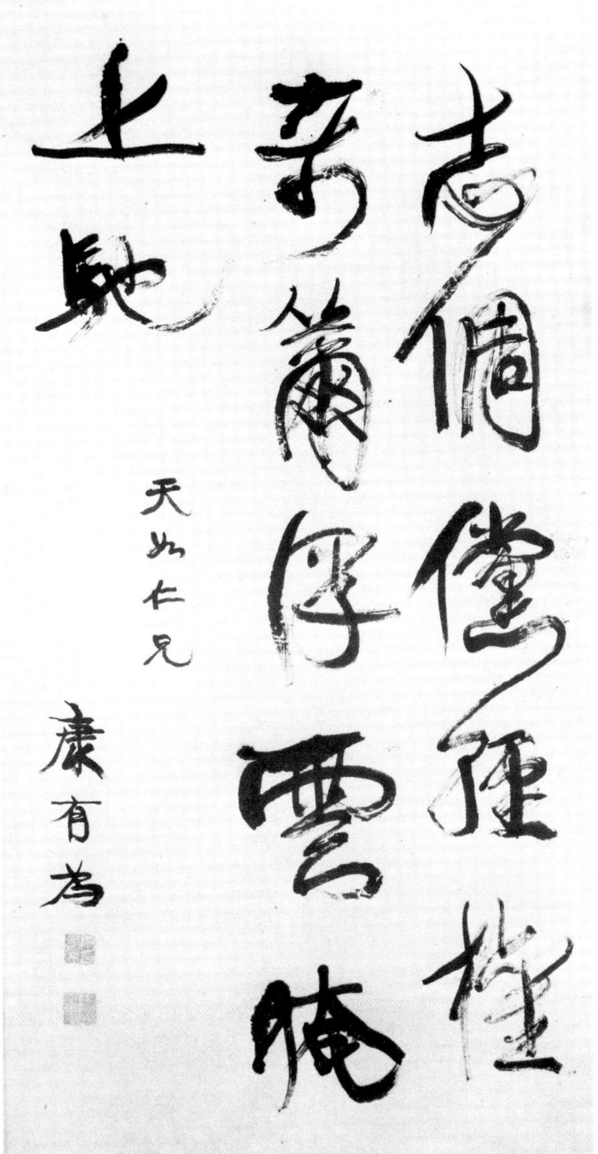

44 RIDING ON THE CLOUDS, Kang Yuwei (1856-1927), China, hanging scroll

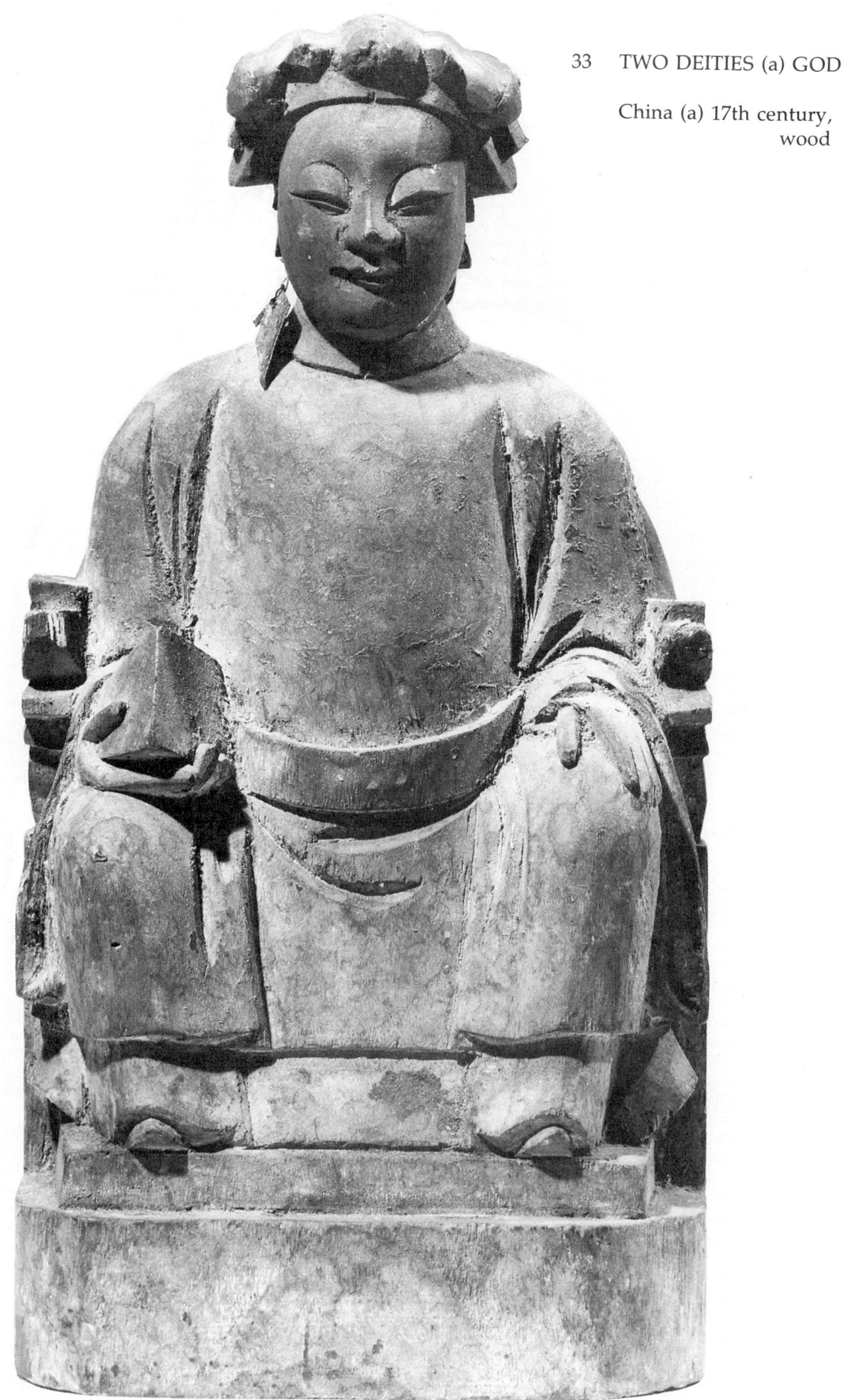

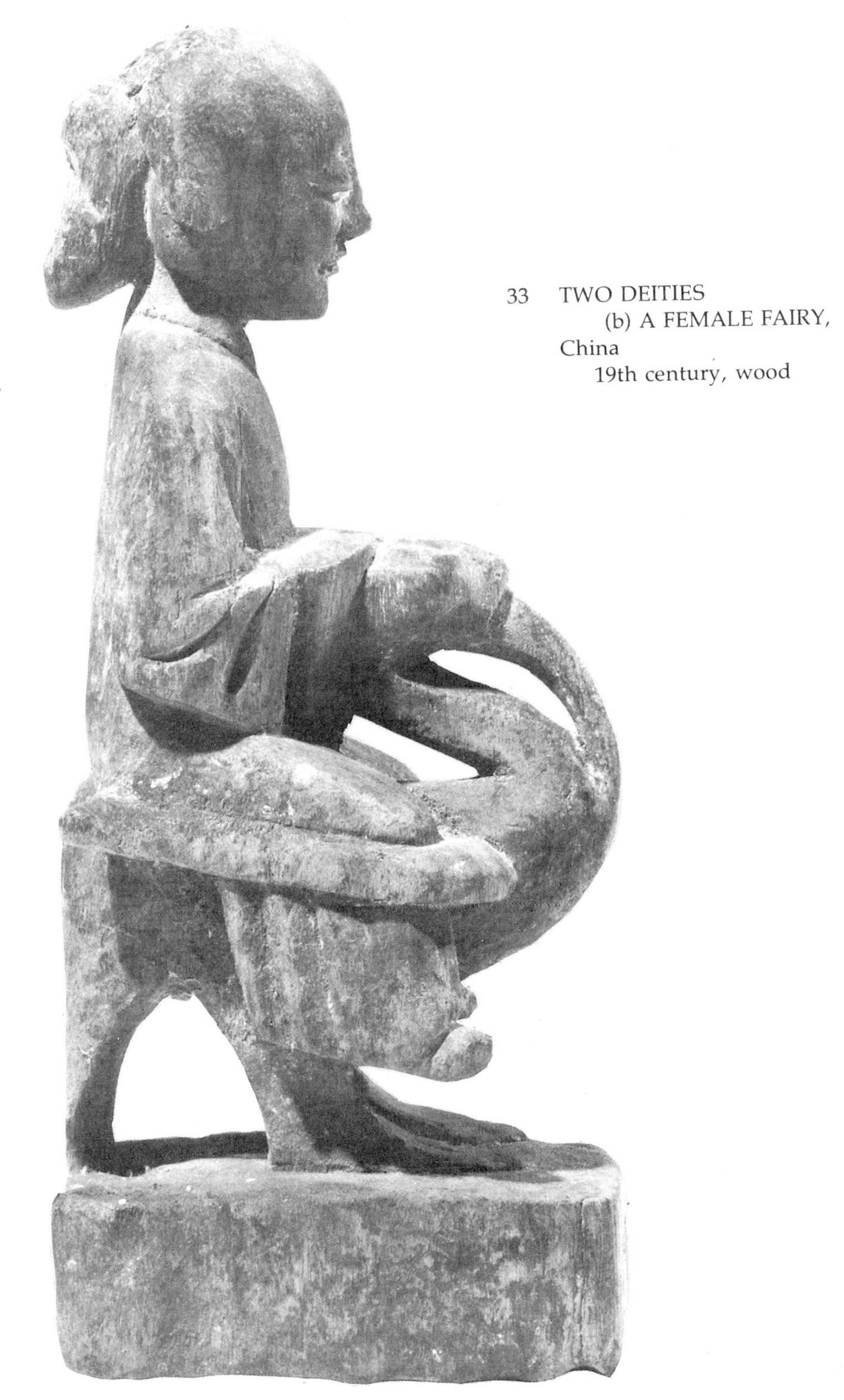

33   TWO DEITIES
       (b) A FEMALE FAIRY,
China
       19th century, wood

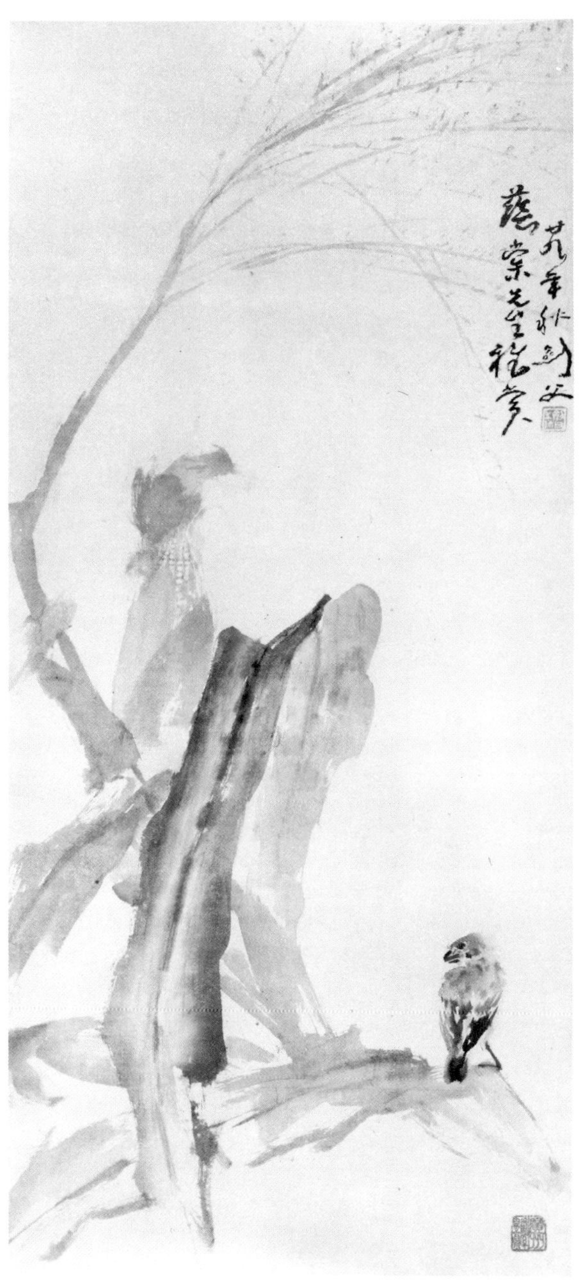

49   SPARROW AND CORN, Gao Jienfu
       (1881-1951), China, dated
       1948, hanging scroll

51   BRUSH HOLDER, China, 1821-1850,
       blue and white porcelain

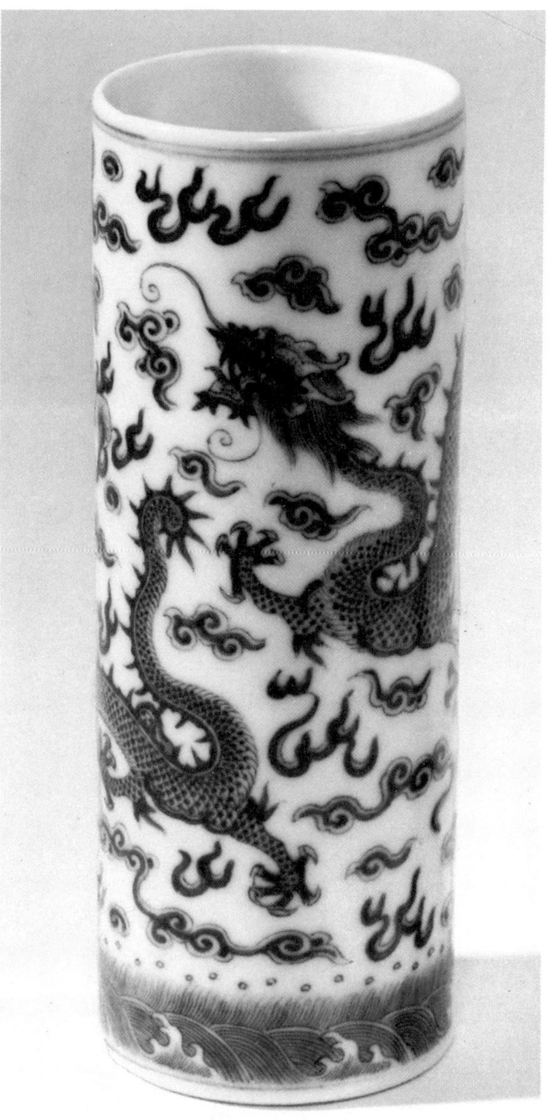

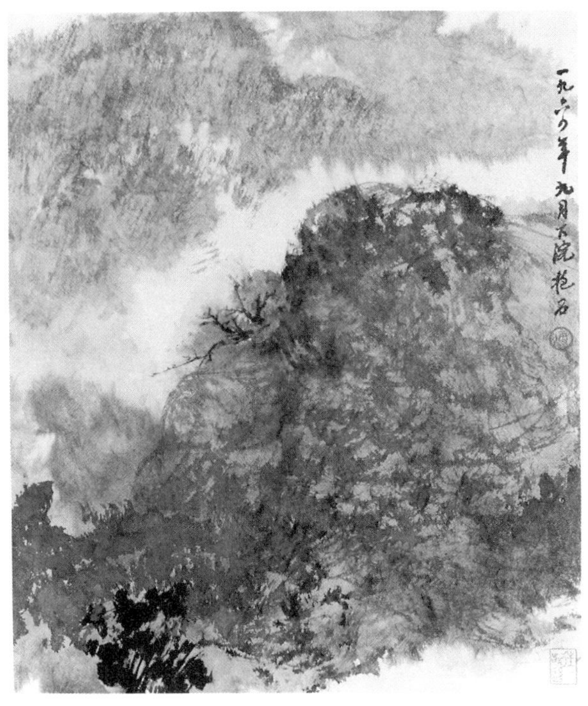

50   LANDSCAPE, Fu Baoshi (1904-1965),
China, dated 1964, framed painting

53   THE SCHOLAR'S DESK, CHINESE AND JAPANESE
ACCOUTREMENTS, 18th and 19th centuries

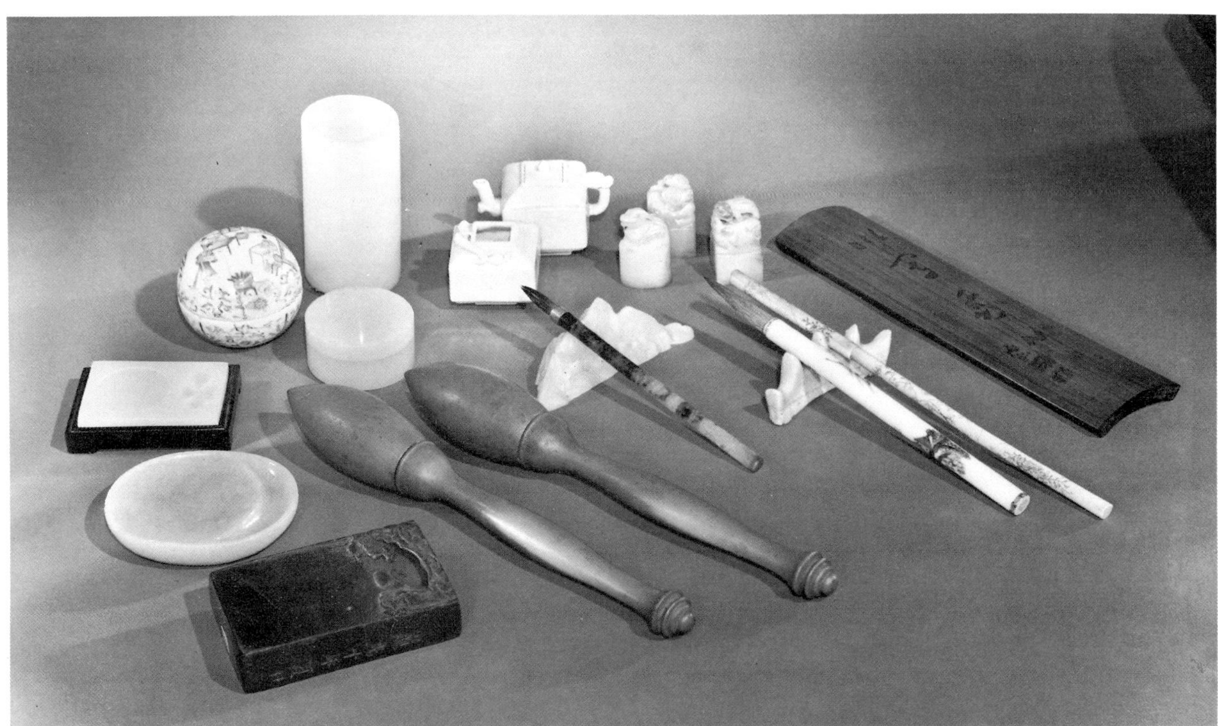

Classical: *Korea*

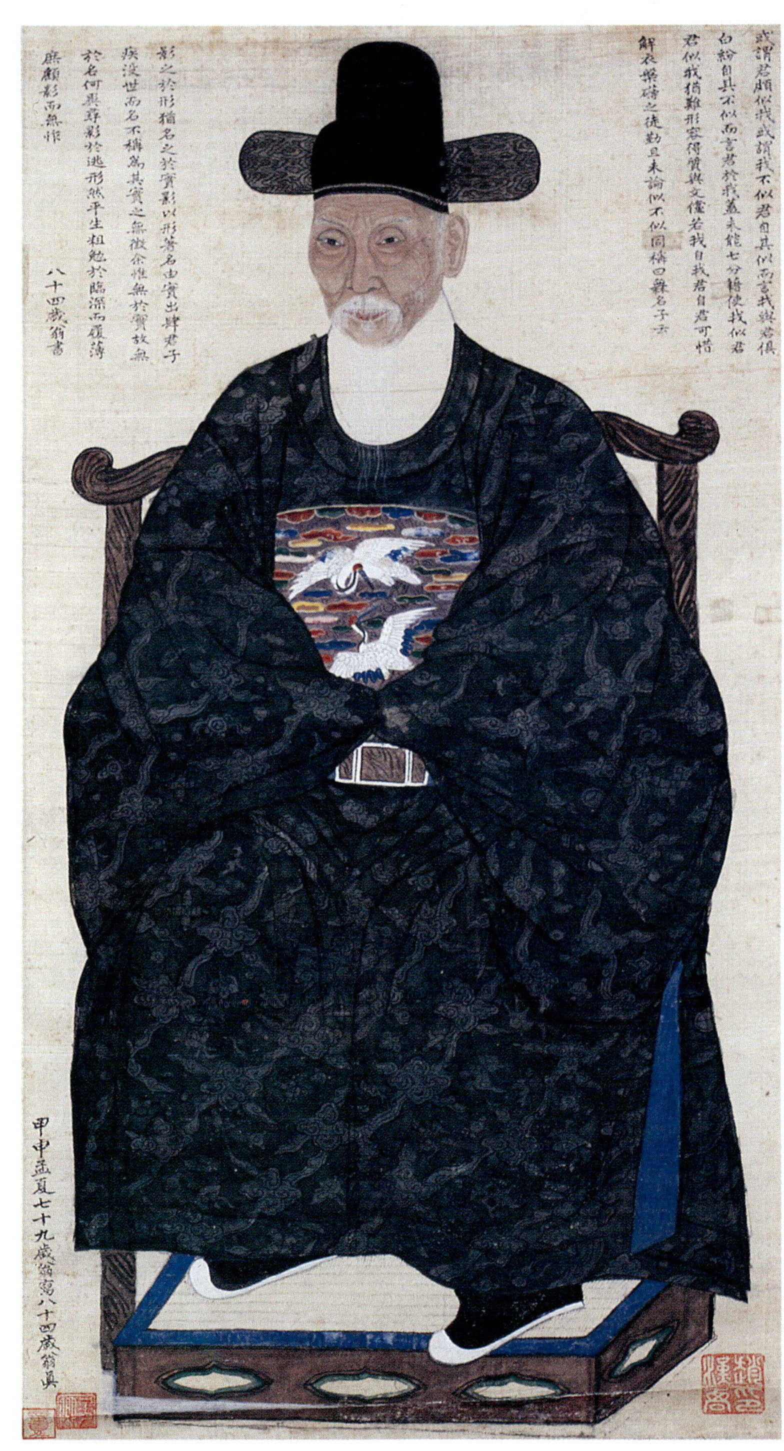

59 PORTRAIT OF AN OFFICIAL, Korea, 19th century, hanging scroll

54   BULBOUS POT, Korea, 1st-4th century,
      grayware matte pottery

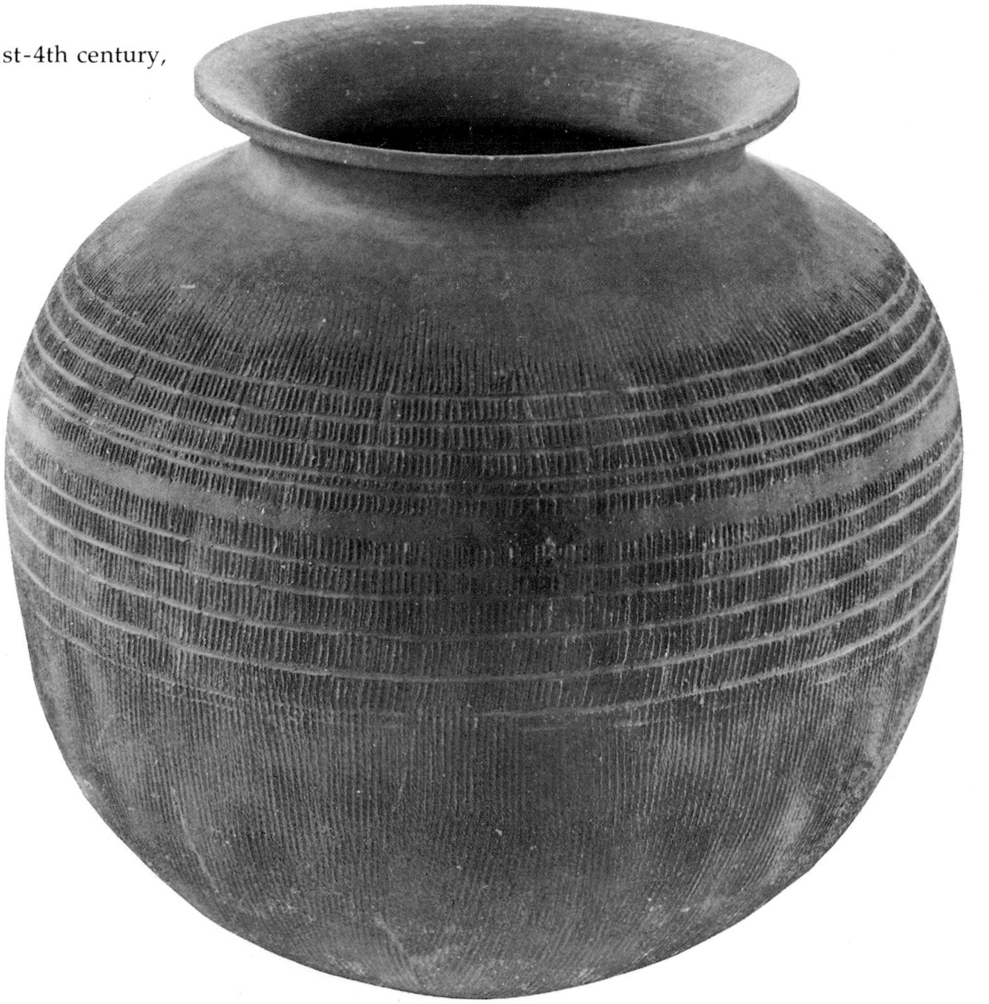

55   MALE AND FEMALE HORSES, Korea, 5th-6th century, clay

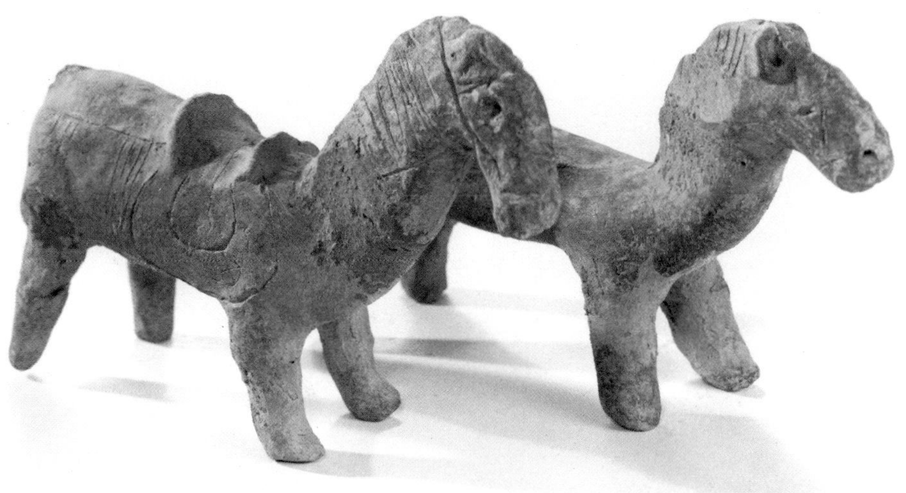

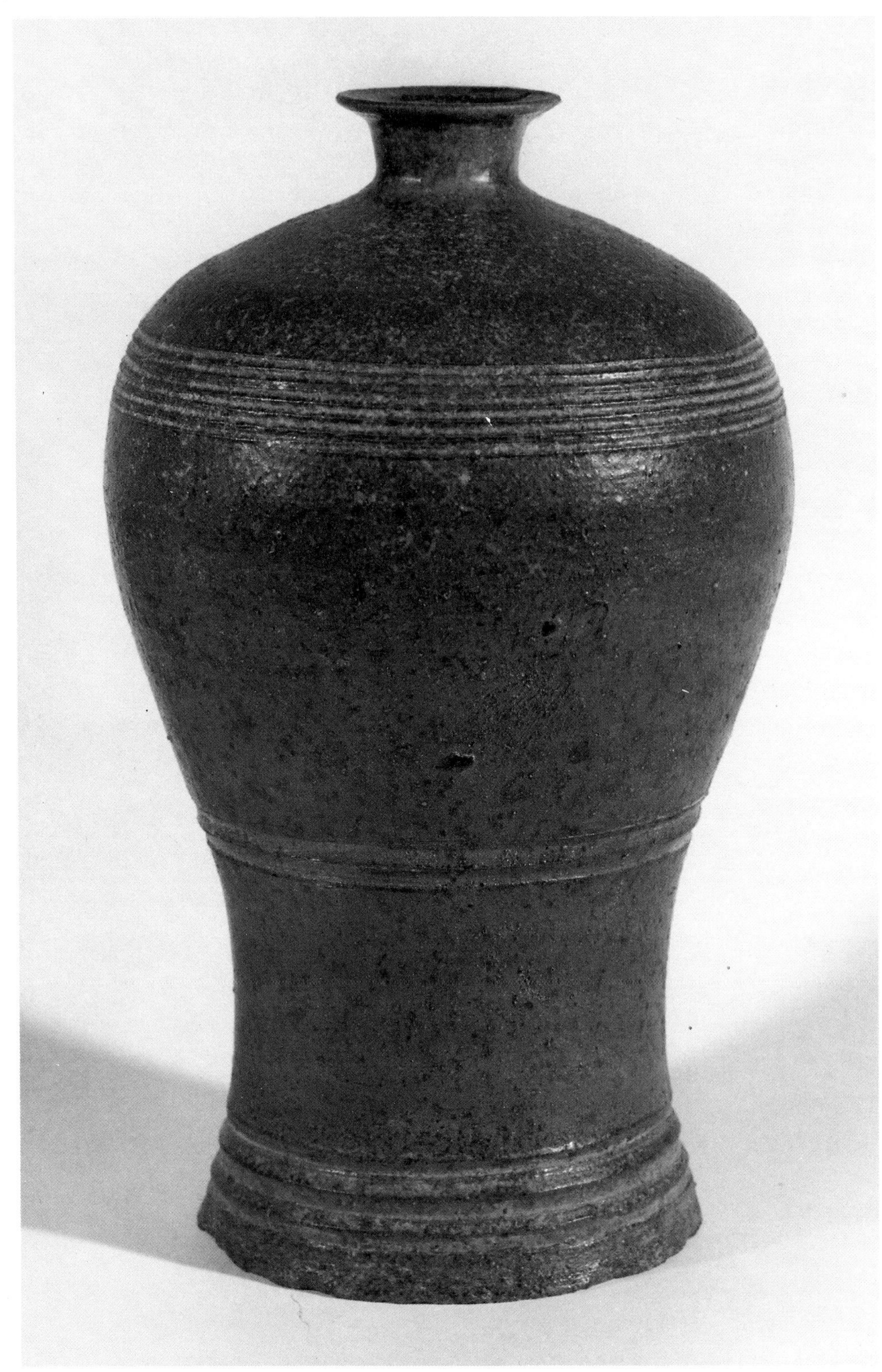

    56   VASE, Korea, 12th century, stoneware

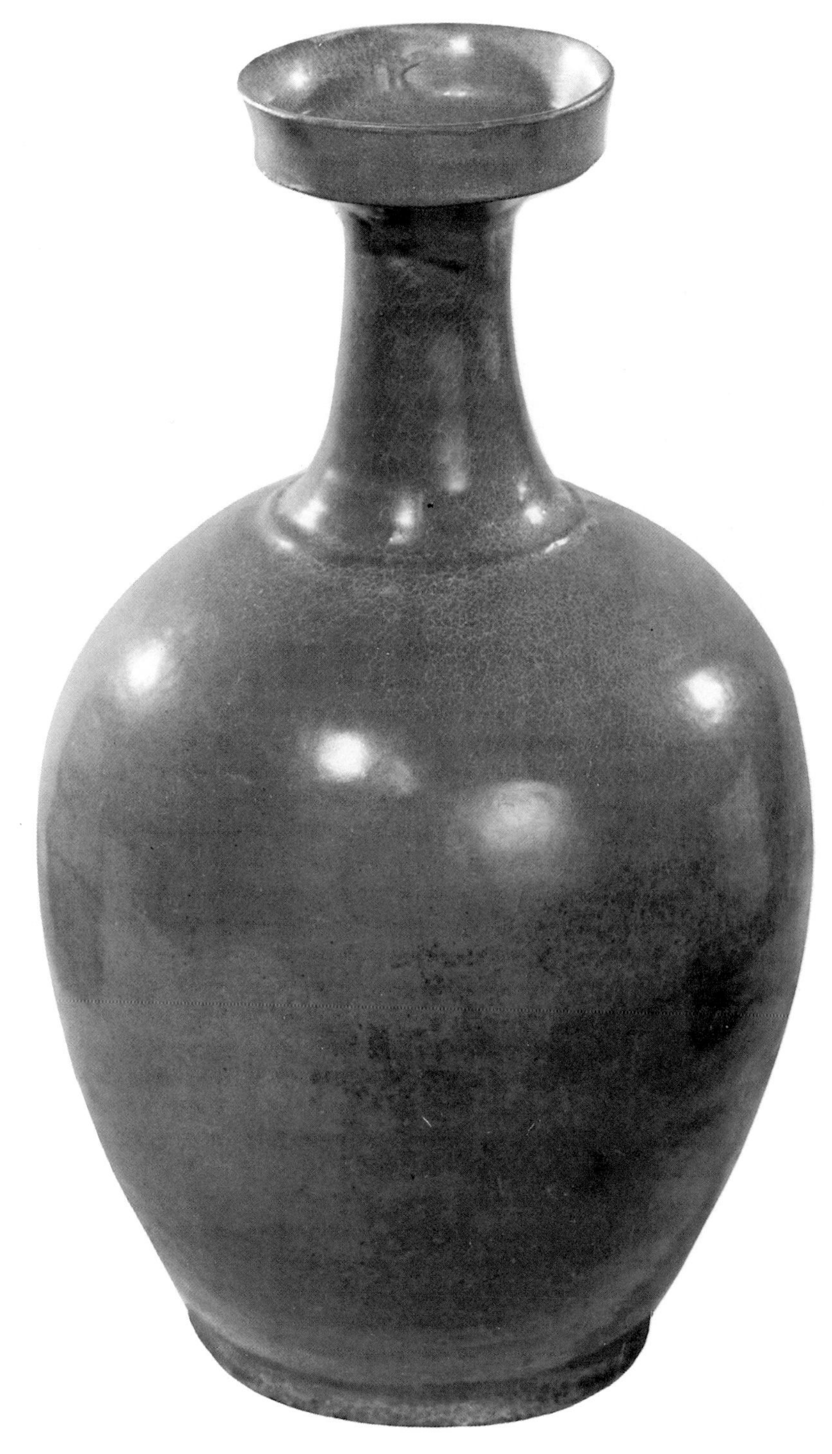

58   (a) BOTTLE, Korea, 11th-12th century, celadon

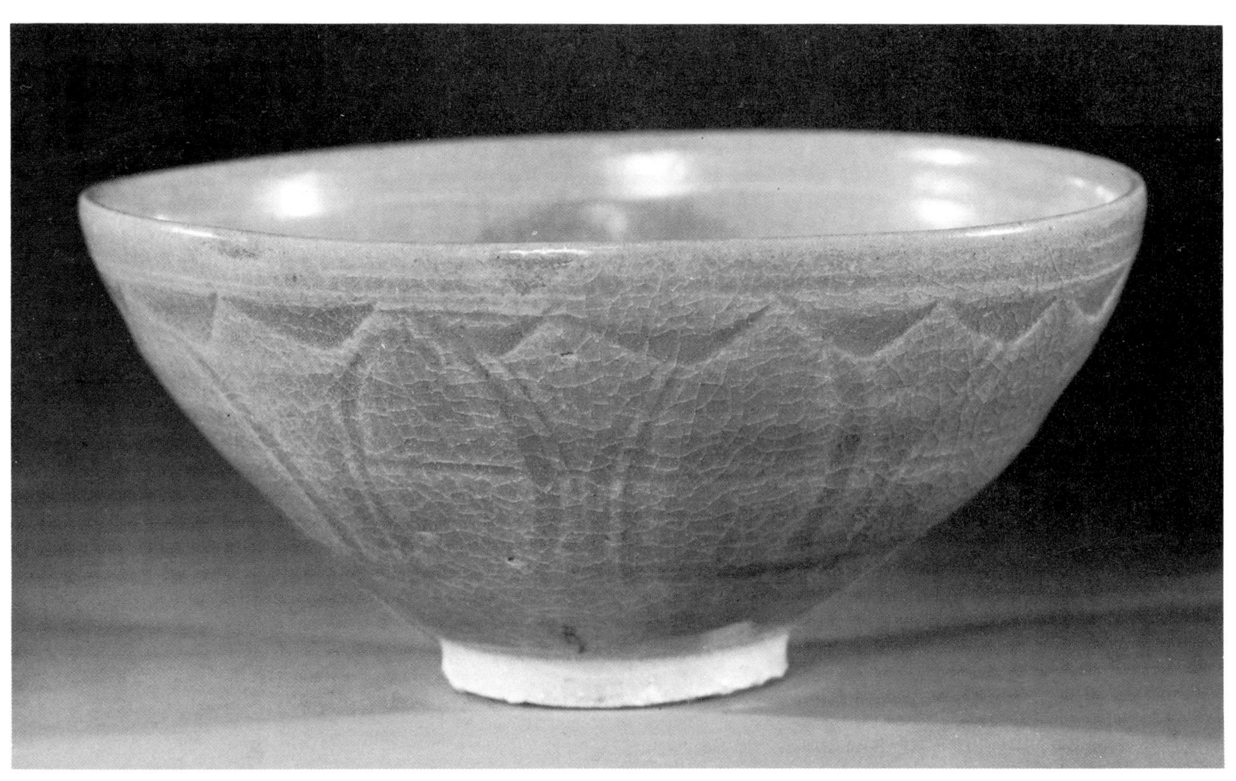

57 BOWL, Korea, 12th century, celadon

58 (b) BOTTLE, Korea,
12th-13th century, bronze

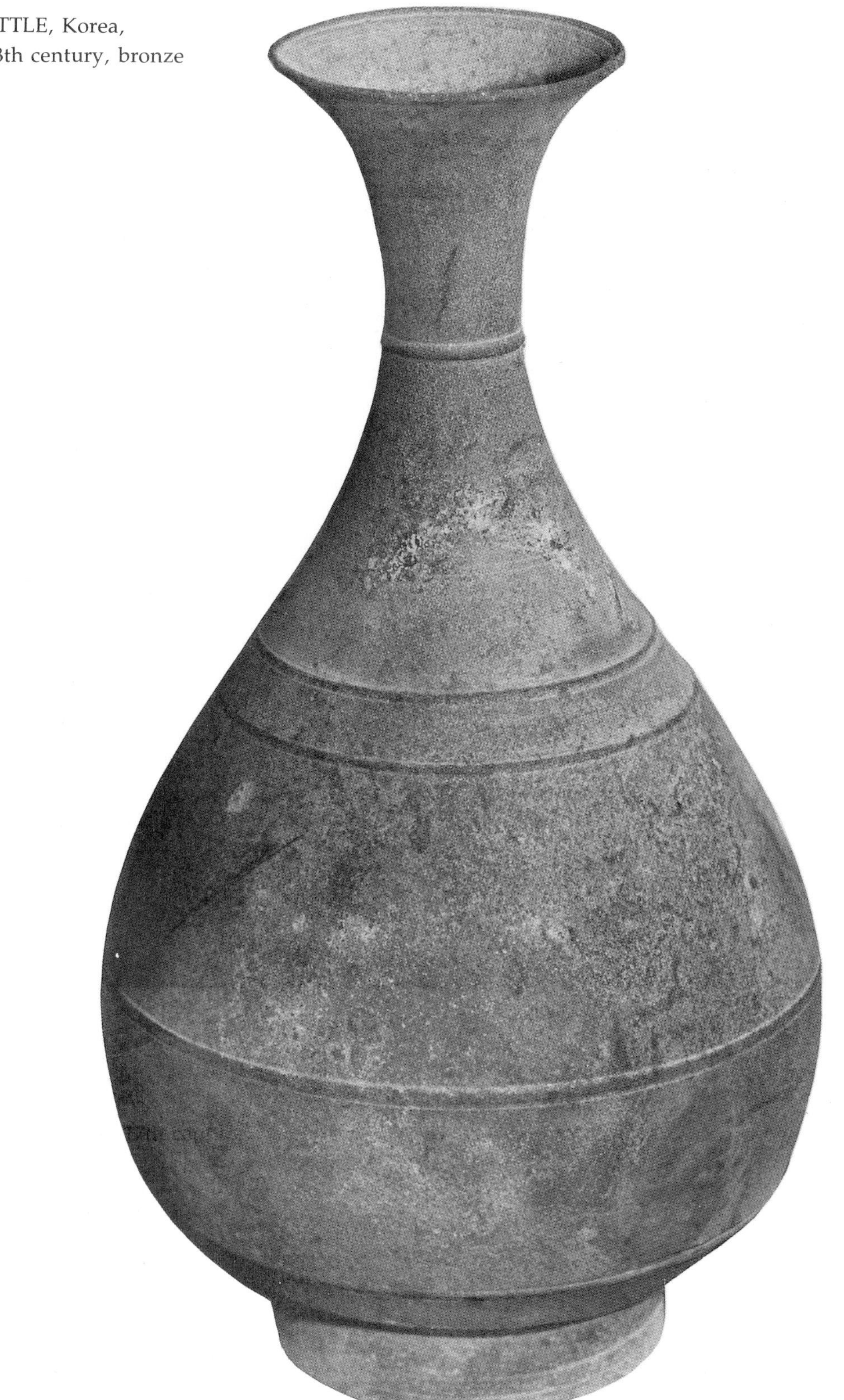

Classical: *Japan*

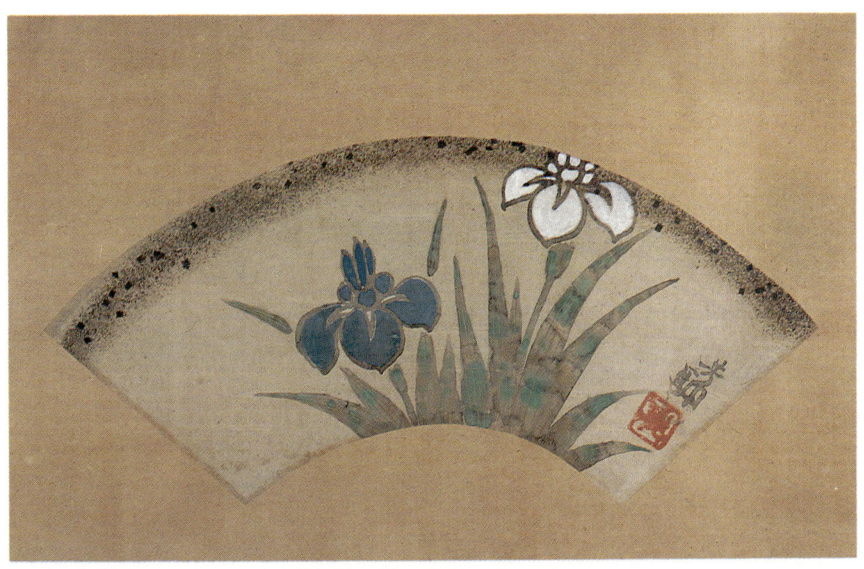

79   WHITE AND BLUE IRIS, Nakamura Hōchu (fl. late 18th-early 19th century), Japan, early 19th century, hanging scroll

69   FLOWER CARTS (detail), Japan, ca. 17th-18th century, one of a pair of six-fold screens

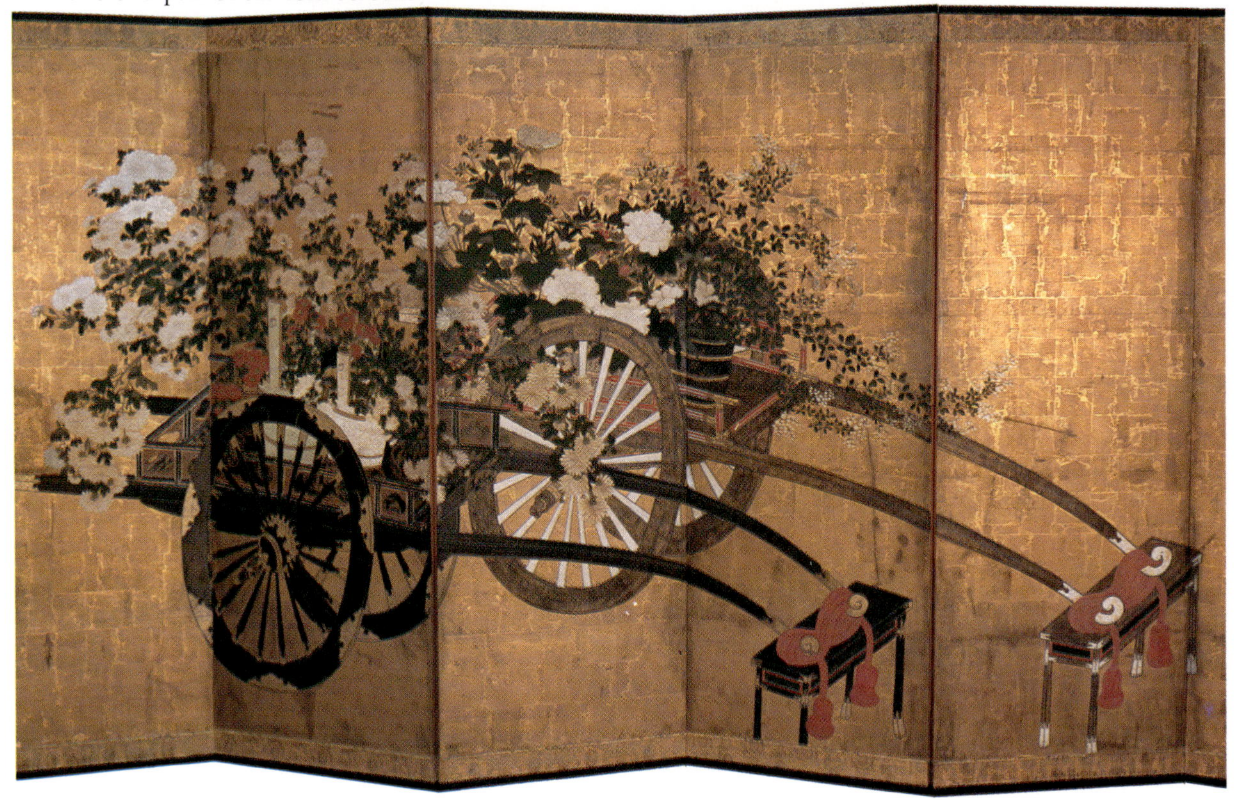

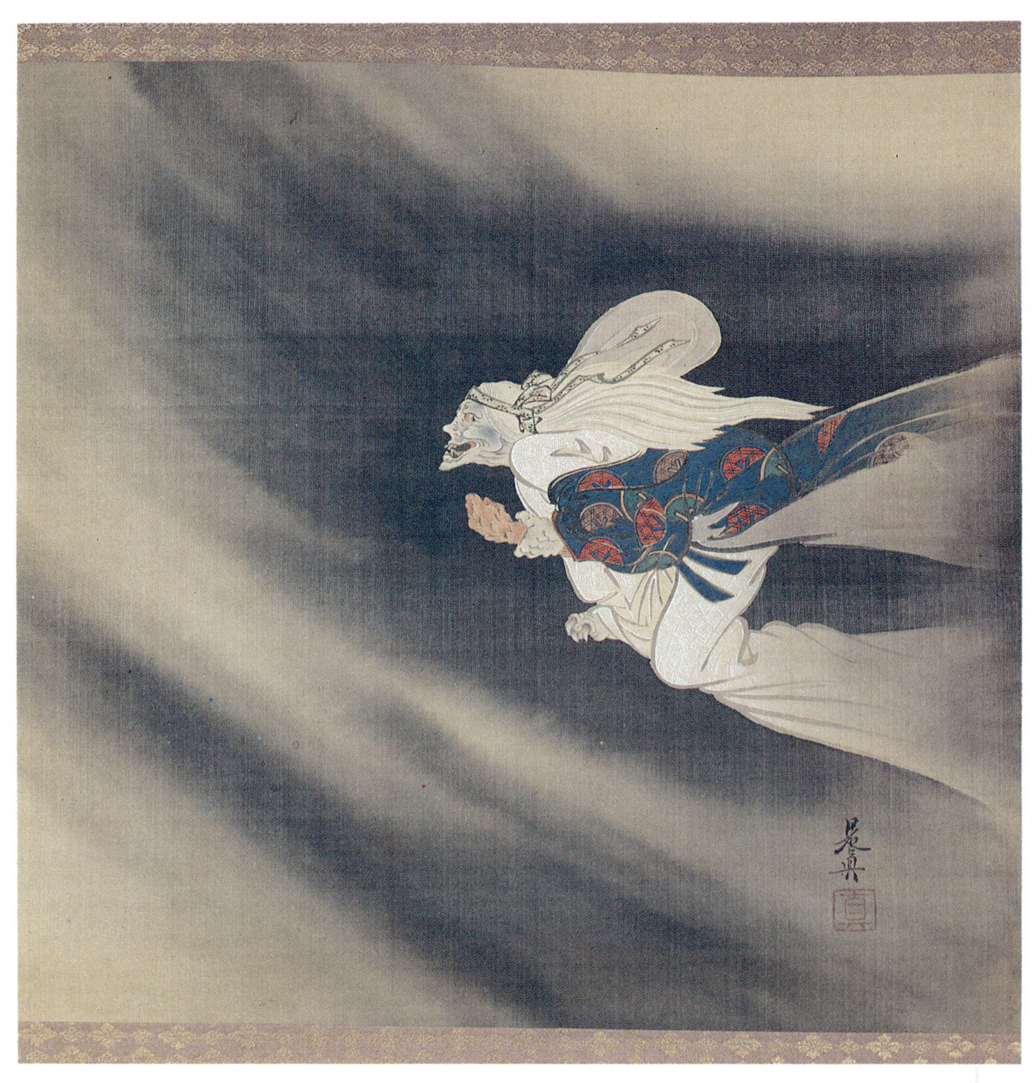

87   RASHOMON WITCH, Shibata Zeshin (1807-1891), Japan, 19th
century, hanging scroll

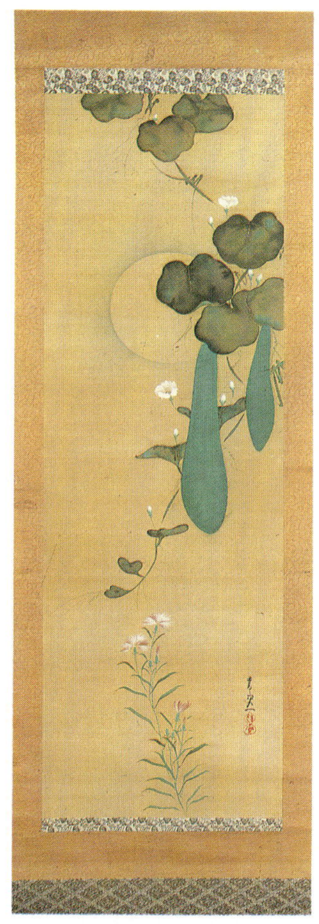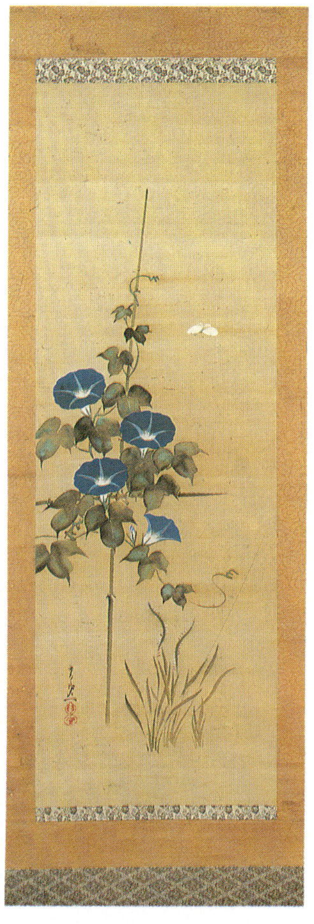

80   MORNING GLORIES AND EGGPLANT, Suzuki Kiitsu
(1796-1858), Japan, ca. 1850, pair of hanging scrolls

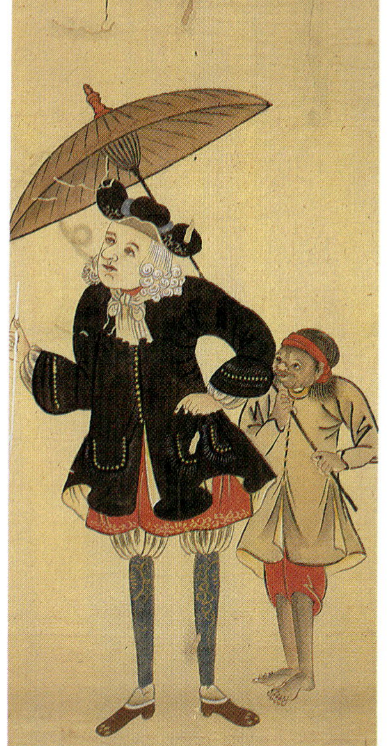

232   DUTCHMAN AND HIS SERVANT, Japan, late 18th century,
woodblock print

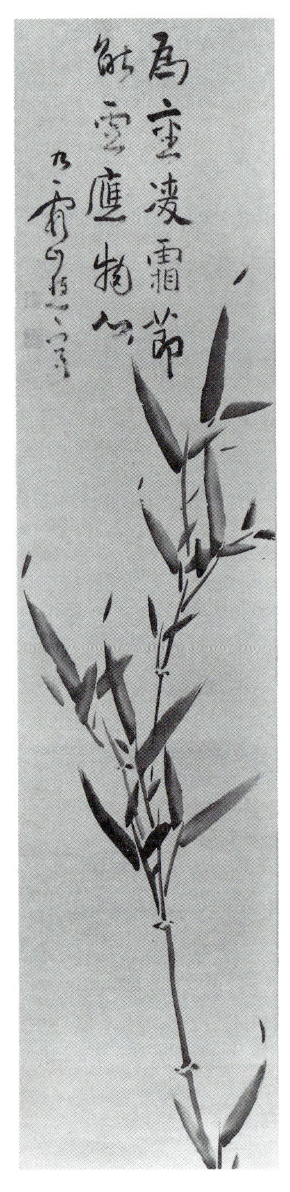

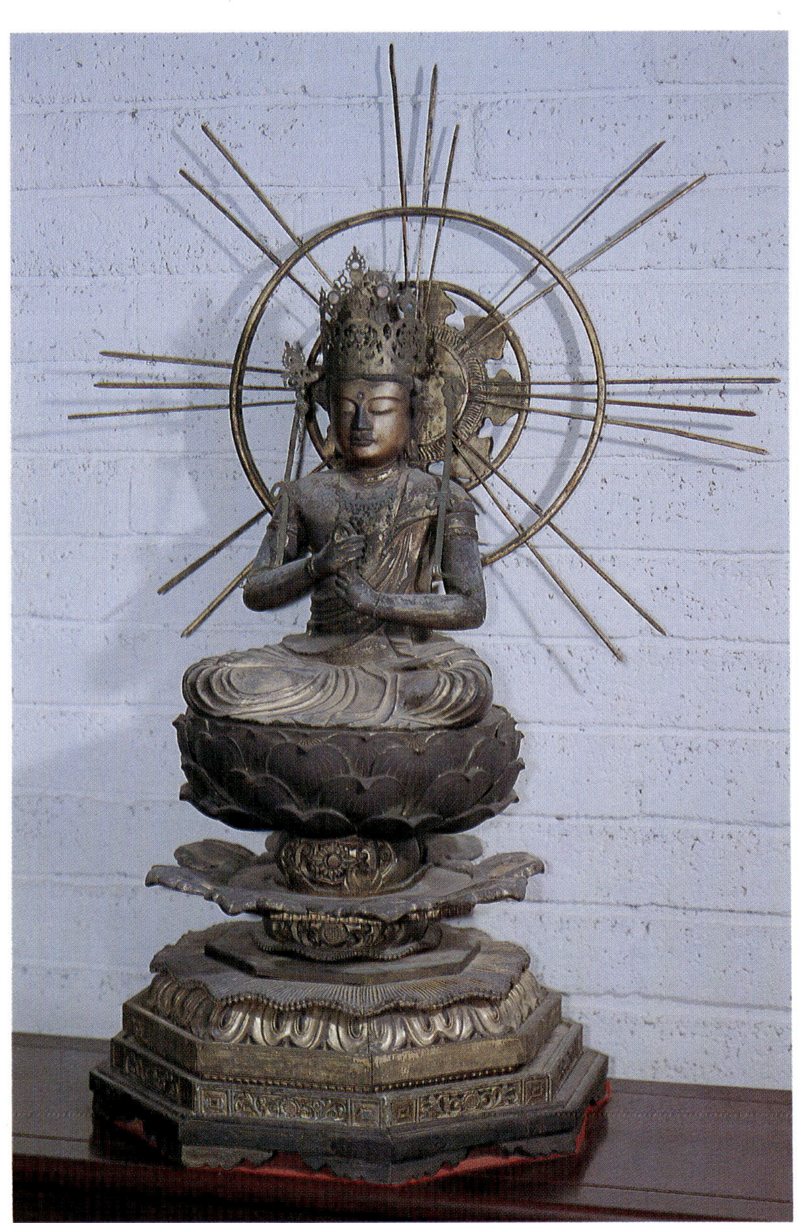

65   DAINICHI, Japan, 14th century, gilt wood

82   BAMBOO, Ike no Taiga (1723-1776), Japan, mid-18th century,
hanging scroll

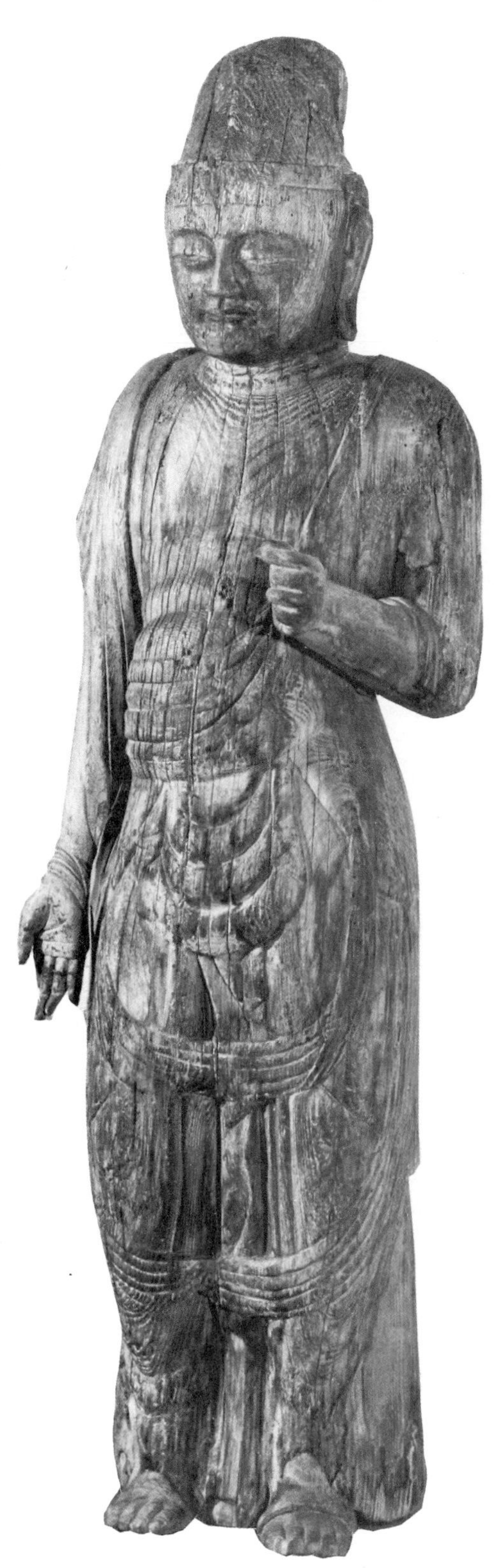

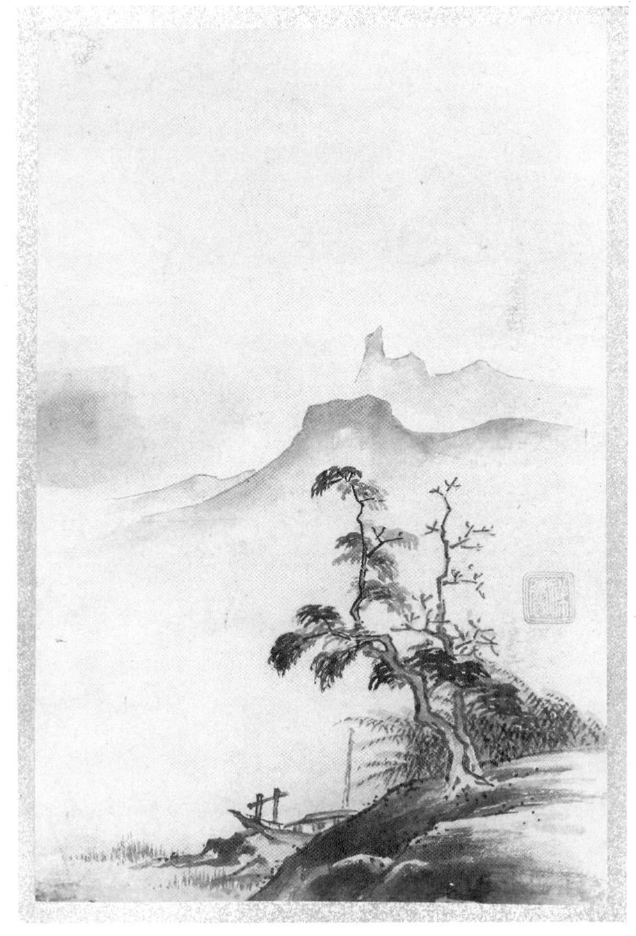

67   NIGHT RAIN AT XIAO-XIANG
     REGION, Japan, ca. 1700, album leaf

62   BODHISATTIVA, Japan, ca. 9th-10th century, wood   117

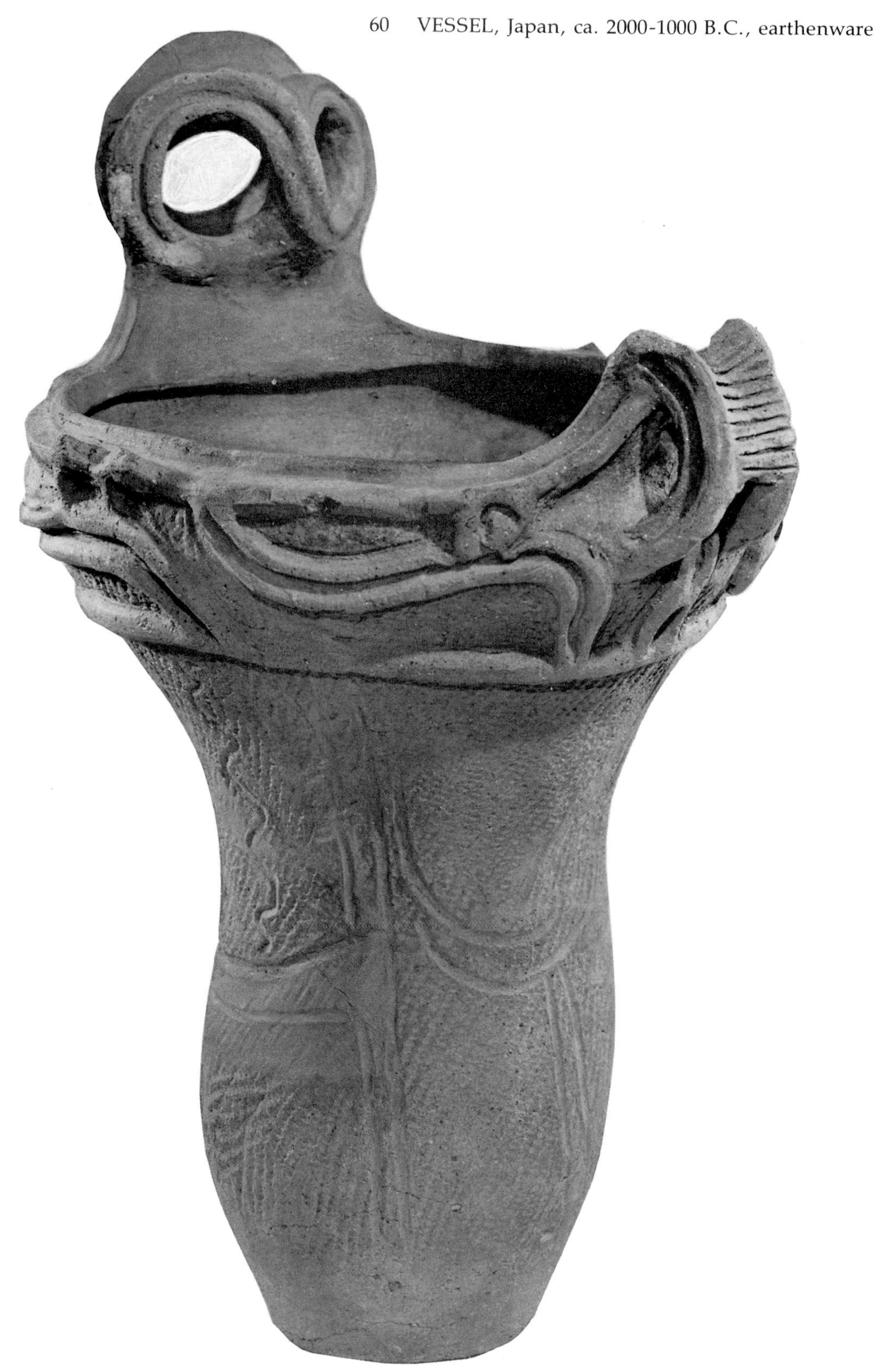

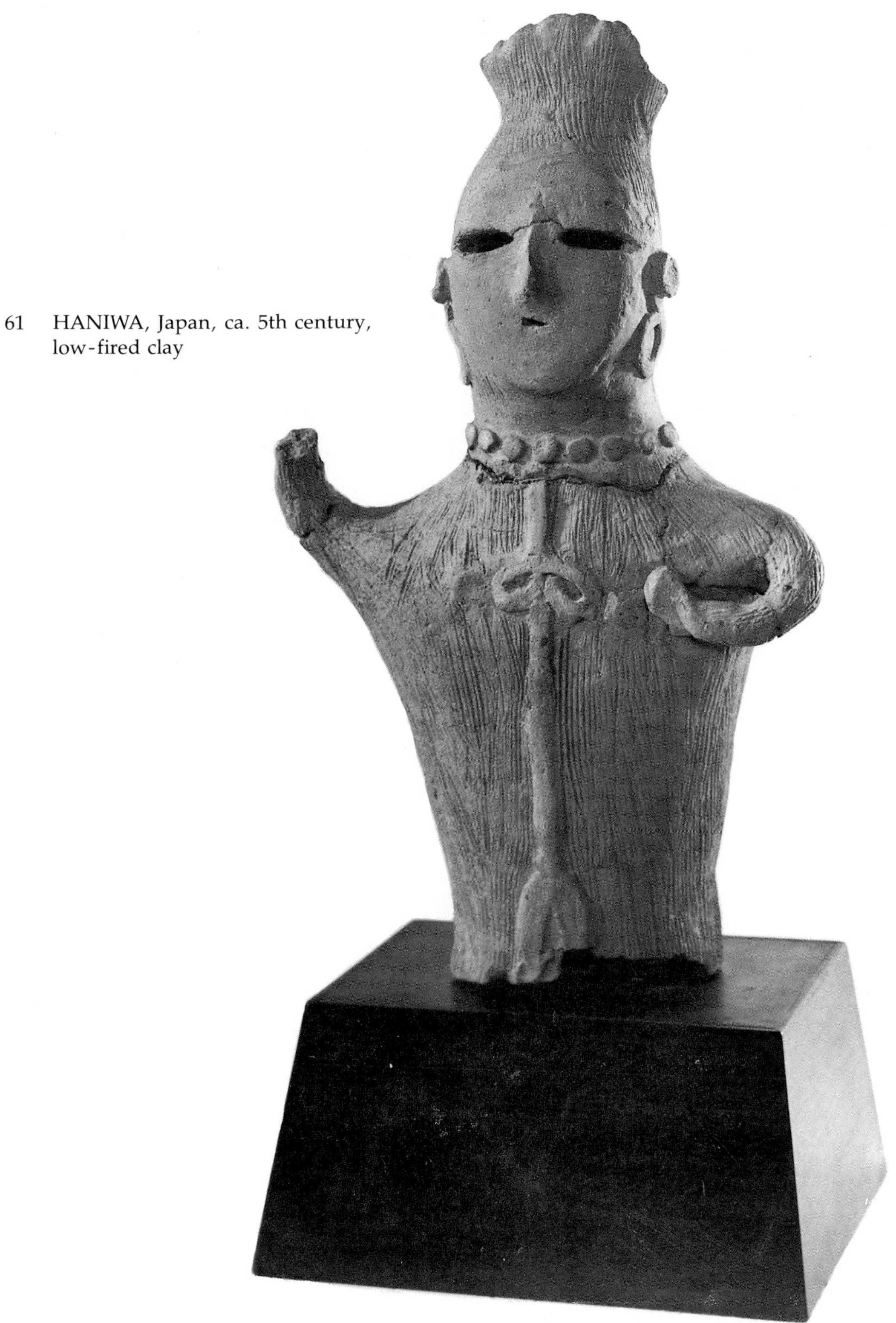

61 HANIWA, Japan, ca. 5th century,
low-fired clay

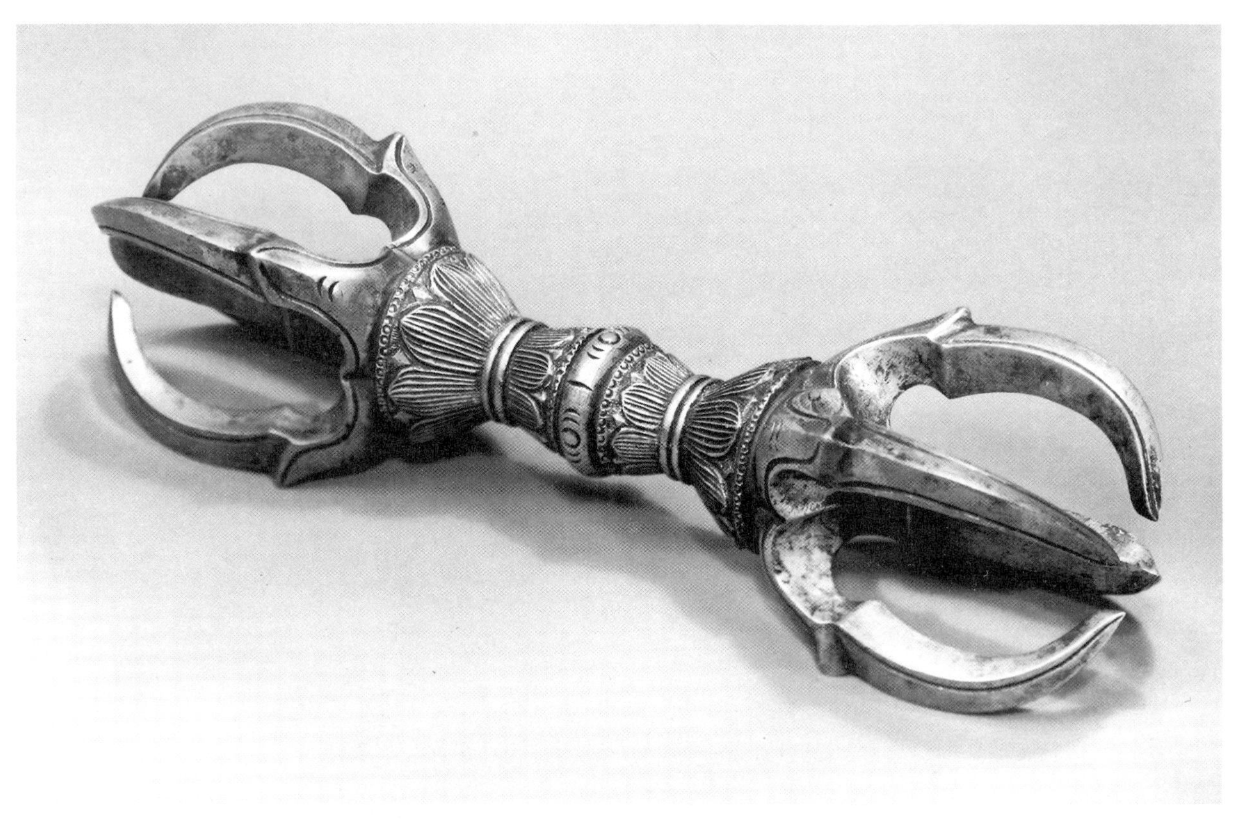

63   FIVE PRONGED VAJRA, Japan, ca. 13th century, gilt bronze

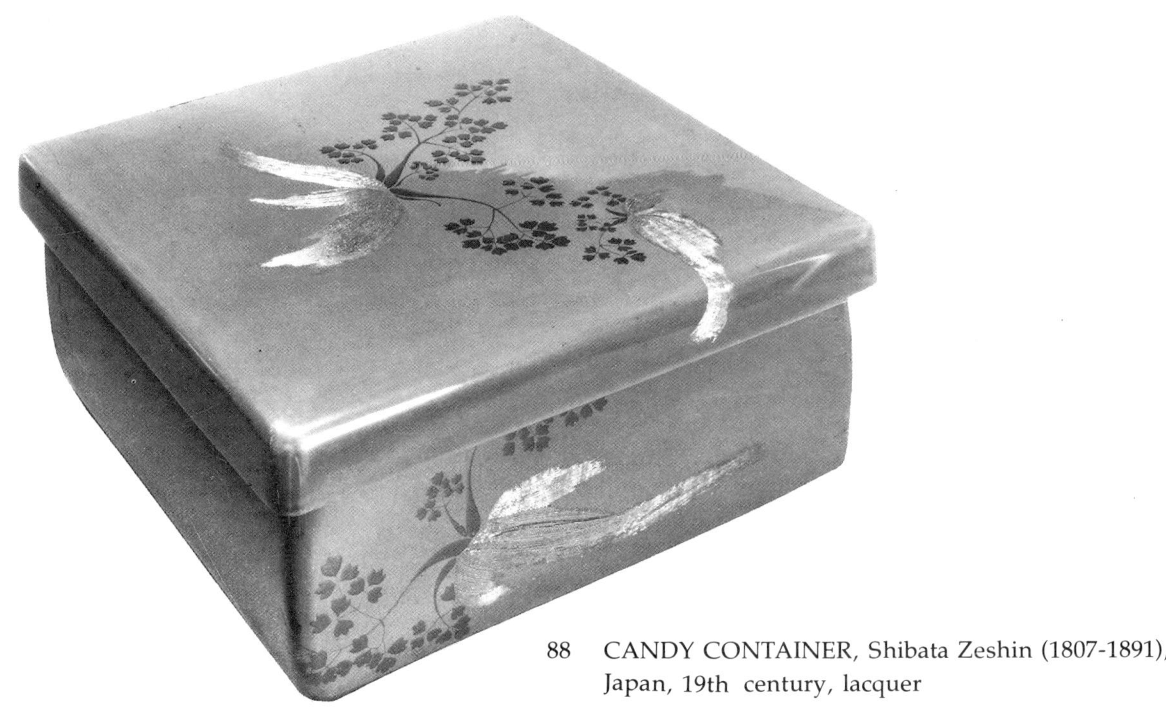

88   CANDY CONTAINER, Shibata Zeshin (1807-1891),
      Japan, 19th century, lacquer

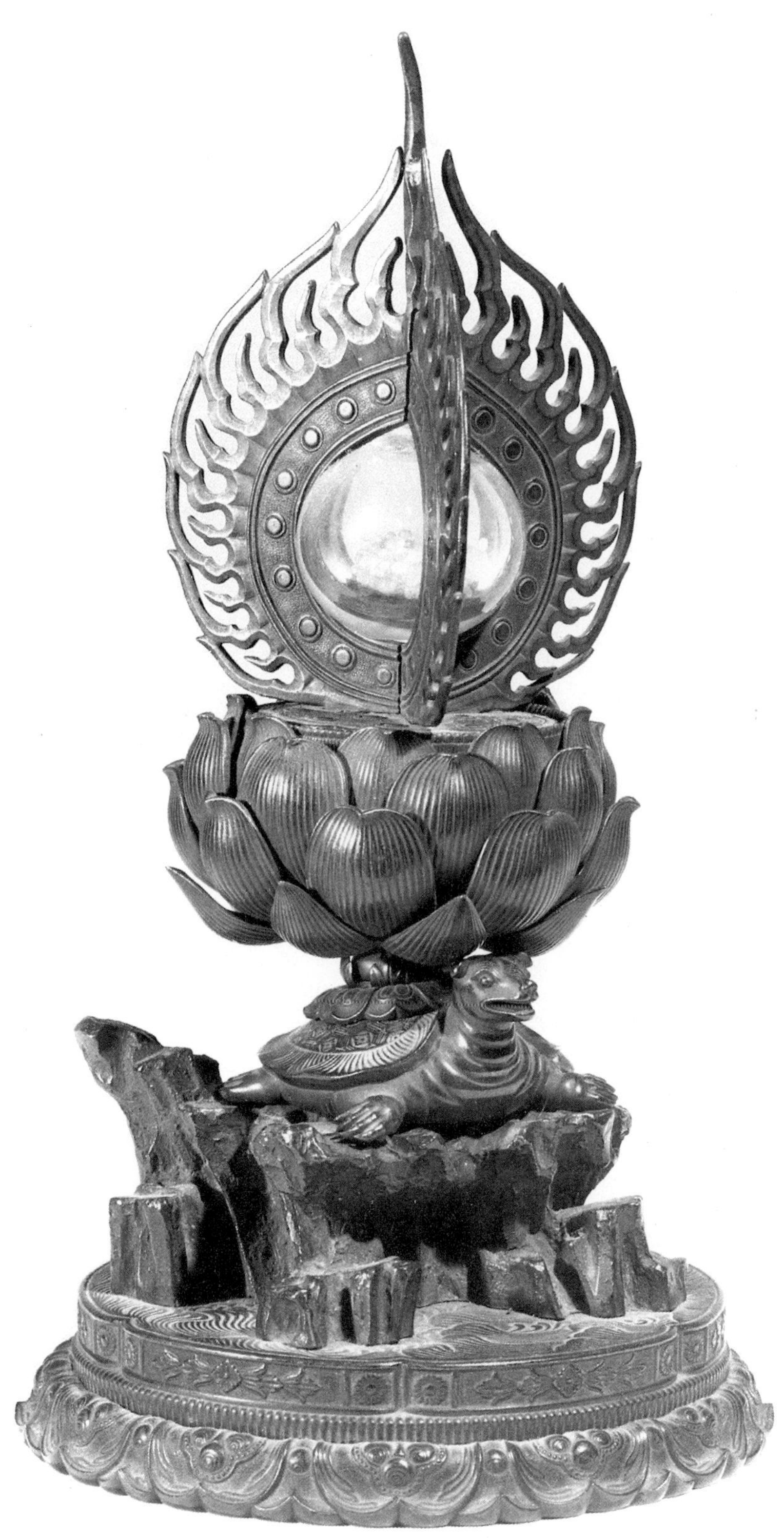

64   SHARITŌ, Japan, ca. 14th-15th century, bronze with crystal

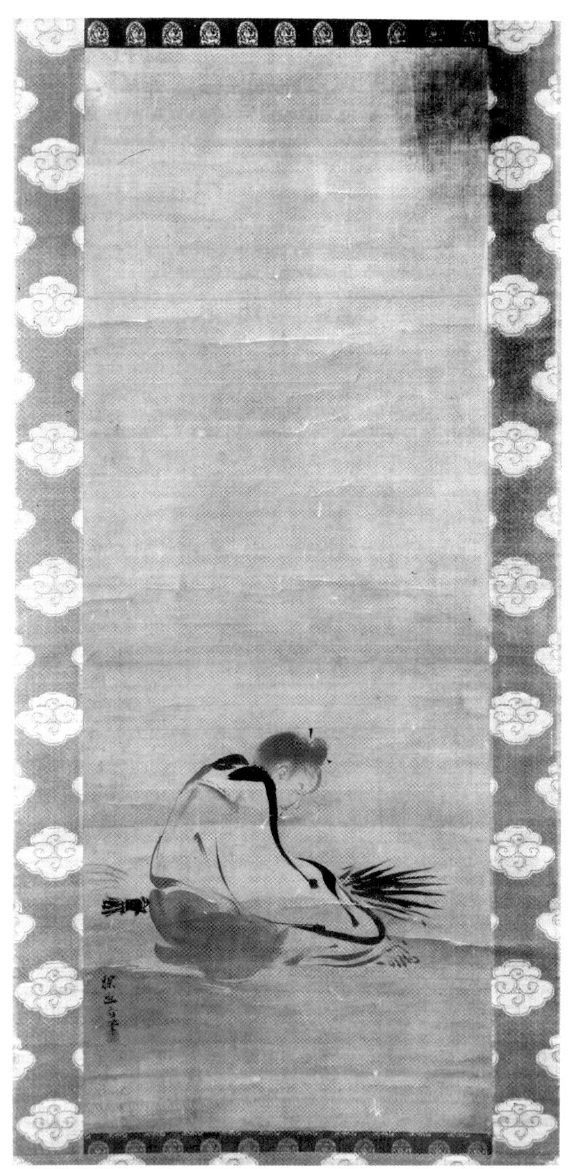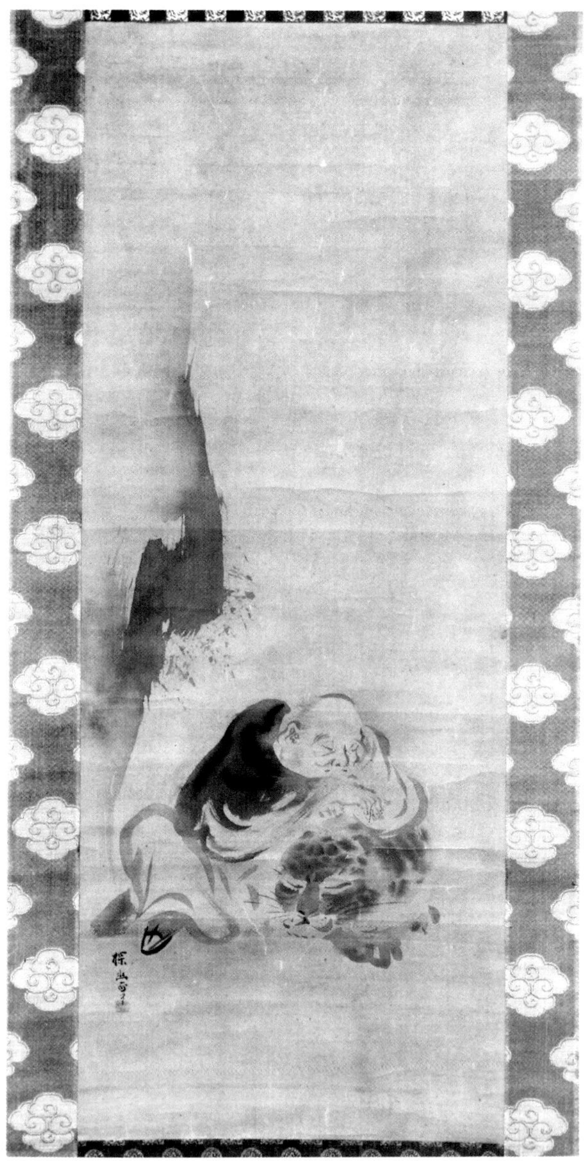

68   BUKAN WITH TIGER AND KANZAN AND JITTOKU, Kanō
Tan'yū (1602-1674),
Japan, 1636-1638, three hanging scrolls

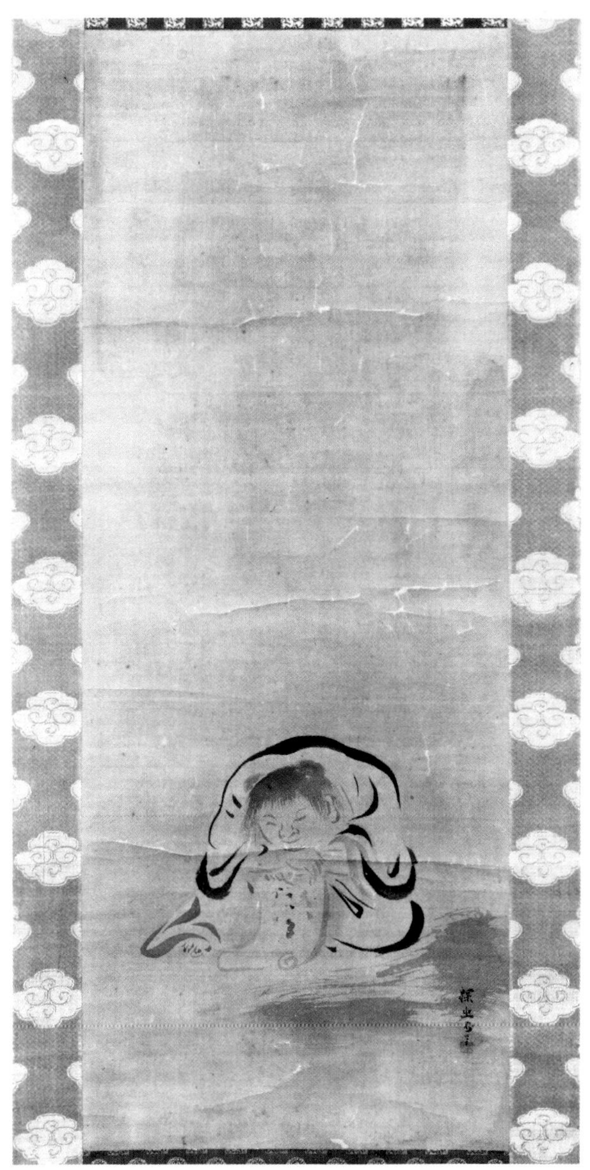

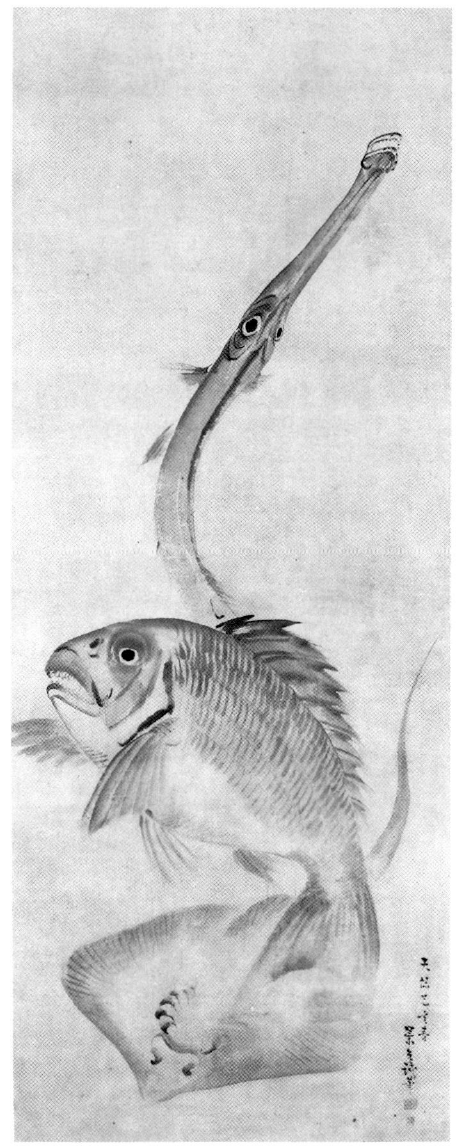

81   THREE FISH, Japan, dated 1839, hanging scroll

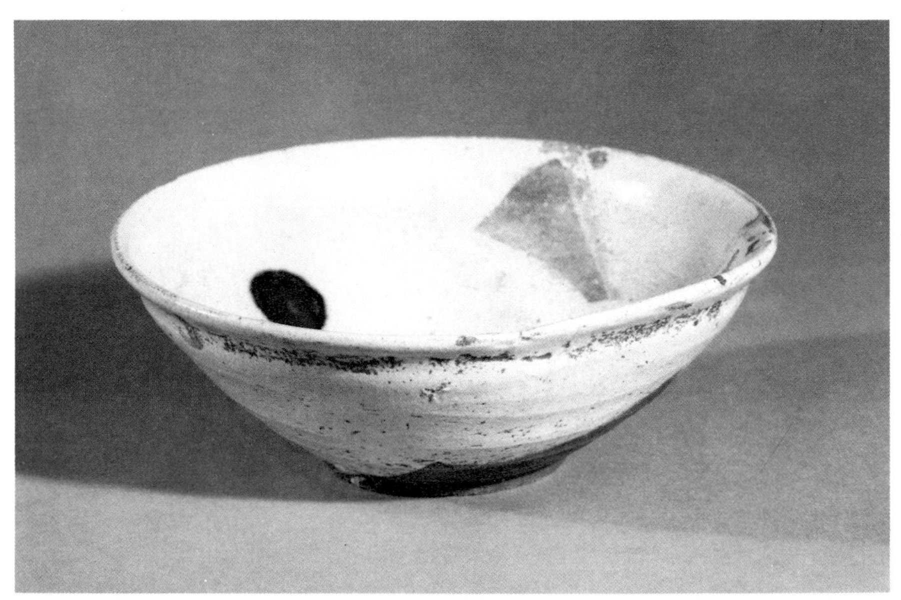

66   TEA BOWL, Japan, ca. 1620's, Mino ware, Ki-seto type

76   TAGASODE, Japan, 19th century, six-fold screen

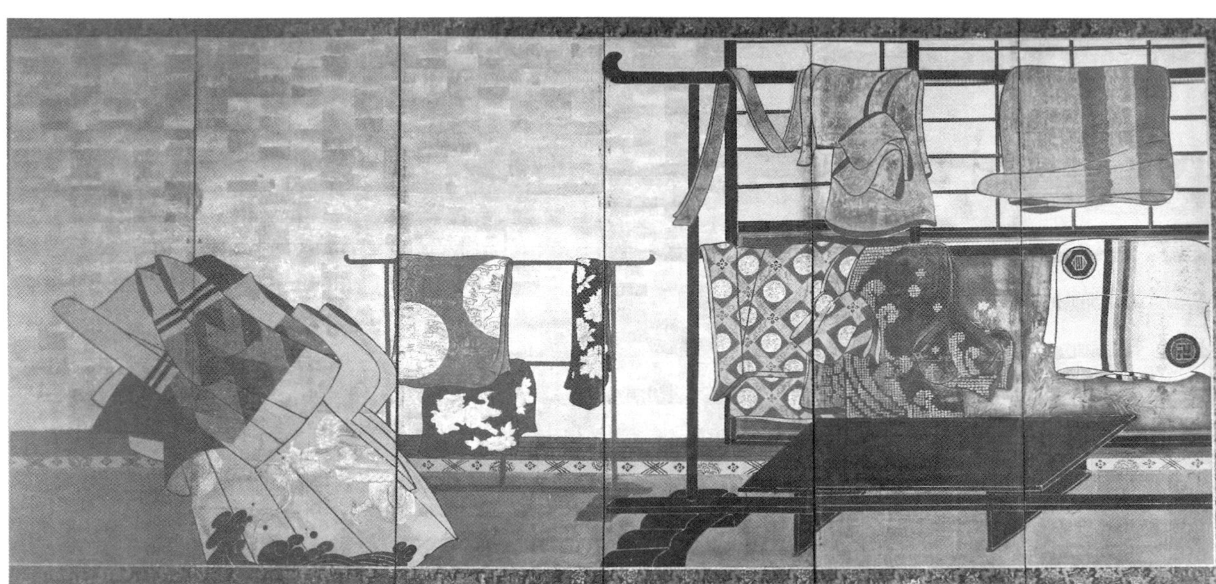

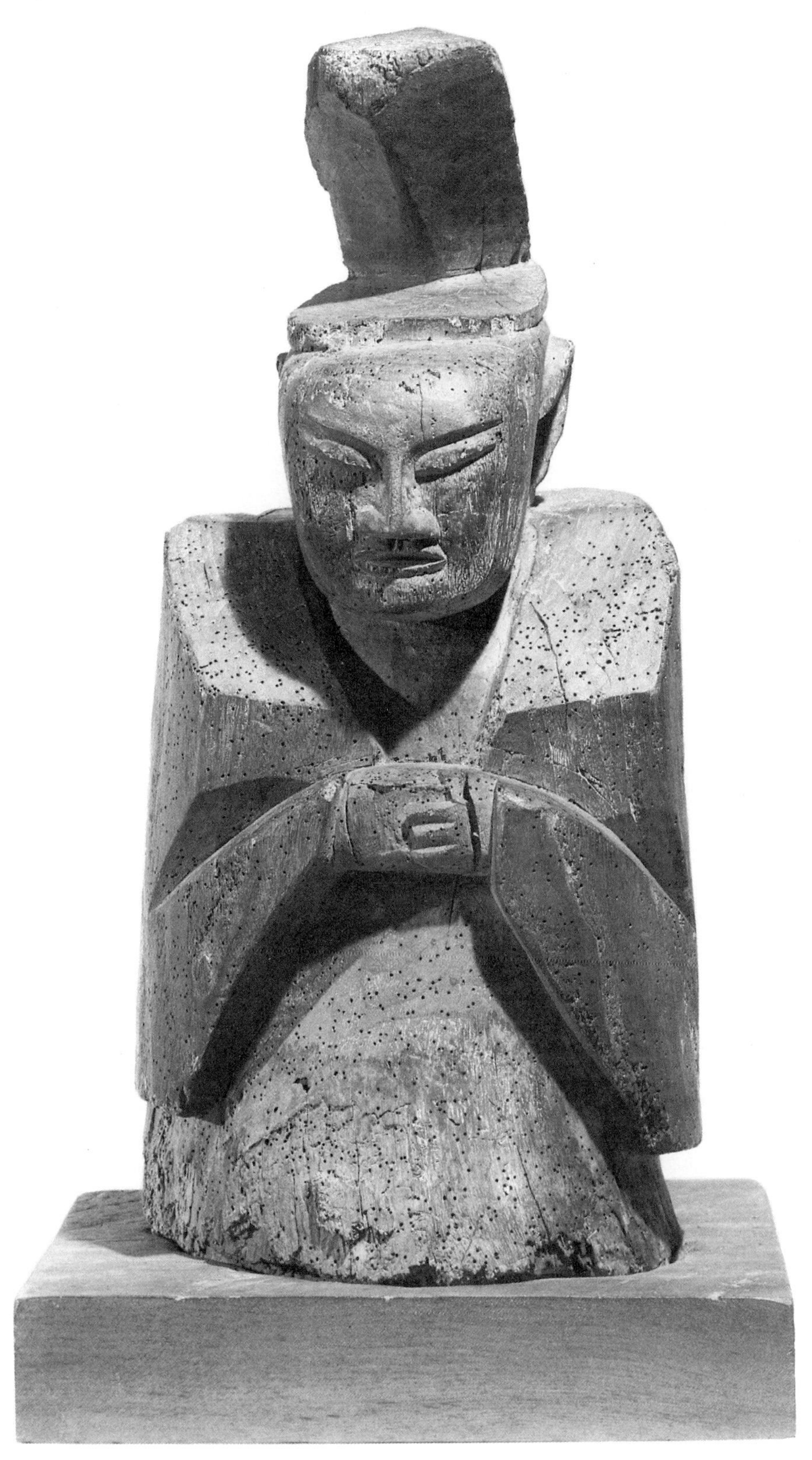

75   SHINTO DEITY, Japan, 18th-19th century, wood

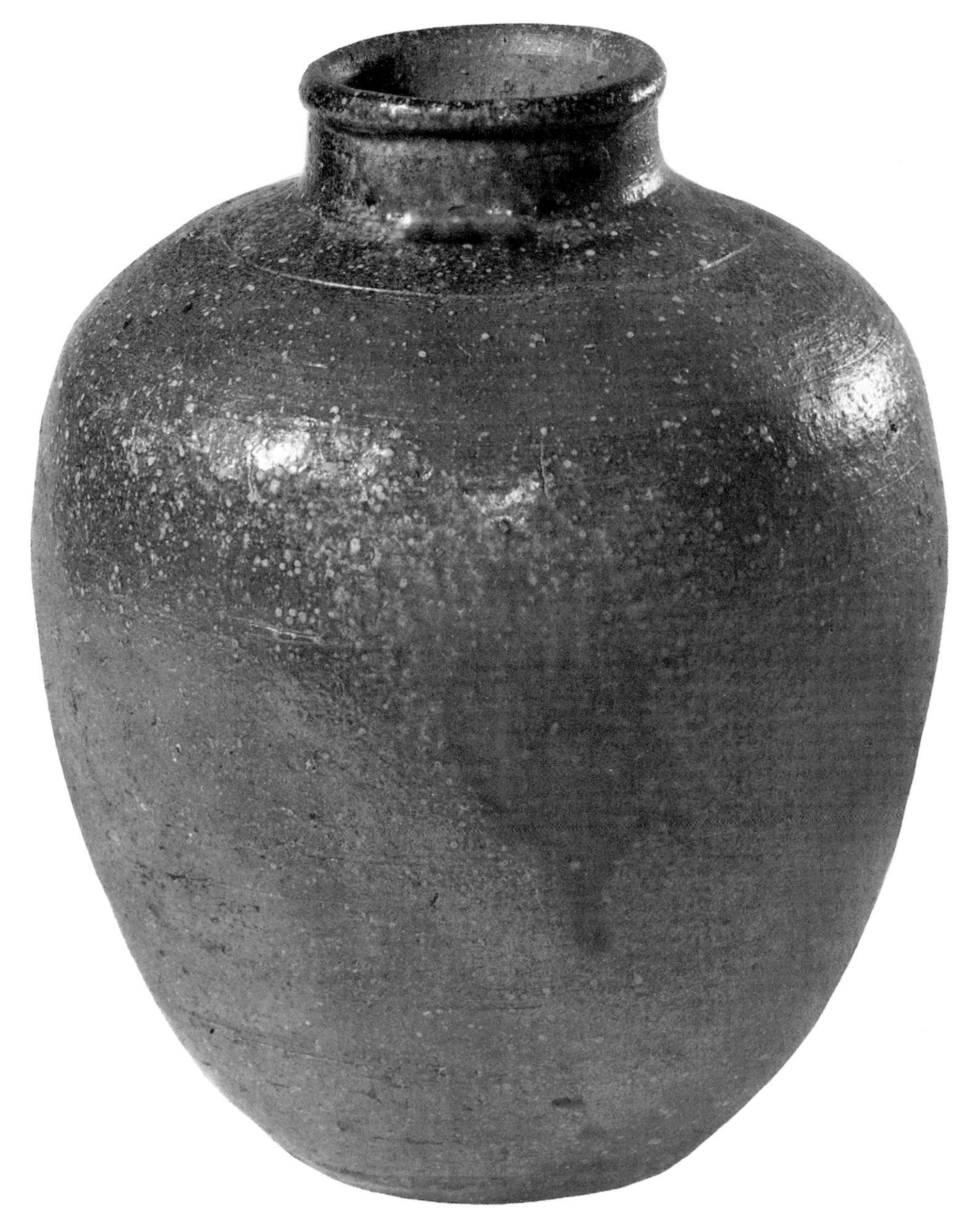

    72   JAR, Japan, 18th century, Shigaraki stoneware

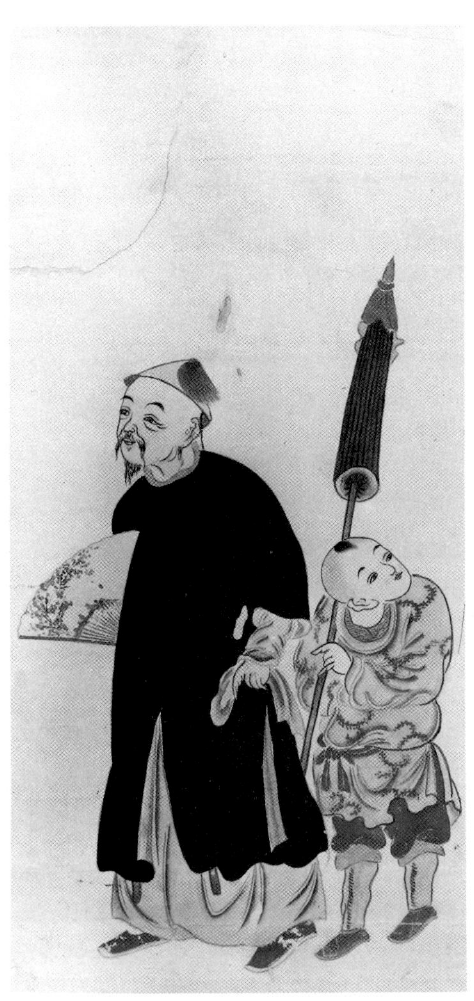

74   CHINESE WITH SERVANT,
Japan, early 19th century,
unmounted painting

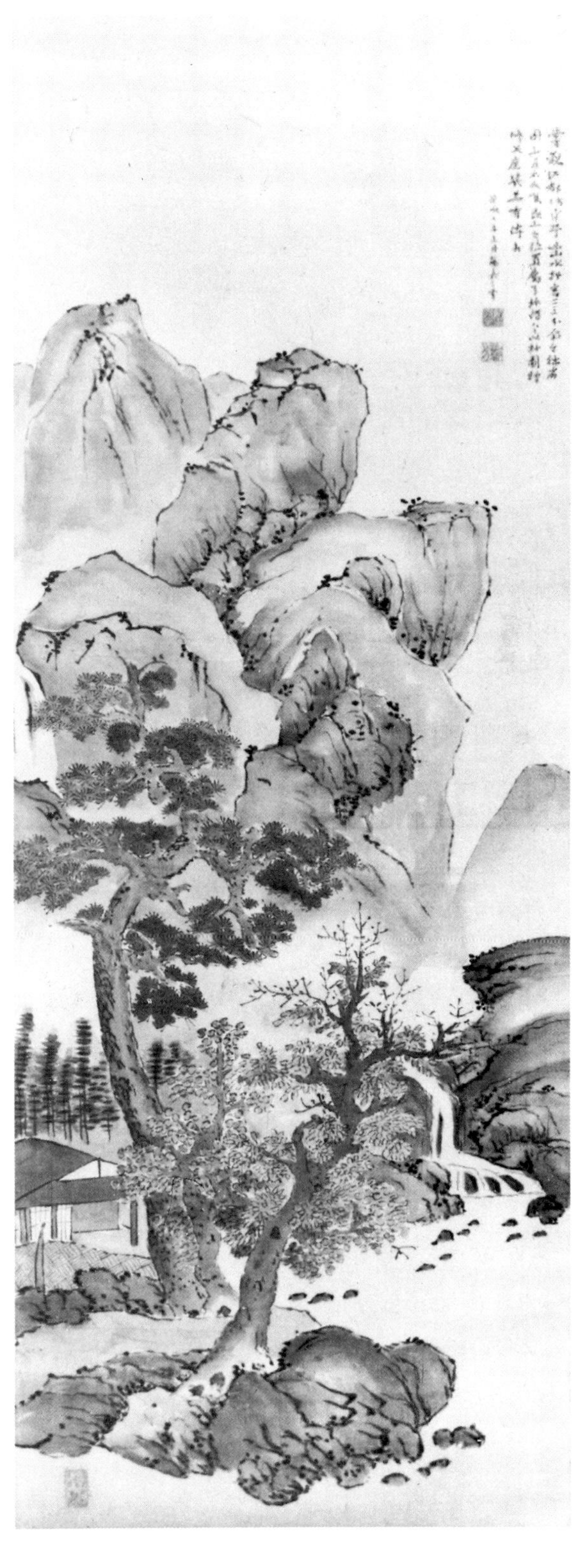

83   AUTUMN LANDSCAPE, Niwa Kagen (1742-1786),
Japan, 18th century, hanging scroll

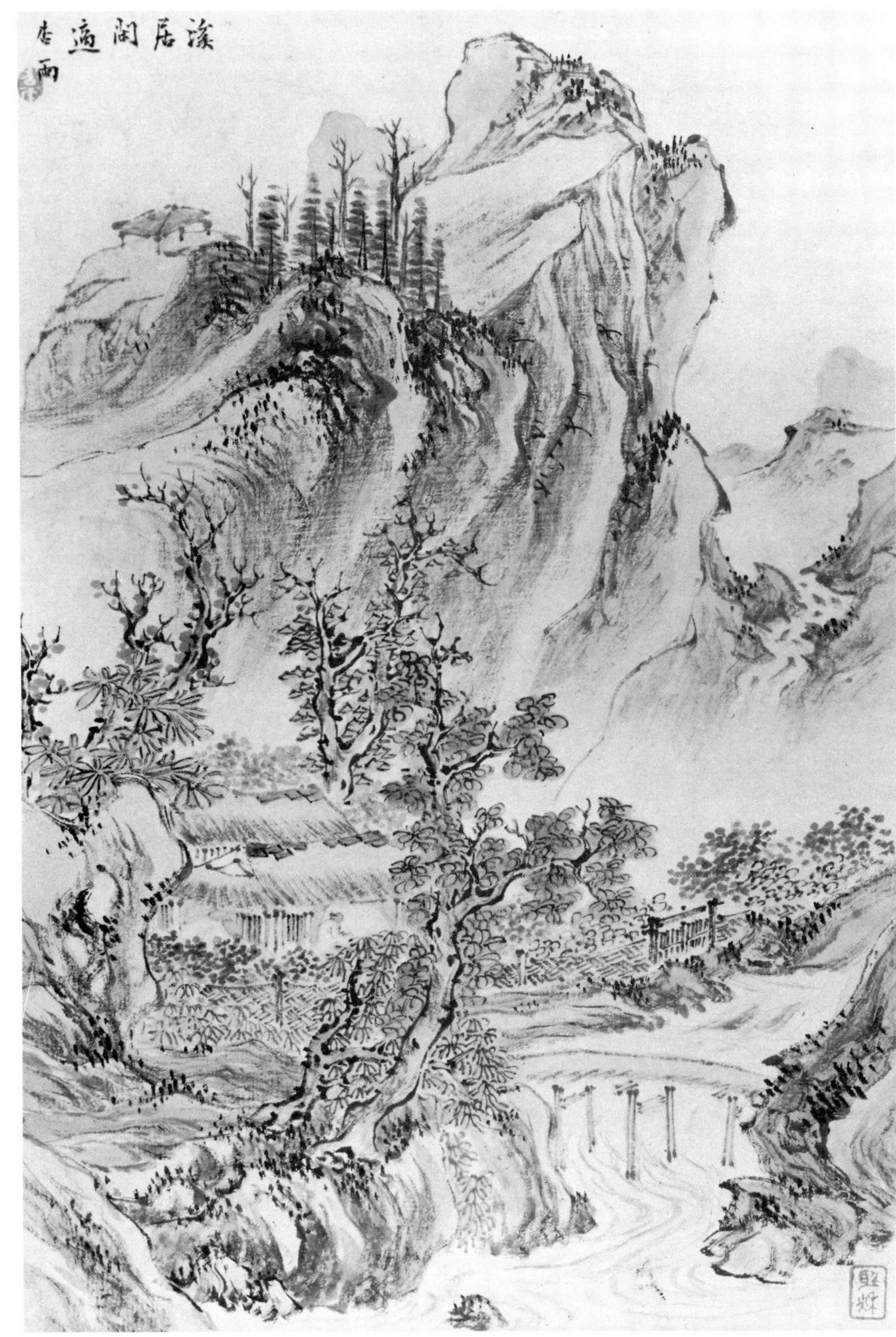

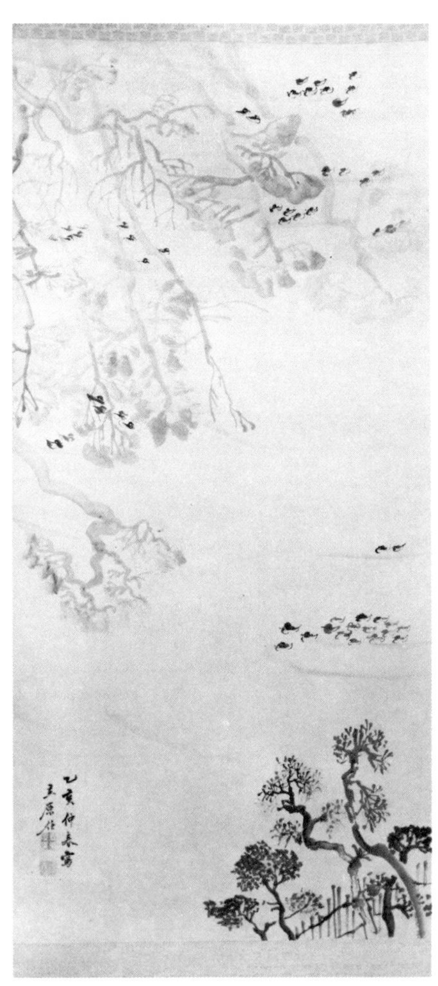

86 LANDSCAPE WITH SHADOWS
AND DUCKS, Tachihara Kyōsho
(1785-1840), Japan, 1815, hanging scroll

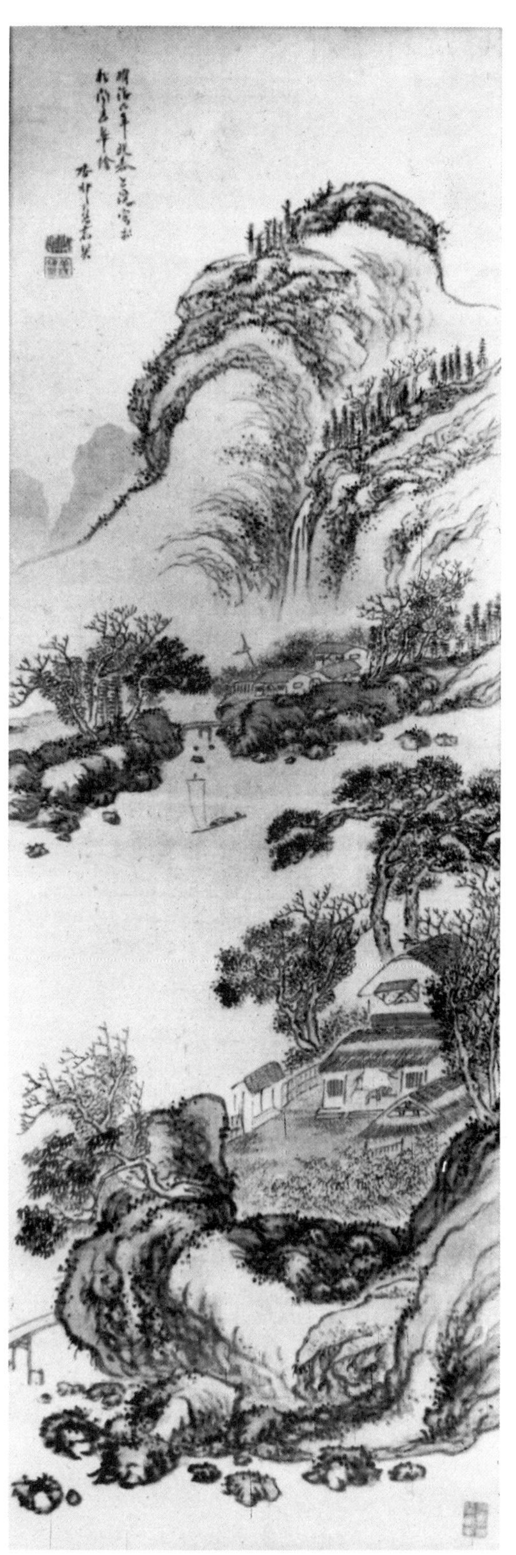

85 AUTUMN LANDSCAPE, Nobusawa Kyōsan (ca. late 19th
century), Japan, dated 1873, hanging scroll

Classical: *India* and *Southeast Asia*

107 BUDDHIST REGULATIONS, Burma, late 19th-early 20th century,
gilt and lacquered wood

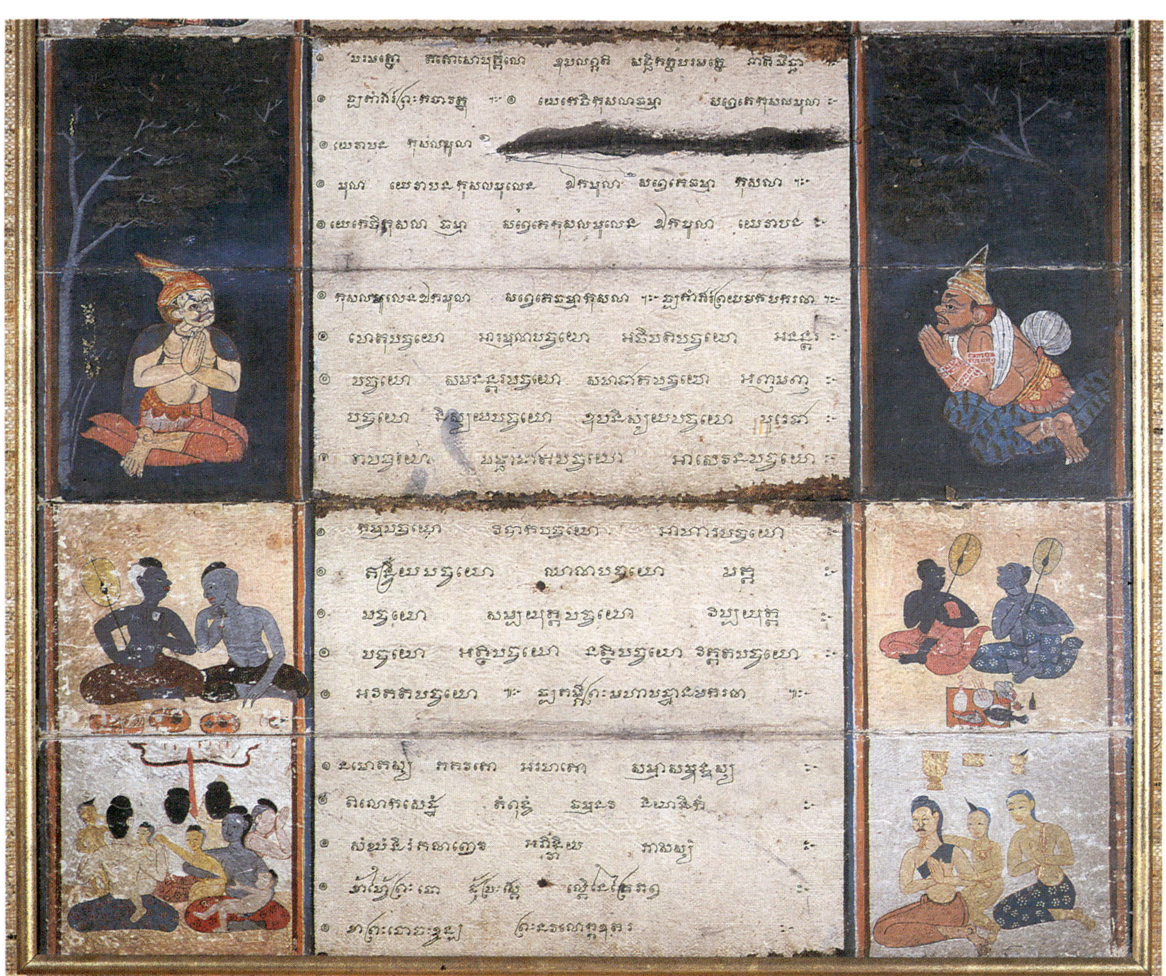

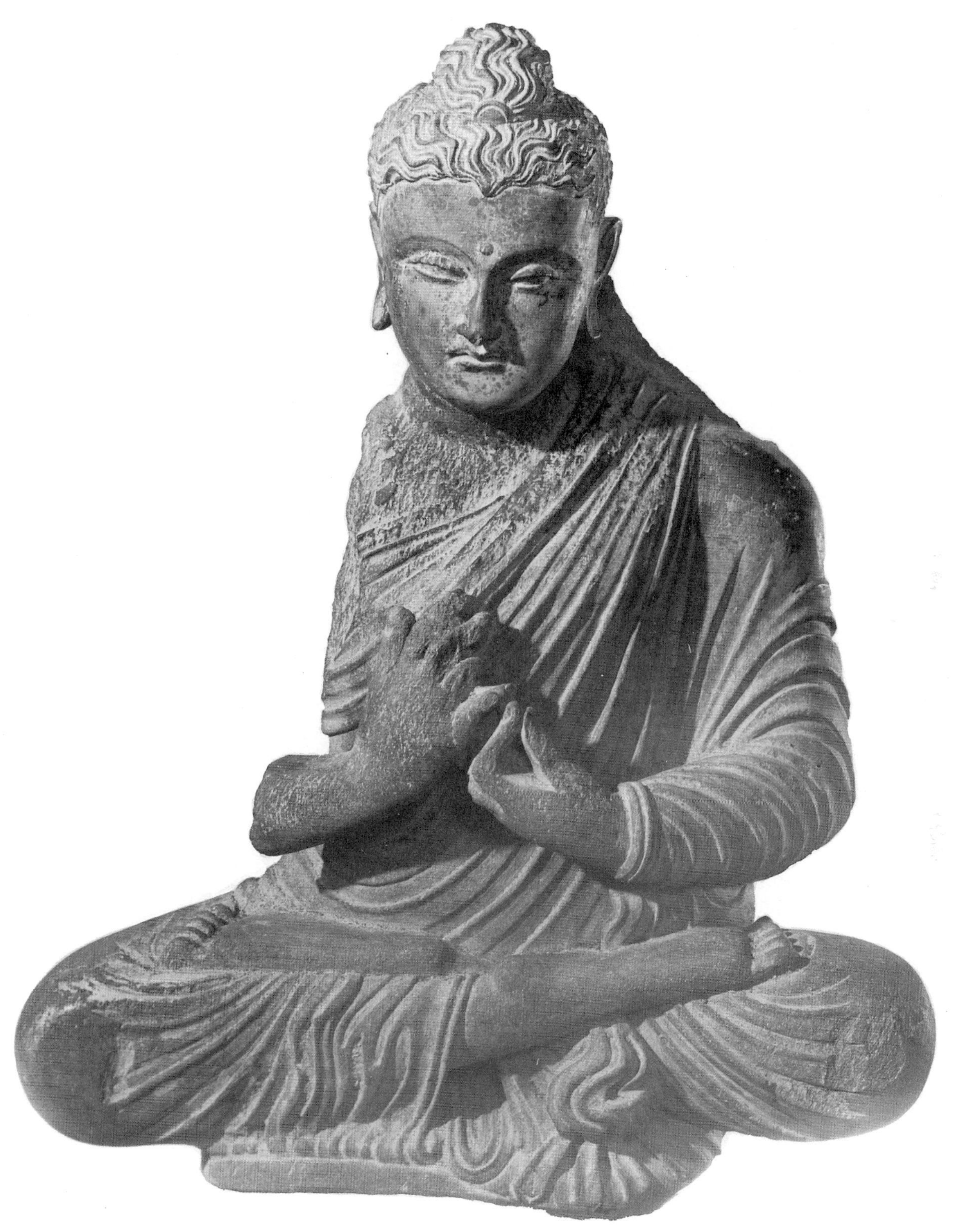

92   SEATED BUDDHA, India, 2nd-4th century A.D., grey schist   131

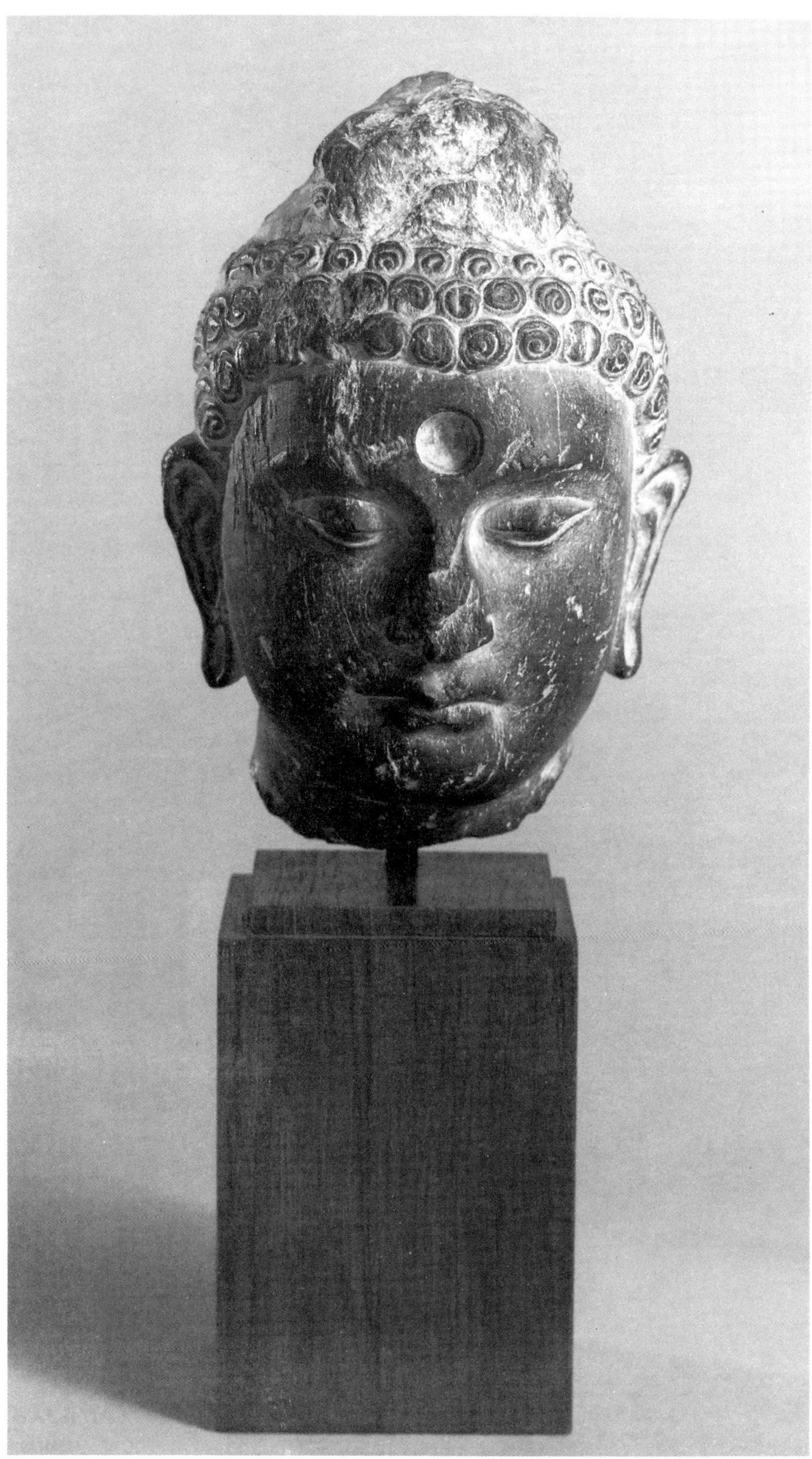

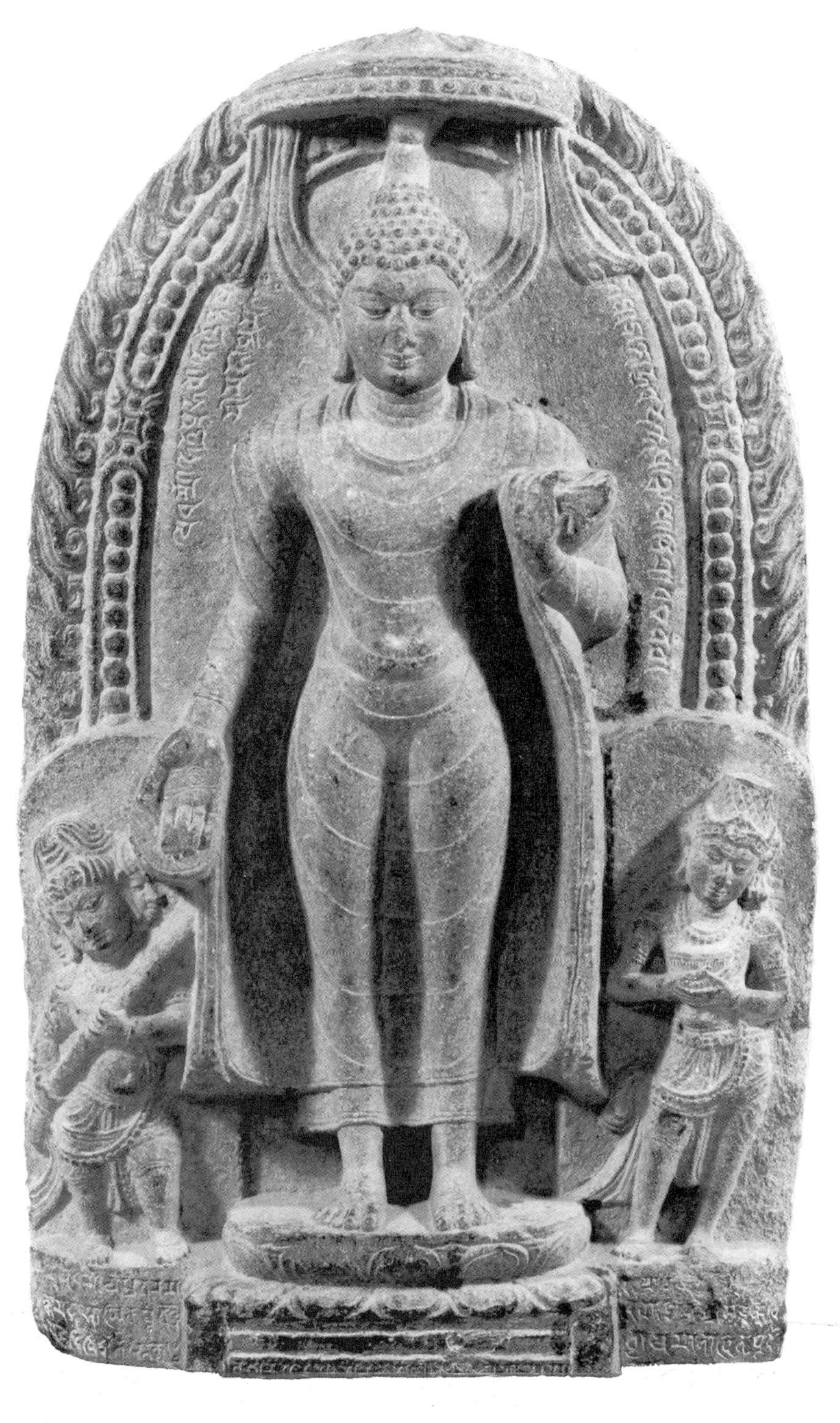

93 STANDING BUDDHA WITH TWO SMALL ATTENDANTS, India,
probably 9th century, grey-black schist

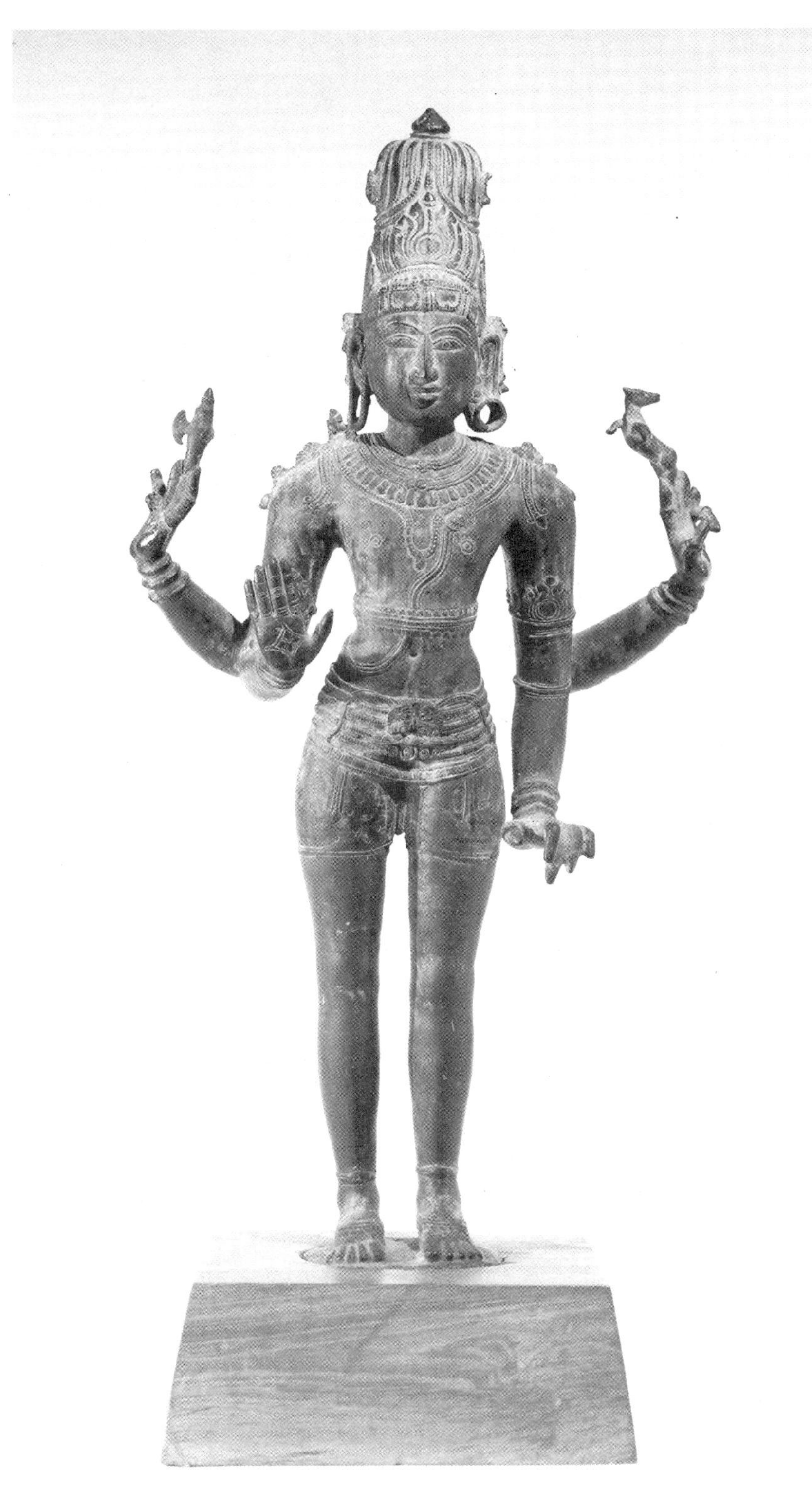

    94   STANDING SHIVA, India, late 15th century, bronze

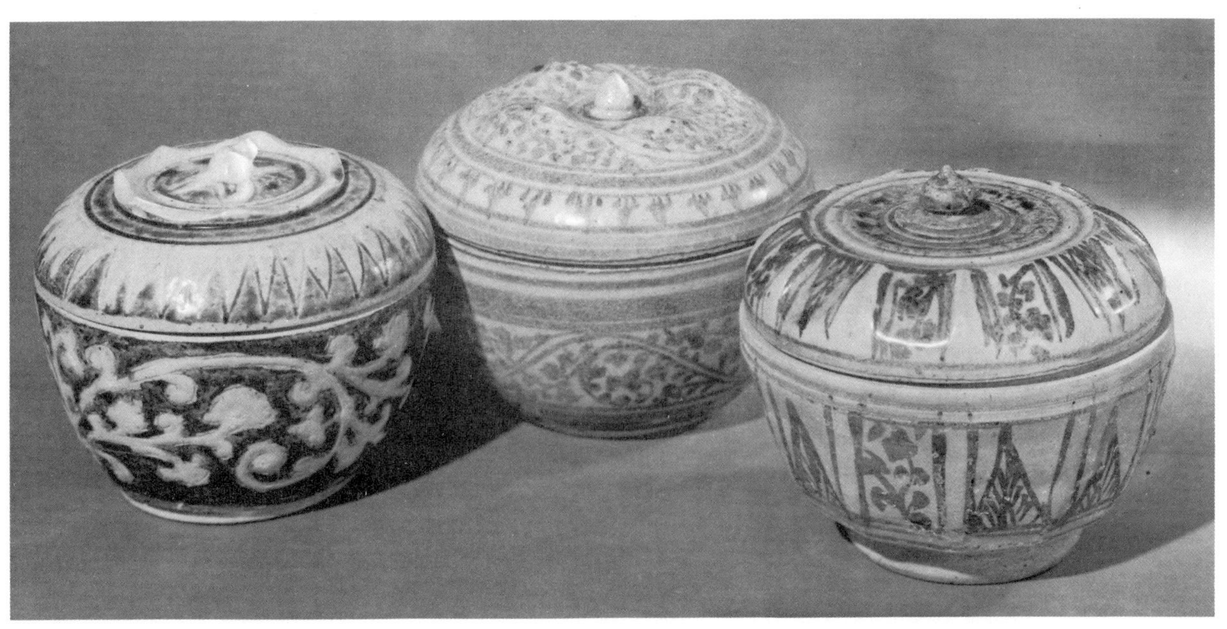

96   THREE CERAMIC BOXES, Thailand, 14th-15th century,
Sawankhalok ware

102 FOUR JARS, Cambodia, 11th-13th century, Khmer ware

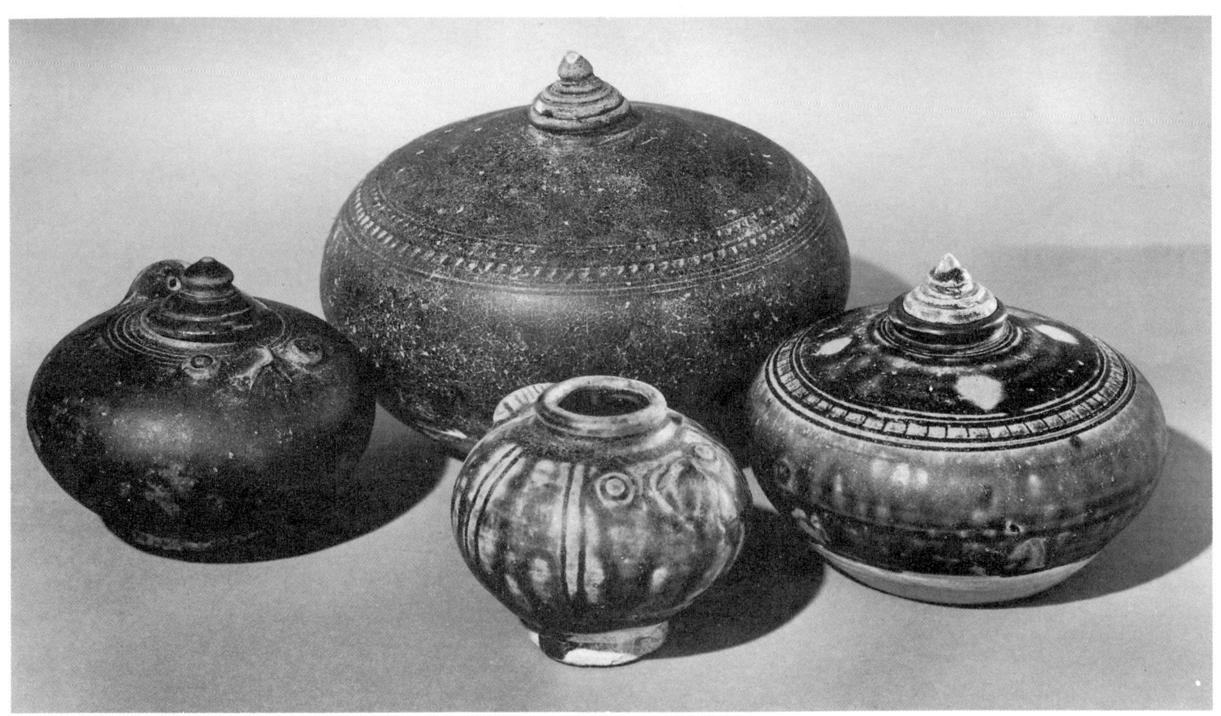

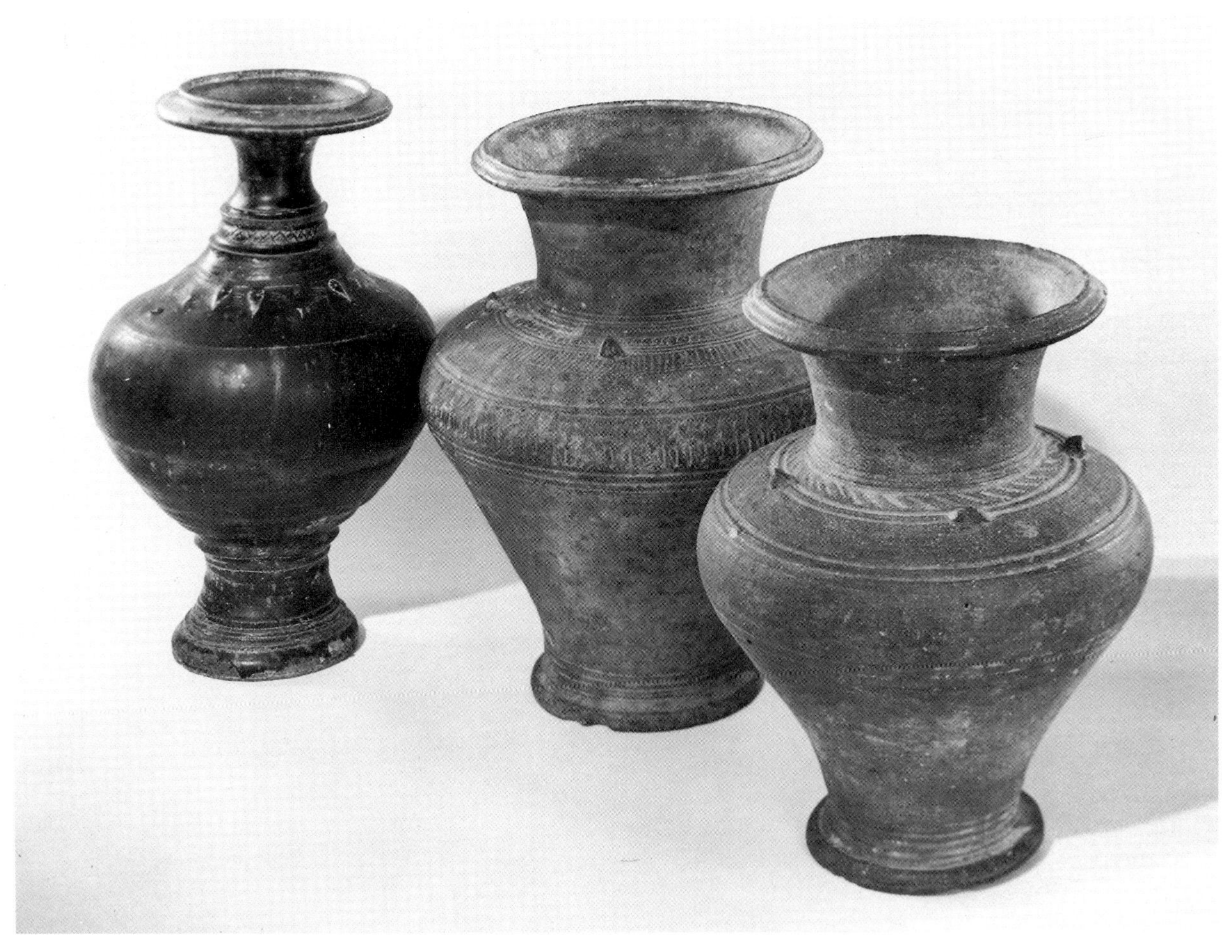

101 THREE JARS, Cambodia, 10th-13th century, Khmer ware

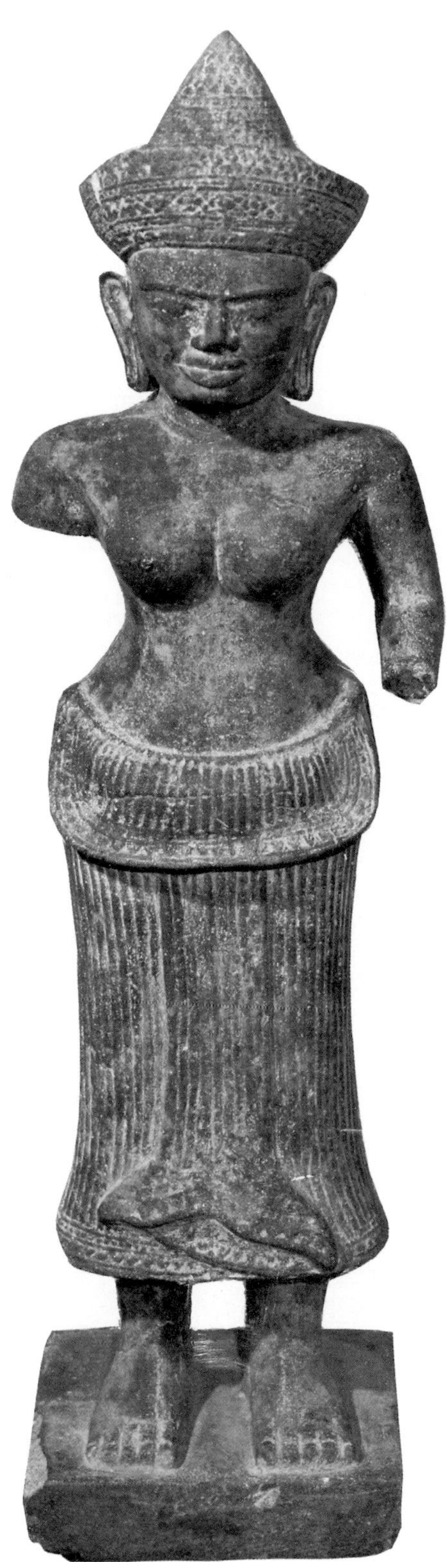

103 STANDING FEMALE FIGURE, Cambodia, 12th-13th century, grey sandstone

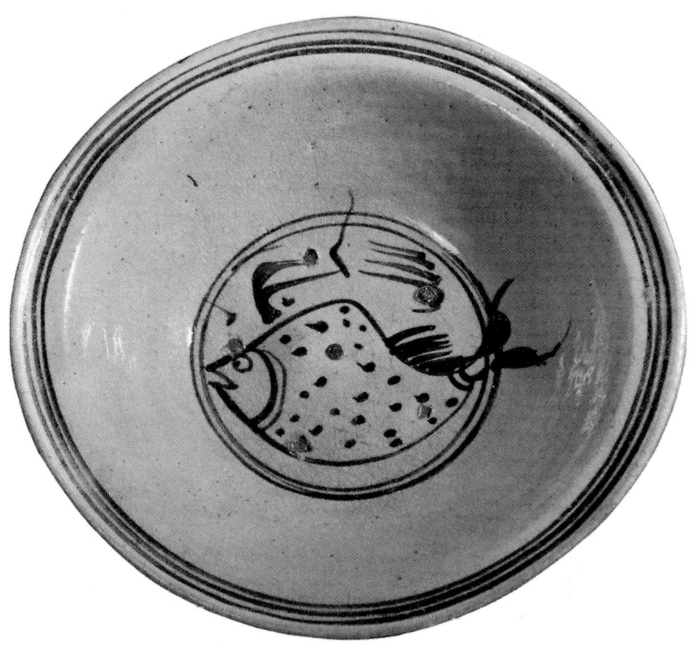

111 BOWL, Thailand, 13th-14th century, Sukhothai ware

109   EPICS AND JATAKA TALES (detail), Thailand, 18th-19th century, panel painting

113   SMALL DISH and TWO WINE CUPS, Vietnam, dated 1847-1883, blue and white porcelain

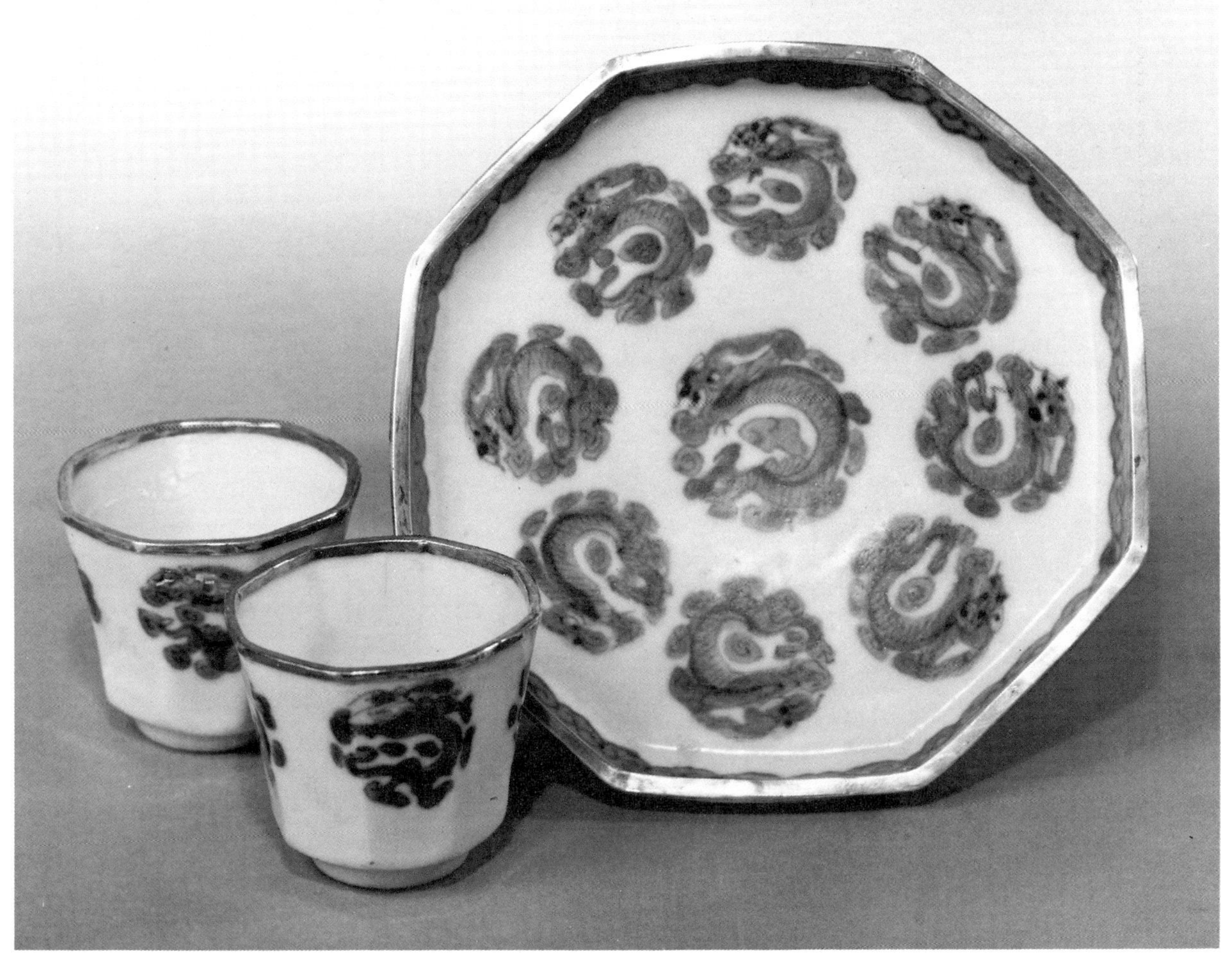

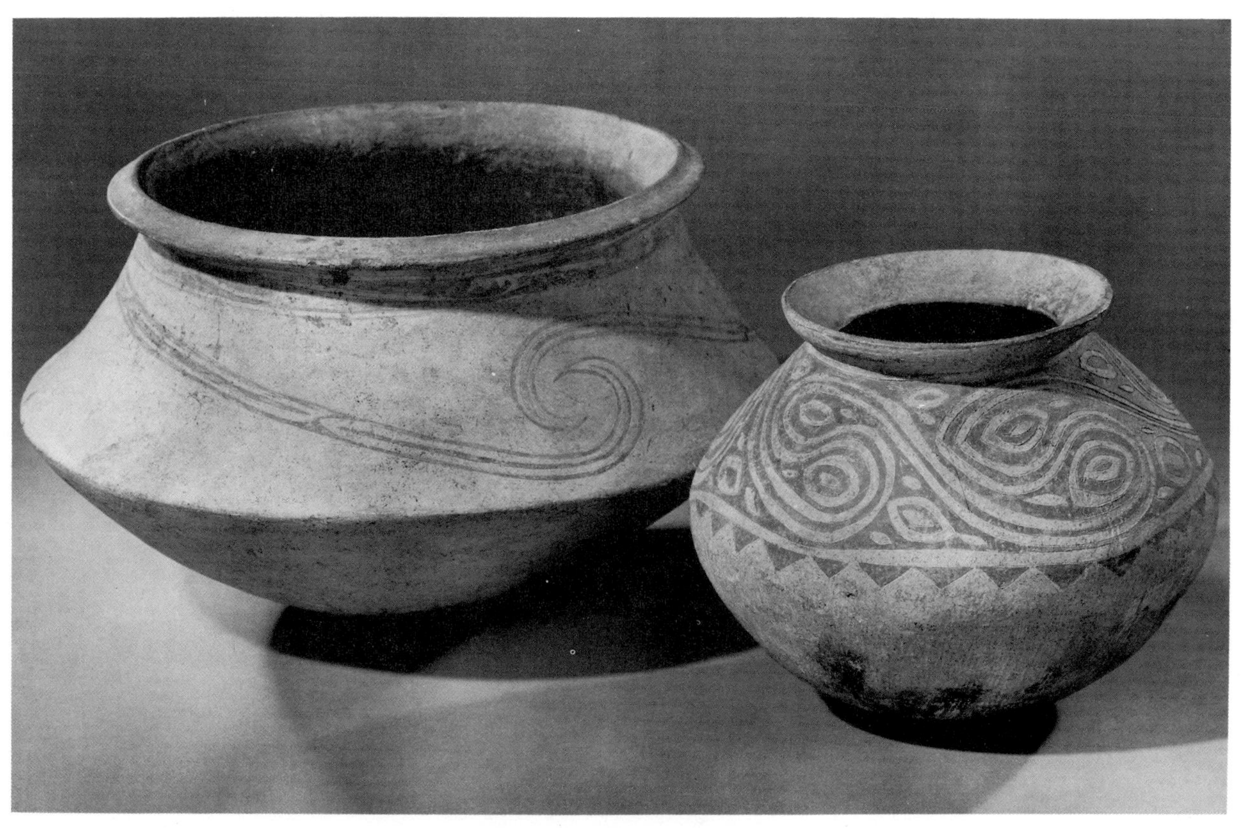

110   TWO POTS, Thailand, ca. 1000 B.C.-400 B.C., Ban Chiang pottery

112   THREE COVERED JARS, Annam, ca. 15th century, blue and white
ceramic

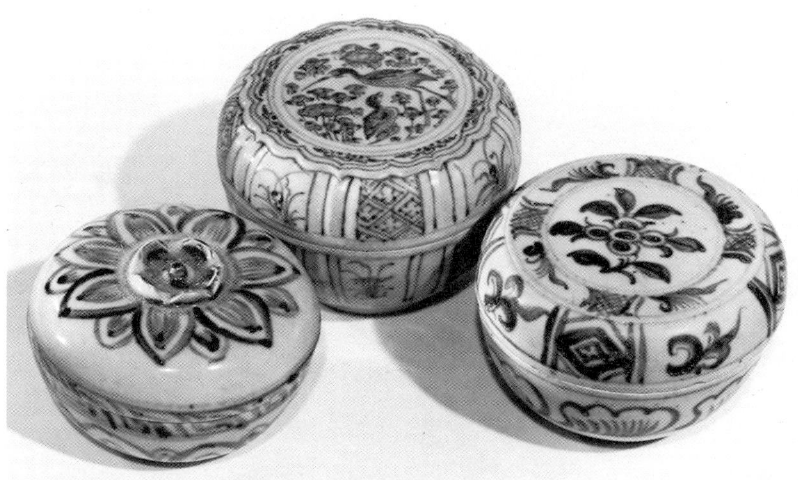

Miniatures: *China*

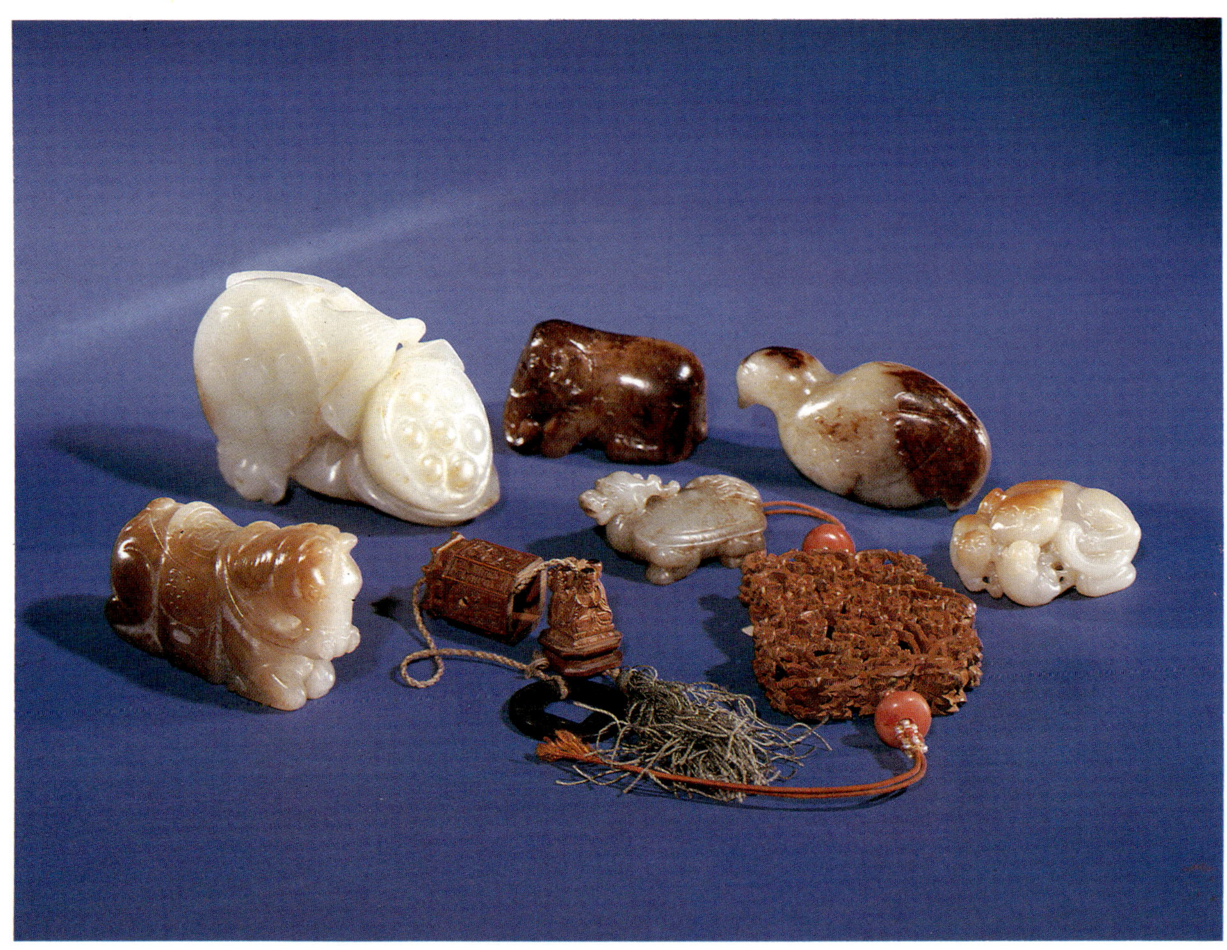

122 a-h MINIATURES, China, 15th through 19th century, a variety of jades and woods

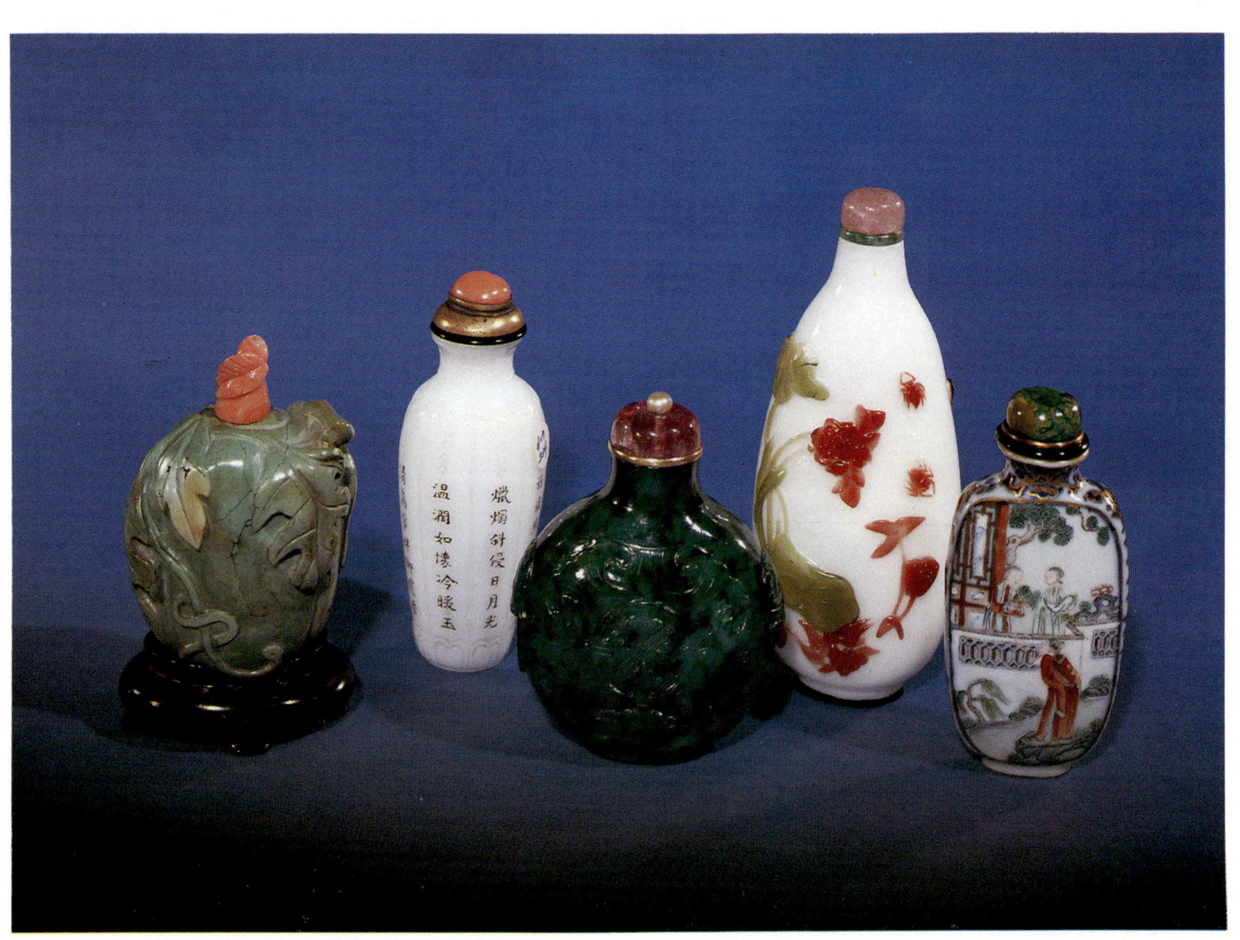

135 a-e SNUFF BOTTLES, China, 18th century, various materials

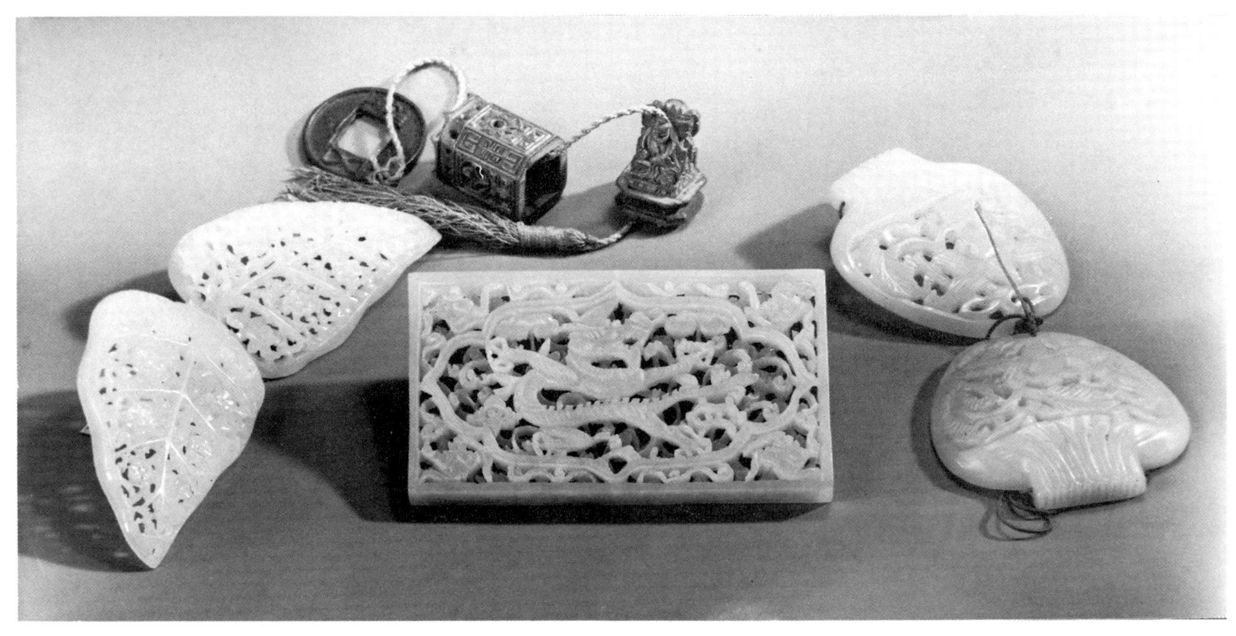

127 a-c PLAQUES AND PERFUMER, China, 15th through 18th
century, jade

119 BI-DISC, China, 1st-2nd century, black jade

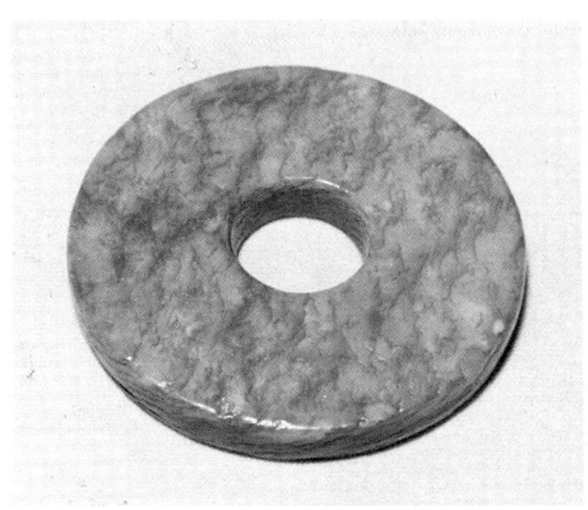

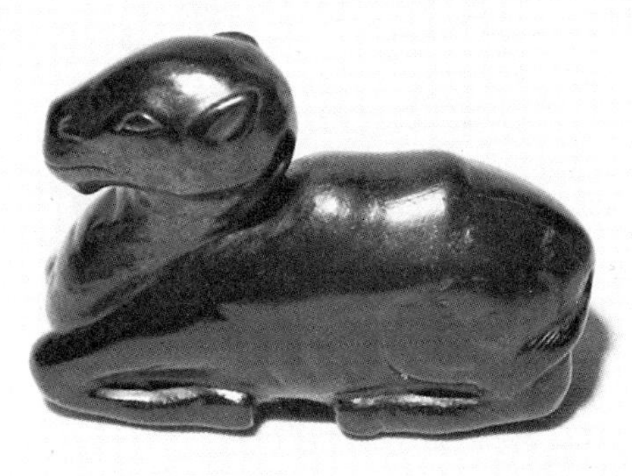

120 CAMEL, China, 4th-6th century, black jade

142

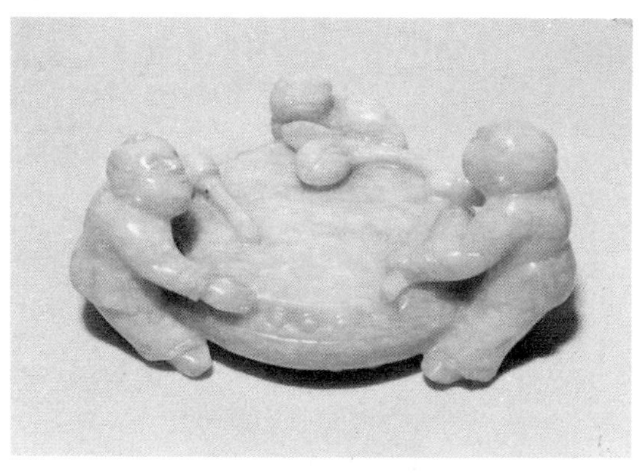

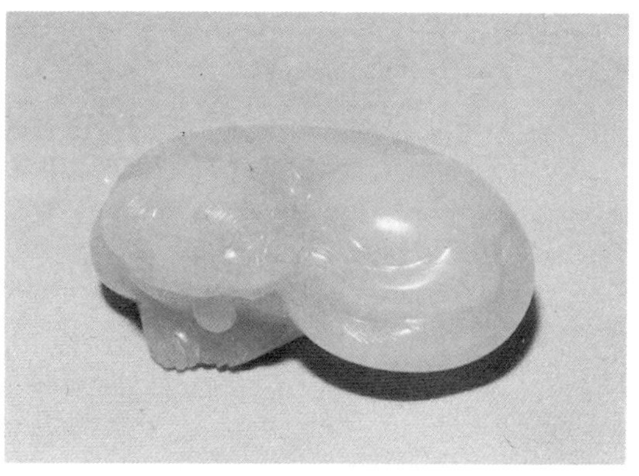

125 TWO BOYS PLAYING THE DRUM,
China, 16th-17th century, jade

128 RECLINING DOG, China, 18th century, jade

134 a-c HAIR PIN, PENDANT AND TWO LOTUS ROOTS, China,
17th through 19th century, jade

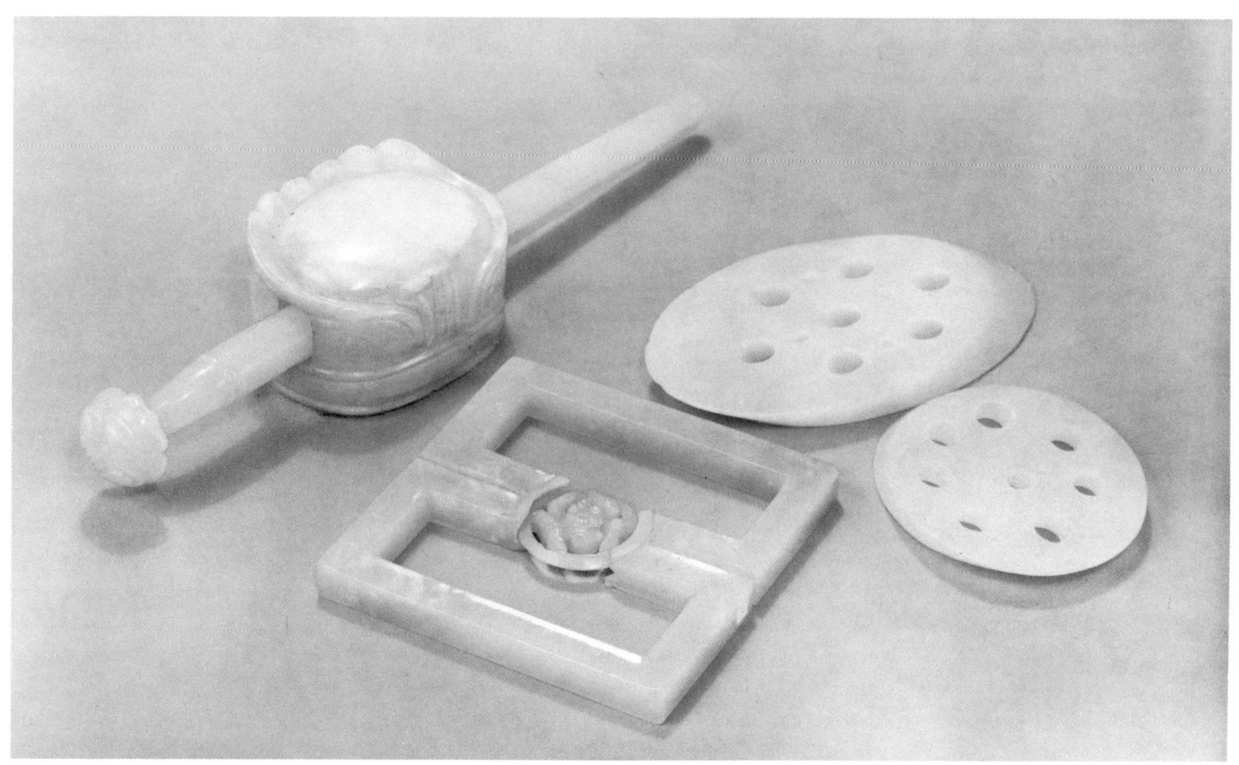

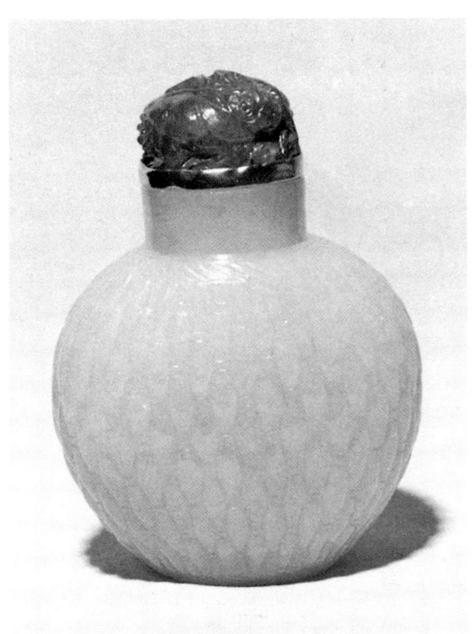

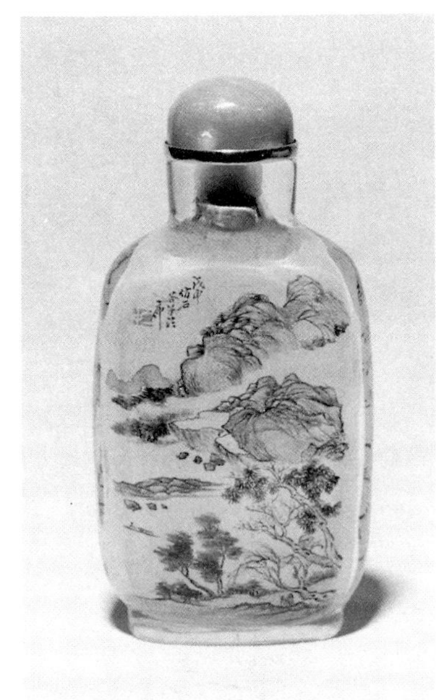

137 SNUFF BOTTLE, China, 18th century, jadeite

141 SNUFF BOTTLE, China, dated 1908, glass

136 SNUFF BOTTLE, China, 18th century, jade

138 SNUFF BOTTLE, China, 18th century,
hair-crystal

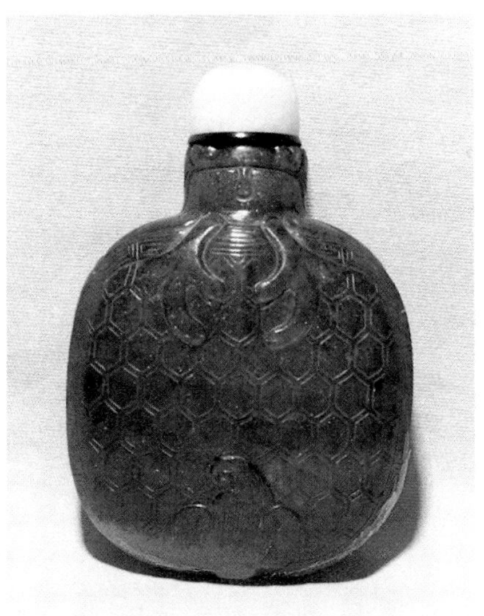

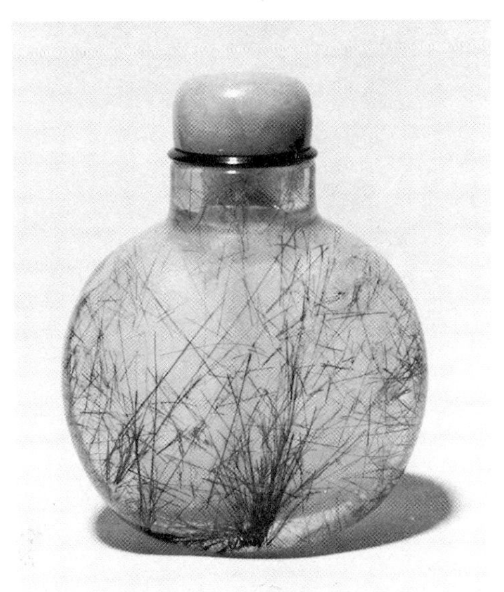

Miniatures: *Korea* and *Japan*

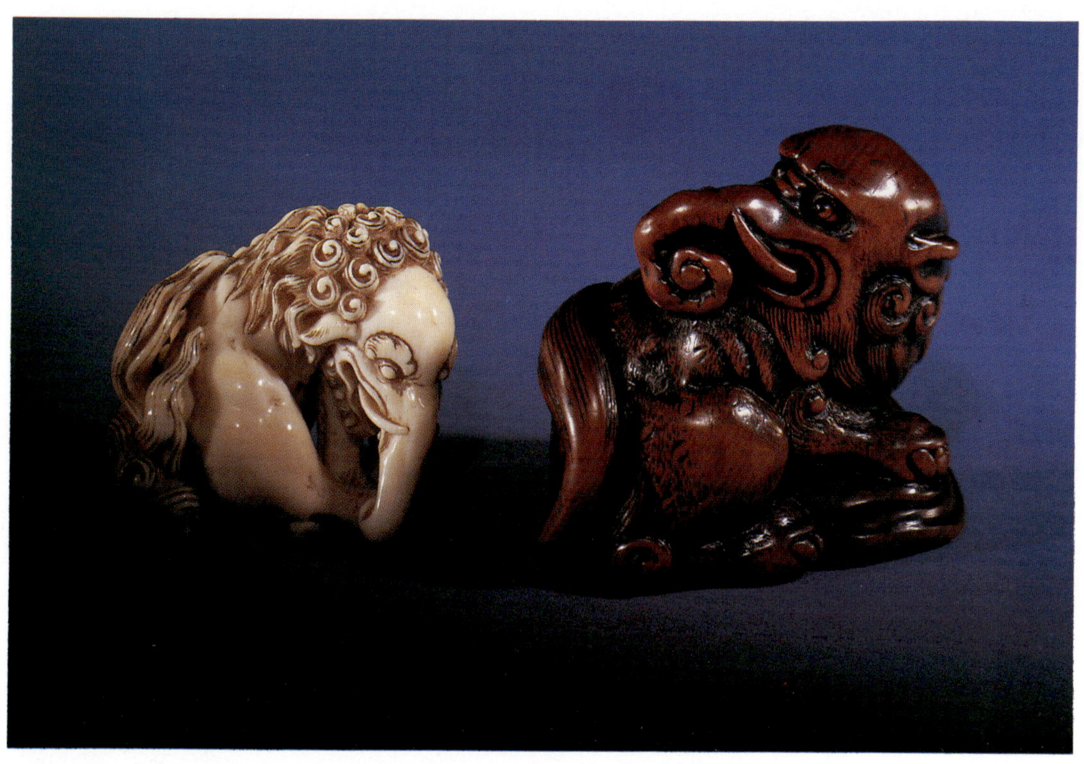

168 TWO ANIMAL GHOSTS, Japan, 18th century, ivory and wood
netsuke

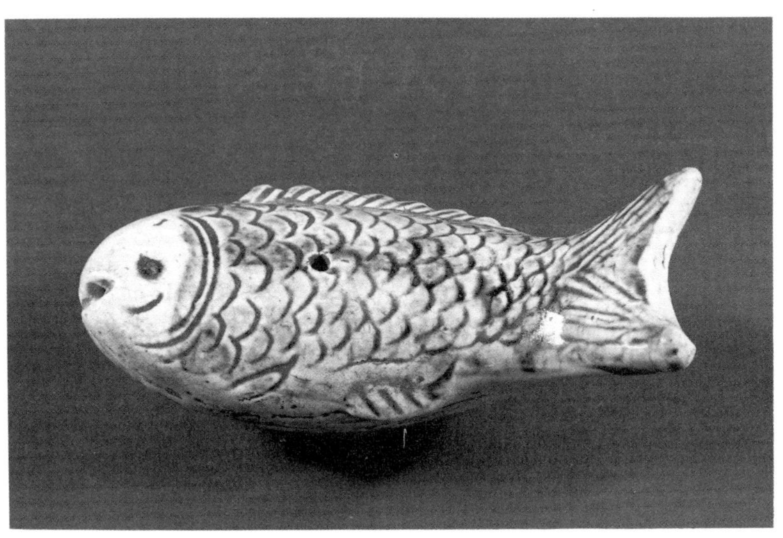

155 CURVED FISH WATER DROPPER, Korea, 17th century, blue and
white porcelain

157 POMEGRANATE WATER DROPPER, Korea, late 17th-early 18th
century, porcelain with purple-red glaze

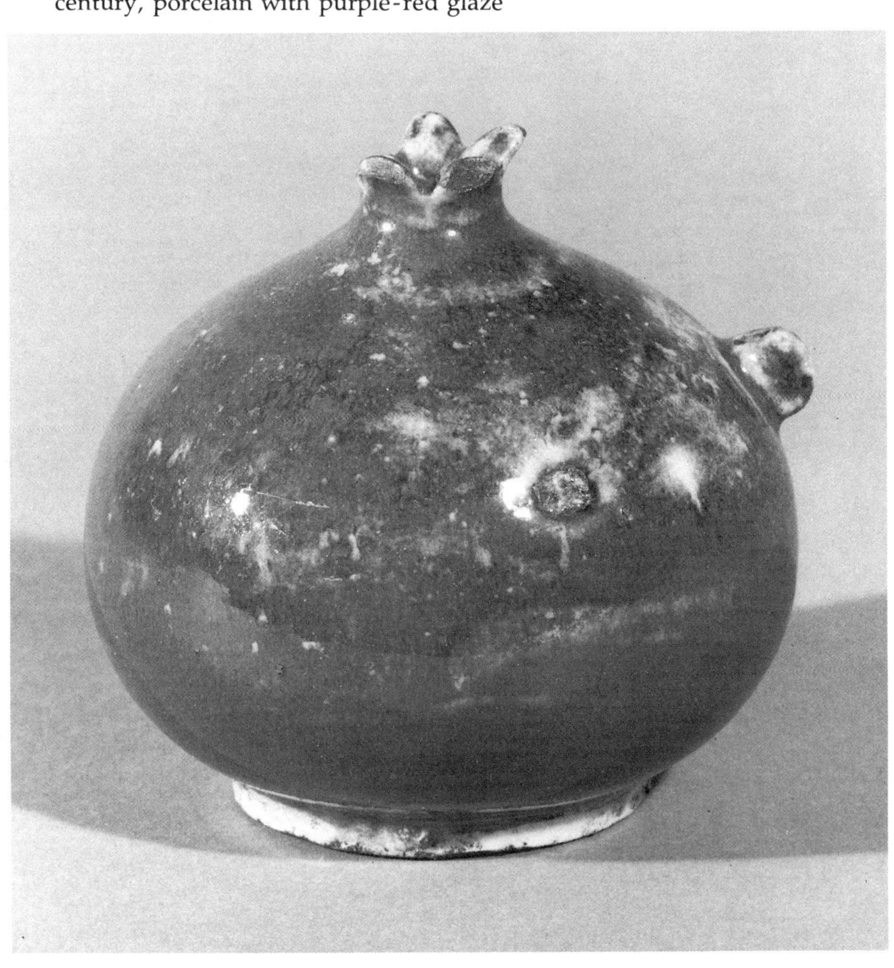

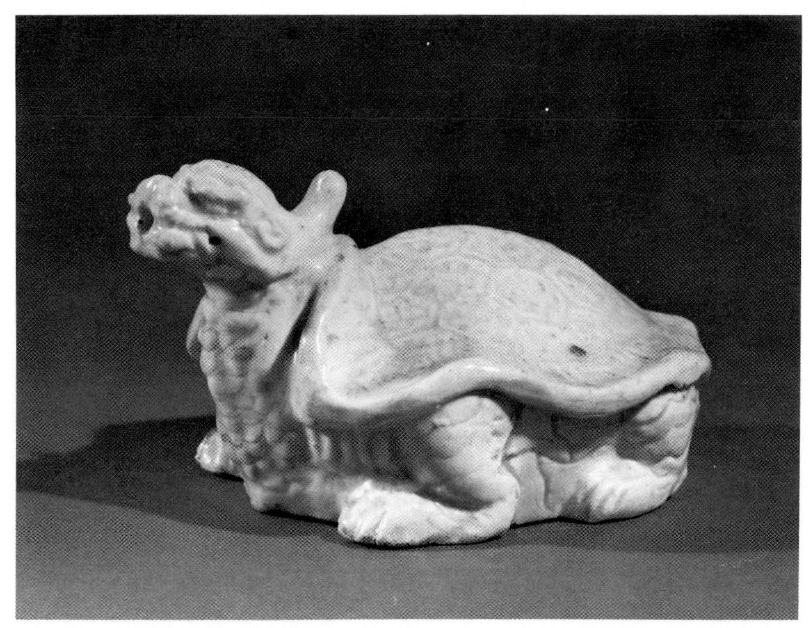

156   TORTOISE WITH DRAGON HEAD WATER DROPPER, Korea,
late 17th-early 18th century, porcelain with celadon glaze

158   MELON WATER DROPPER, Korea, late 17th-early 18th century,
porcelain

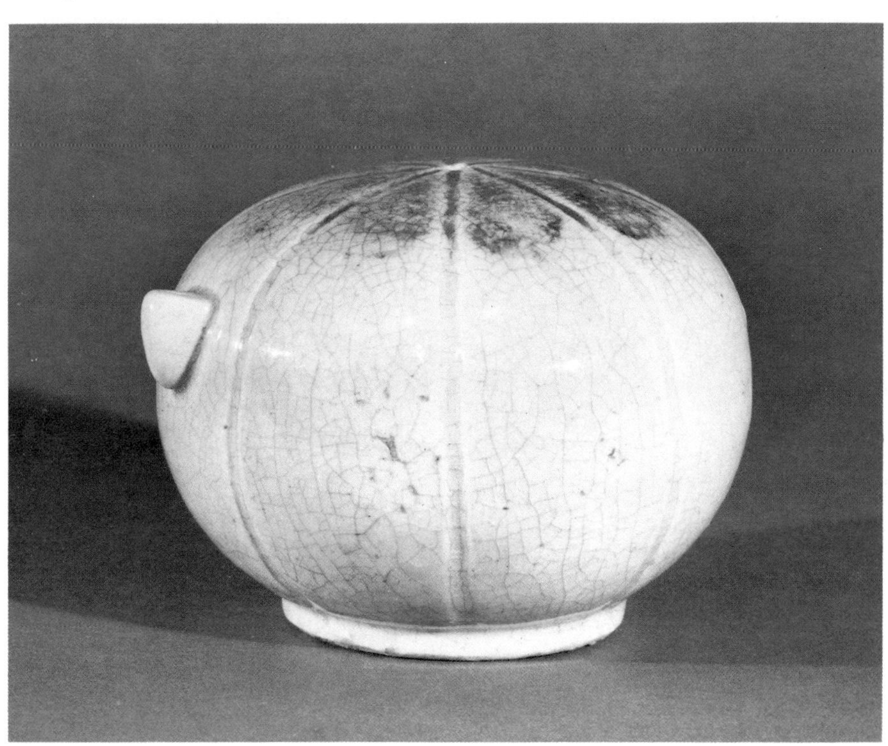

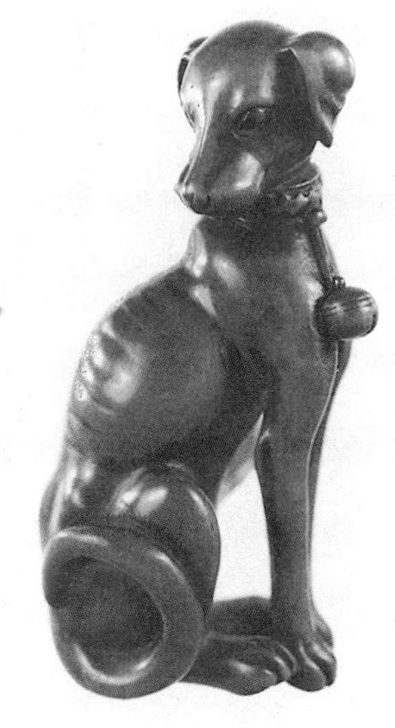

183 DOG, Japan, 18th century,
boxwood netsuke

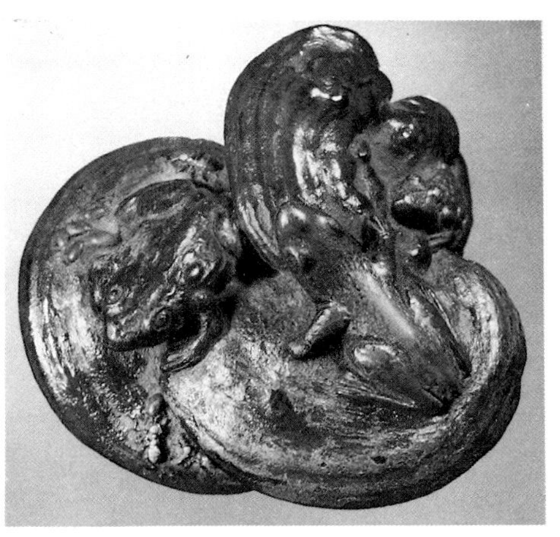

170 FROGS AND REISHI FUNGUS,
Japan, dated 1723, wood netsuke

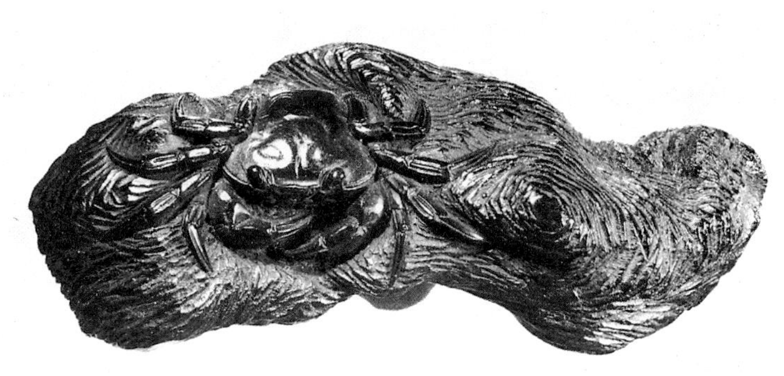

180 CRAB ON MOKUME BASE,
Japan, 18th century, wood netsuke

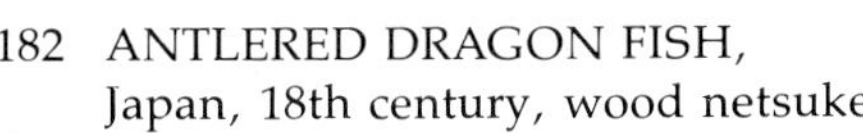

182 ANTLERED DRAGON FISH,
Japan, 18th century, wood netsuke

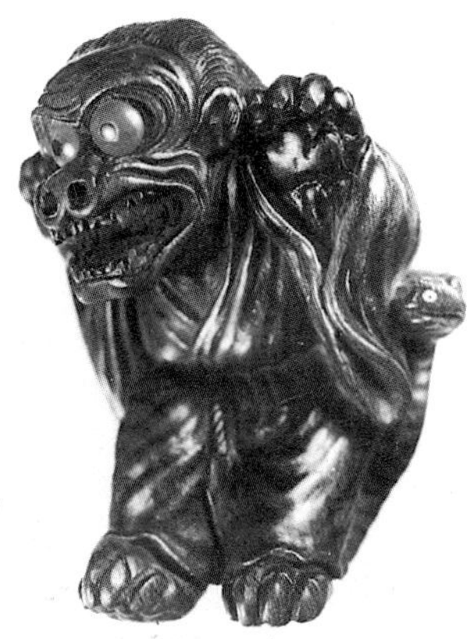

181 NUE, Japan, 18th century,
wood netsuke

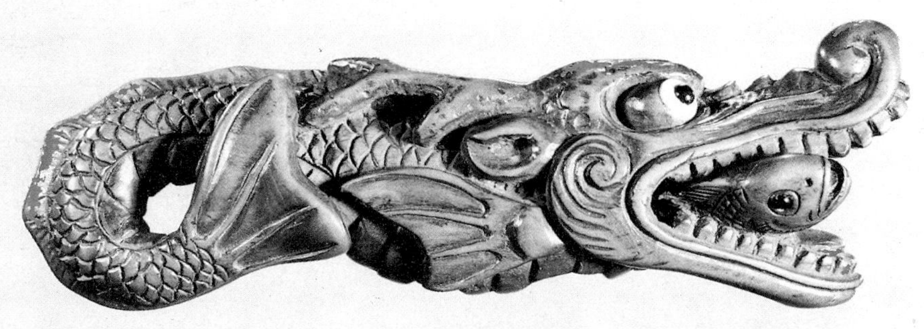

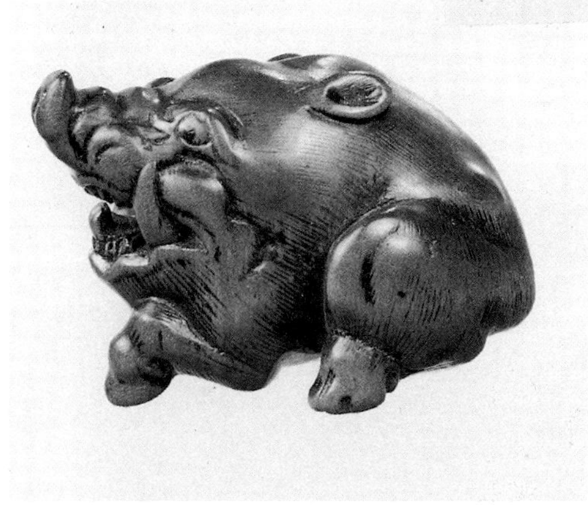

191 BOAR, Japan, late 18th-
early 19th century, wood netsuke

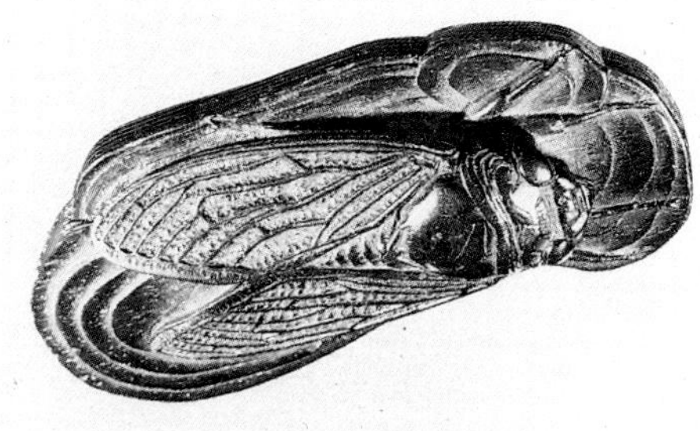

192 CICADA ON MOKUME BASE,
Japan, late 18th-early
19th century, wood netsuke

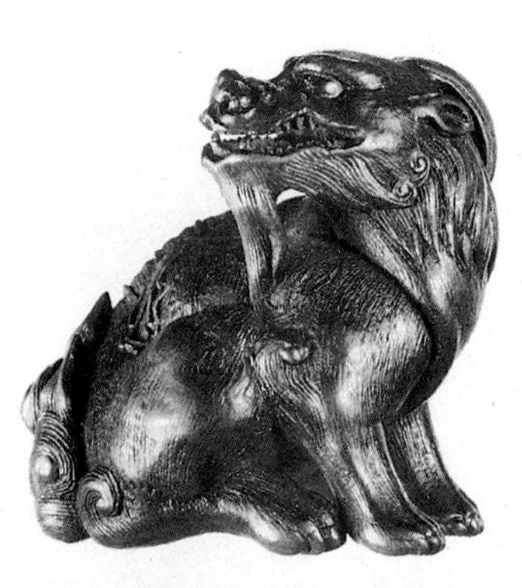

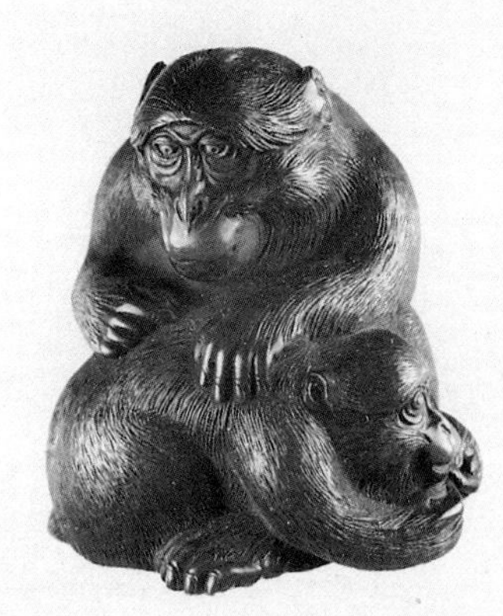

193 MONKEY WITH ITS BABY, Japan, late 18th-early
19th century, metal alloys
and gold netsuke

194 SEATED KIRIN, Japan, early 19th
century, black wood netsuke

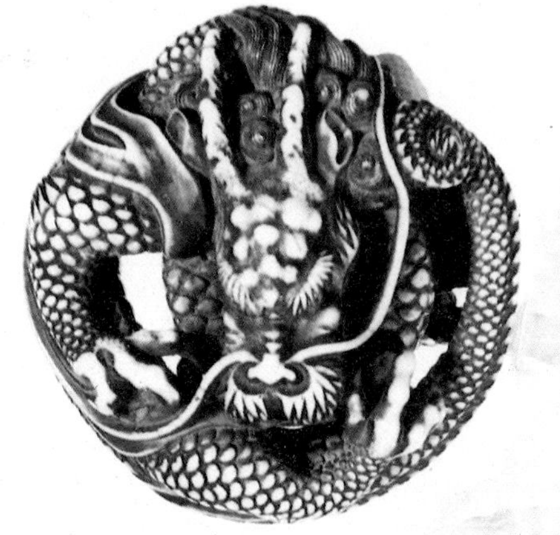

203 COILED DRAGON, Japan,
early 19th century, ivory netsuke

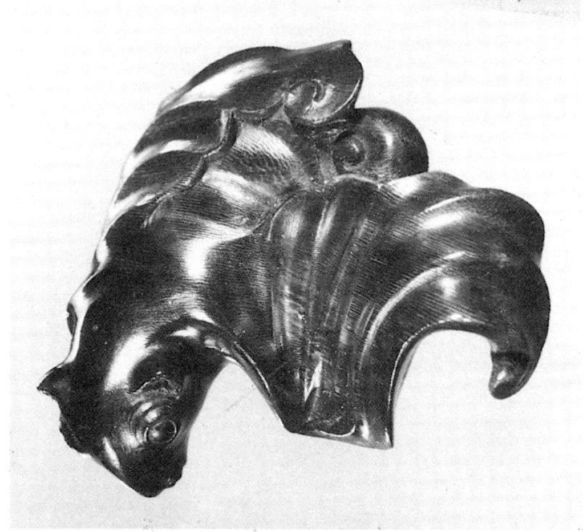

204 BAT, Japan, 19th century,
rhinoceros horn netsuke

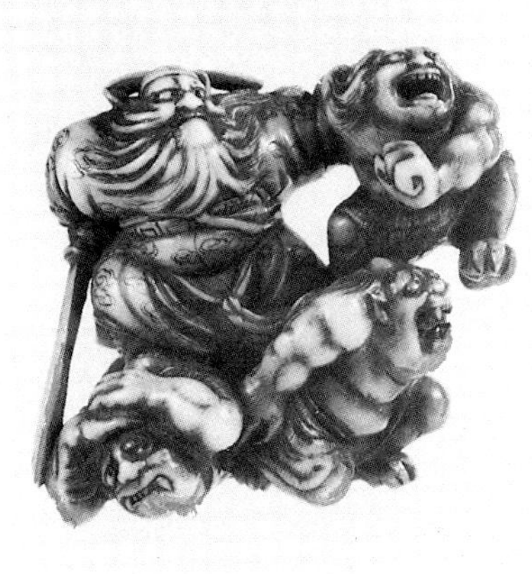

205 SHŌKI WITH THREE ONI,
Japan, 19th century, ivory netsuke

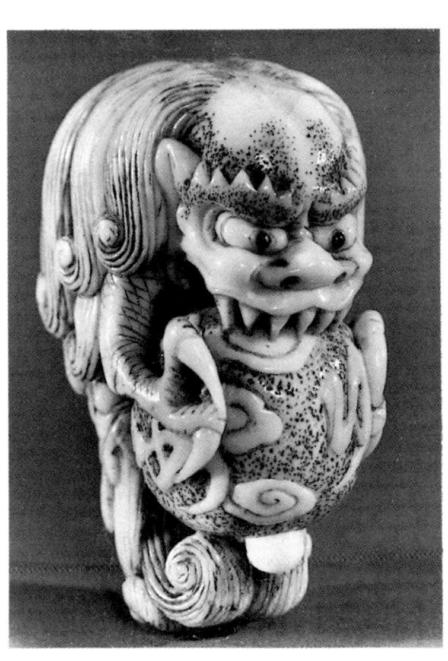

206 ANIMAL GHOST, Japan,
19th century, ivory netsuke

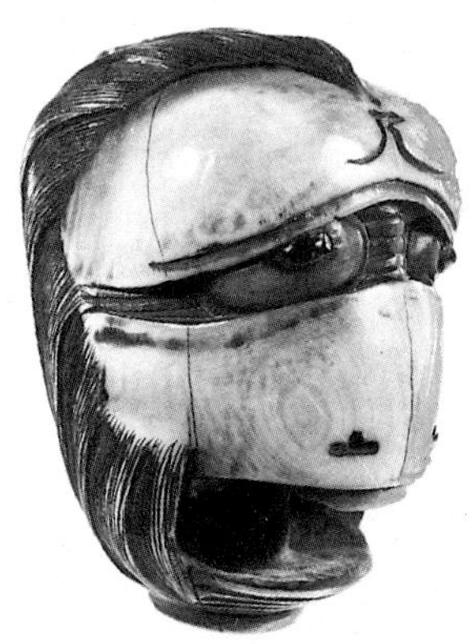

207 OIWA, Japan, 19th century,
ivory netsuke

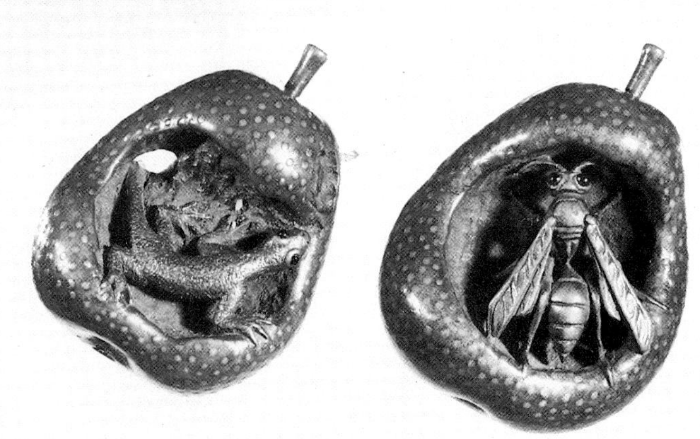

208 PEAR AND SALAMANDER,
Japan, 19th century, wood netsuke

Prints: *China* and *Japan*

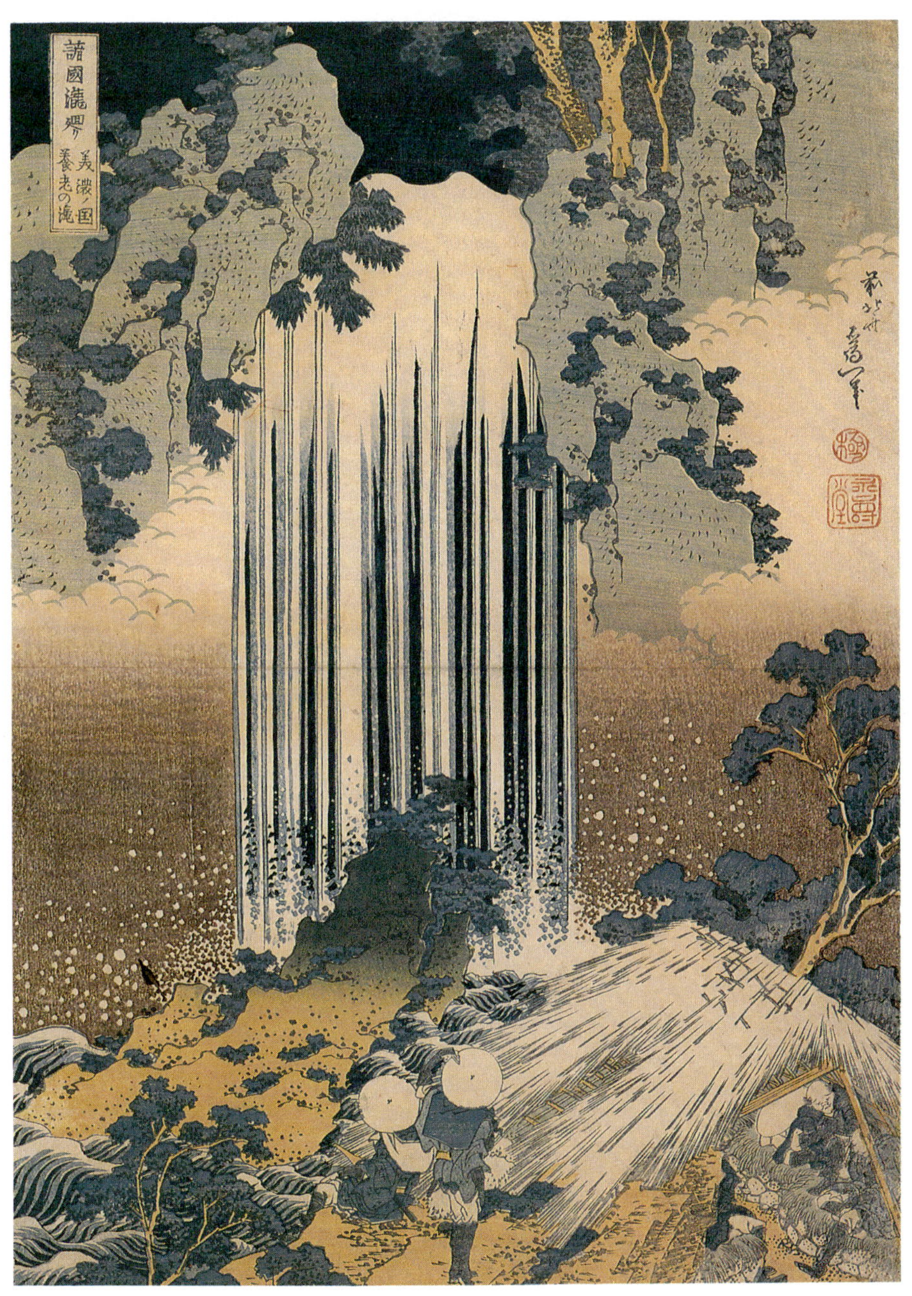

226 YORO WATERFALL, Katsushika Hokusai (1760-1849), Japan, ca. 1833, woodblock print

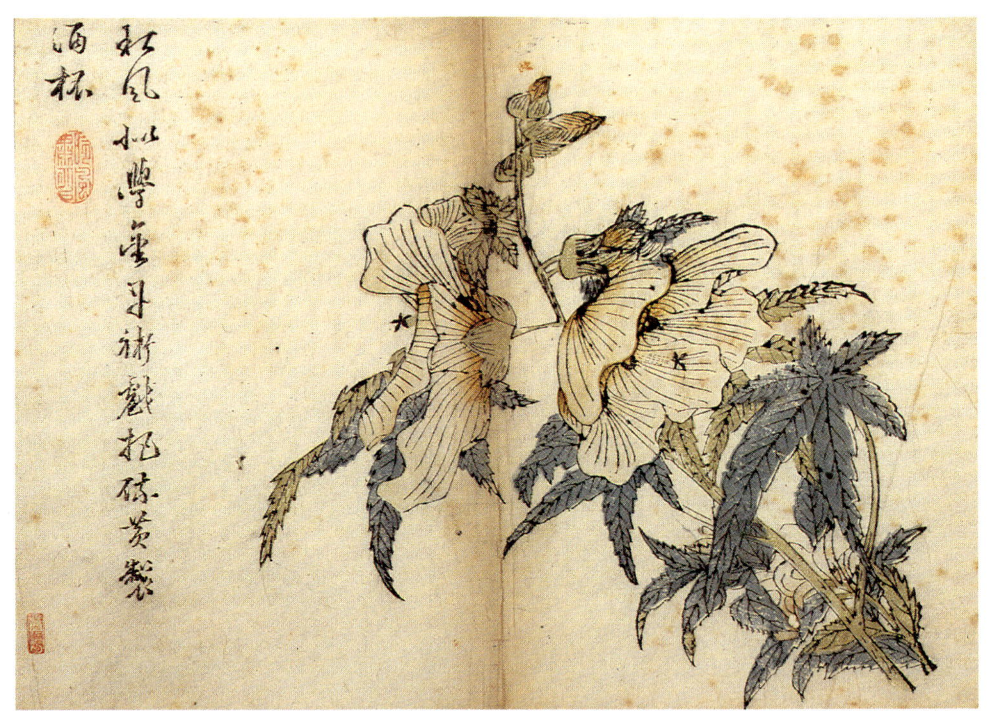

212 THE MUSTARD SEED GARDEN MANUAL, Two Pages, China,
18th century, woodblock print

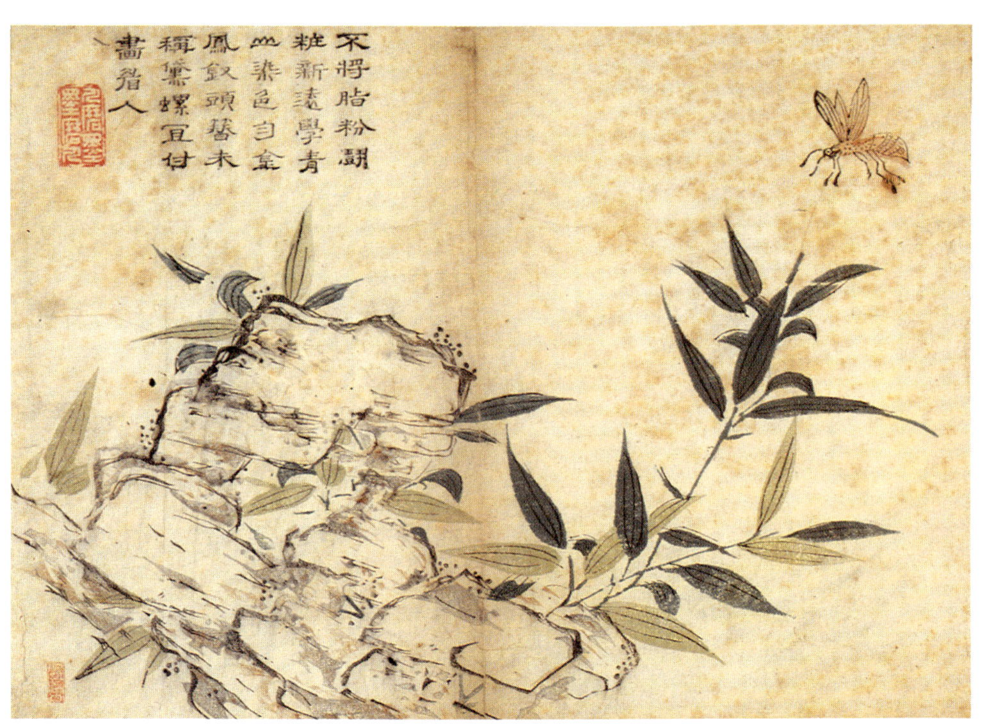

152

214 THE ACTOR NAKAMURA TOMIJŪRŌ I,
Torii Kiyohiro (fl. 1750's-1760's), Japan,
ca. late 1750's-early 1760's, woodblock print

213 CARRIAGE STOPPING SEQUENCE,
Torii Kiyomasu II (fl. 1720's-1760's),
Japan, ca. early 1740's, woodblock print

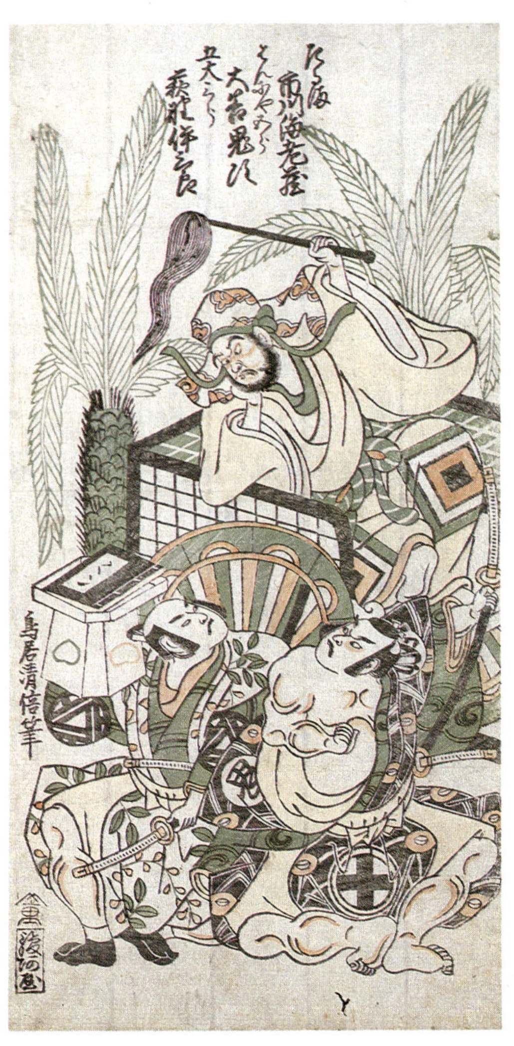

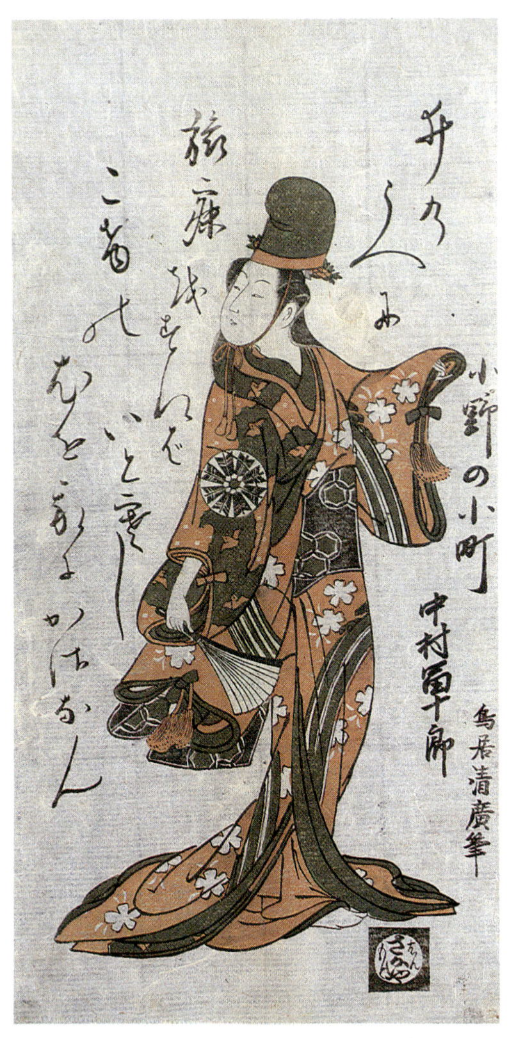

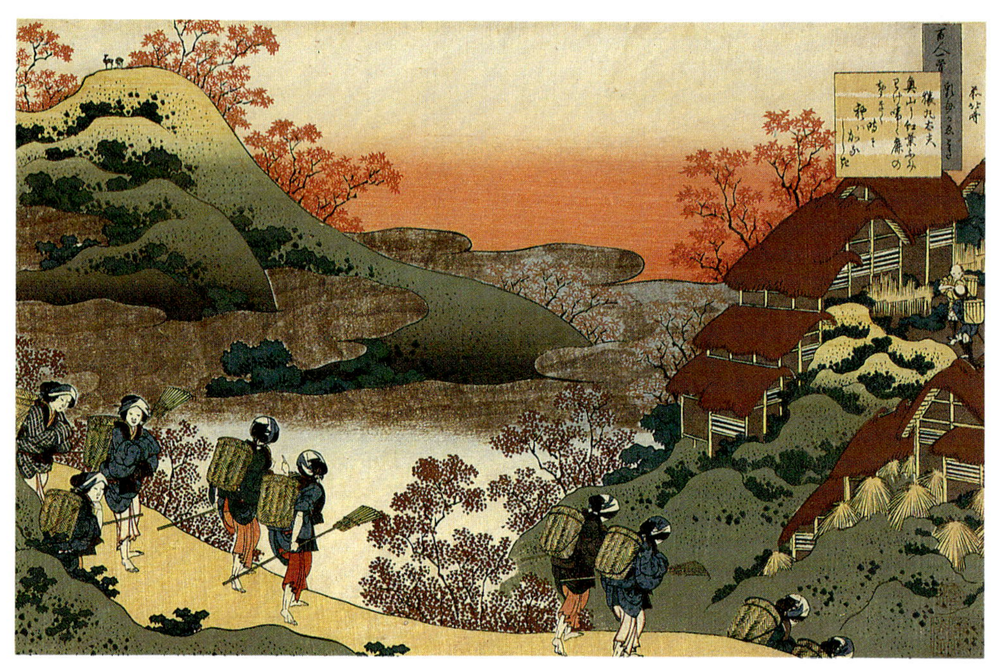

229 SARUMARU DAIYU, Katsushika Hokusai (1760-1849), Japan, ca.
1835, woodblock print

220 KAJIKAZAWA, Katsushika Hokusai (1760-1849), Japan, 1823-1831,
woodblock print

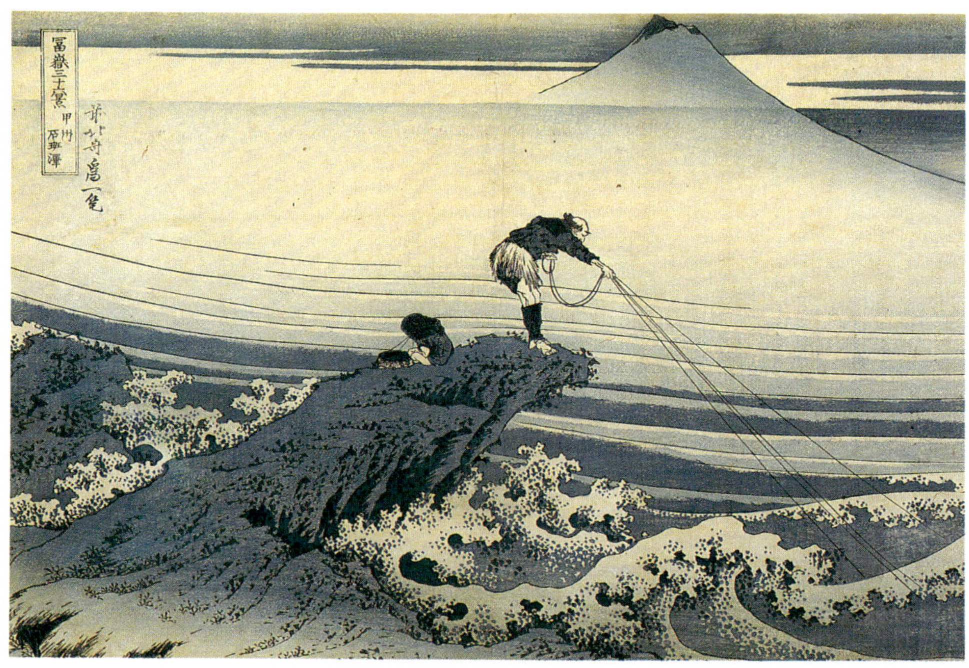

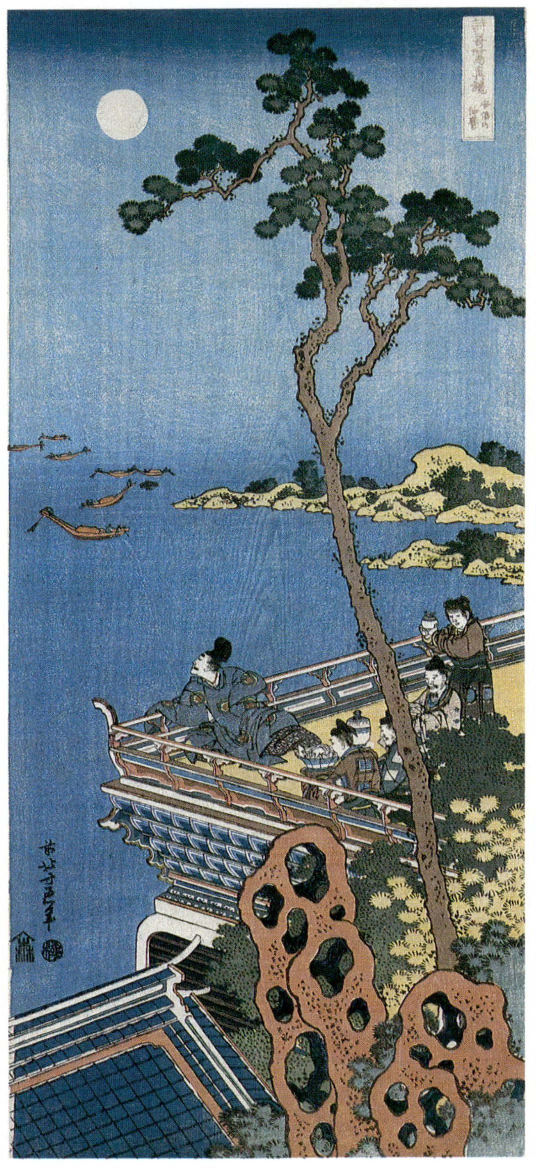

223 THE POET ABE NO NAKAMARO,
Katsushika Hokusai (1760-
1849), Japan, early 1830's, woodblock print

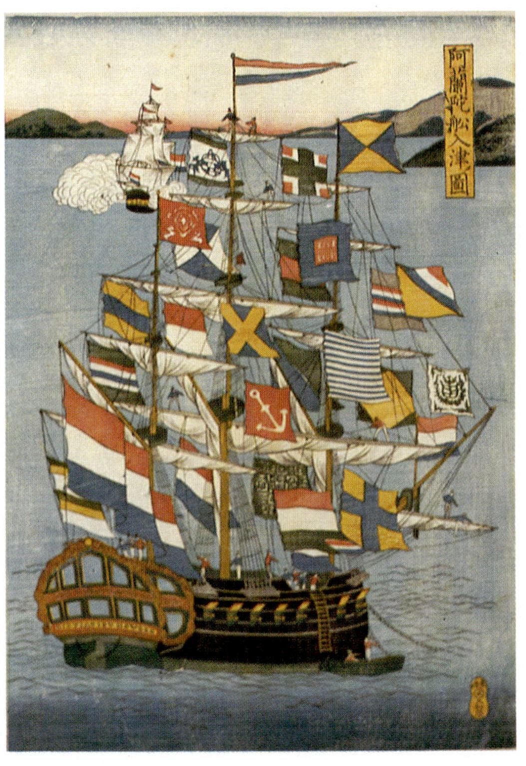

241 DUTCH SHIP, Japan, early 19th century,
woodblock print

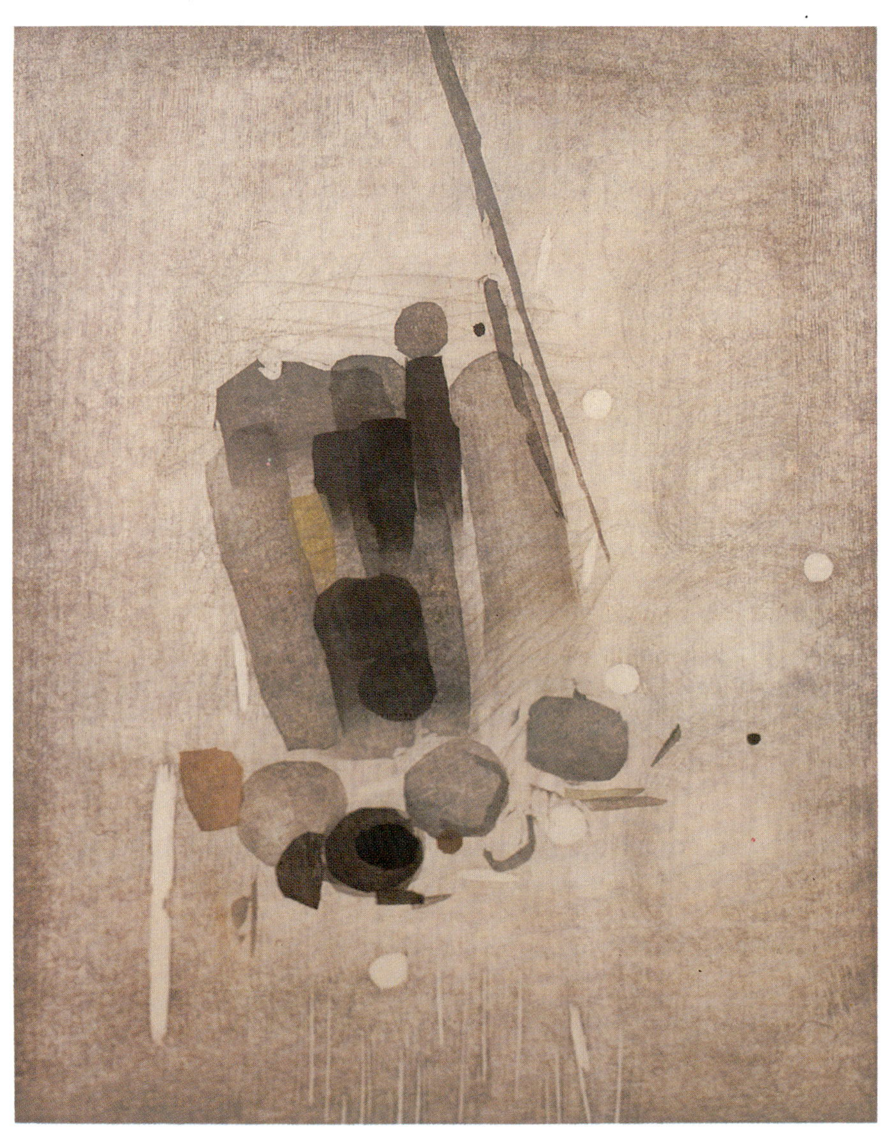

243 MISTY MORNING, Ansei Uchima, Japan, 1964, woodblock print

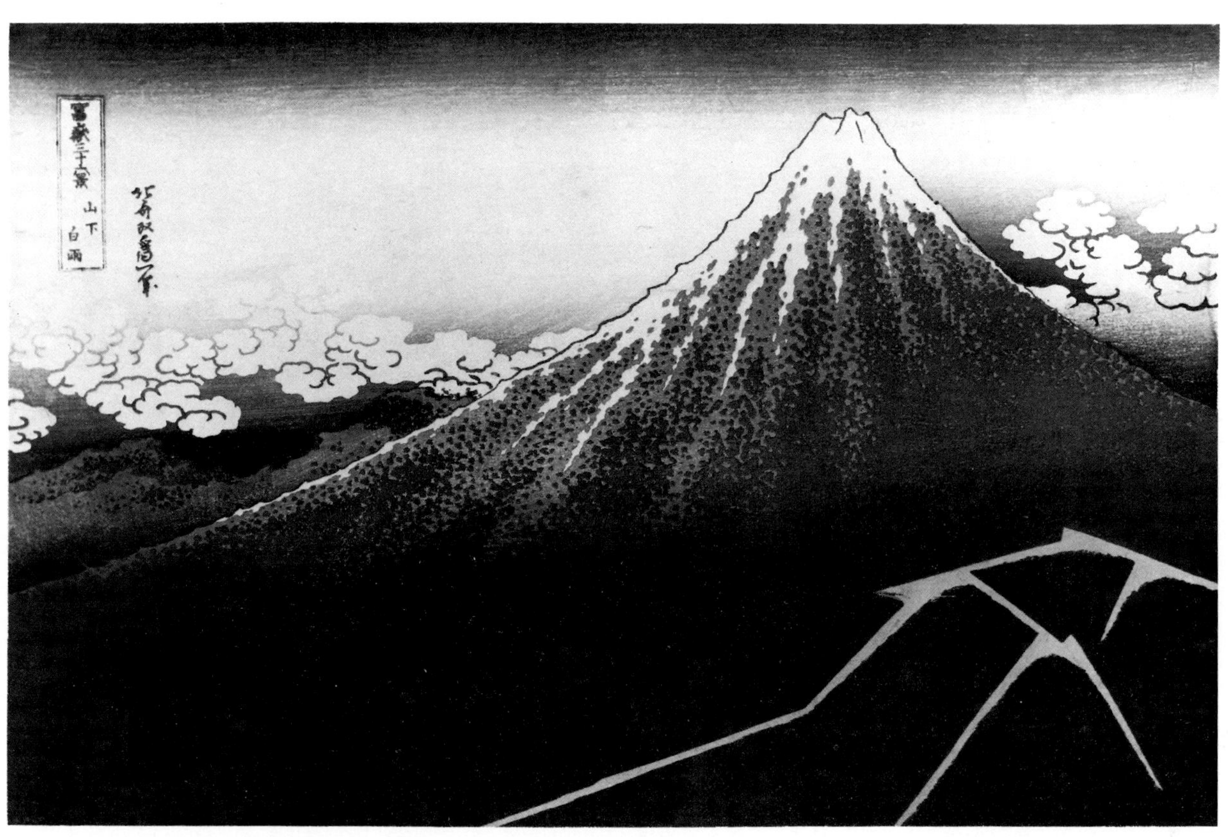

218 THUNDERSTORM BELOW THE MOUNTAIN, Katsushika
Hokusai (1760-1849), Japan, 1823-1831, woodblock print

216 FIGURE STUDY, Katsushika Hokusai (1760-1849), Japan, 1796, woodblock diptych

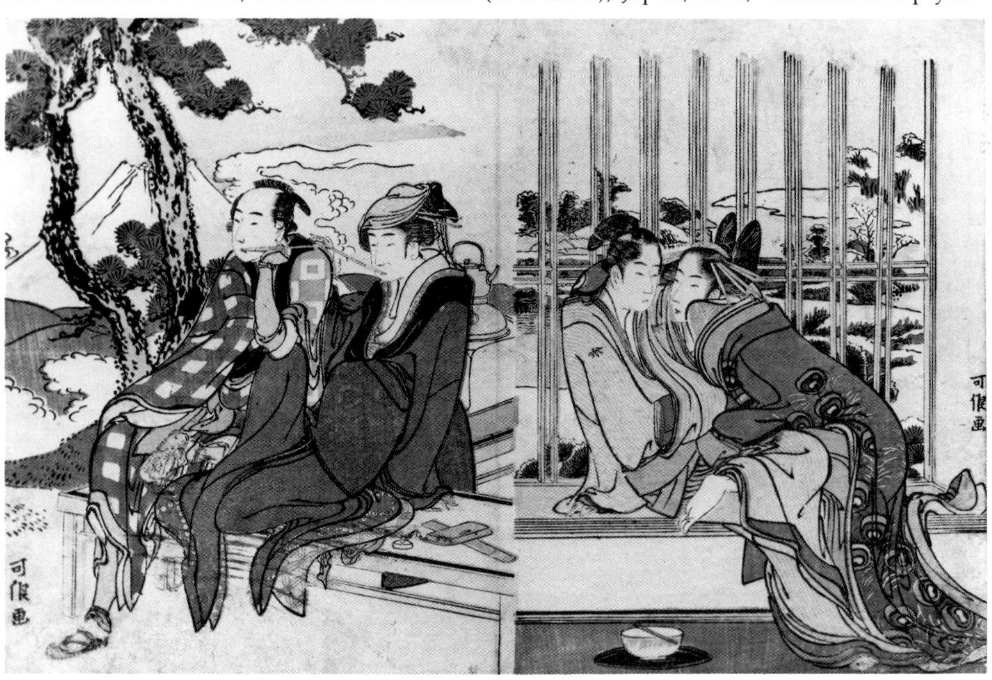

215 THE ACTOR ŌTANI HIROJI III,
Katsukawa Shunsen
(fl. 1780's-1790's), Japan, ca. 1796,
woodblock print

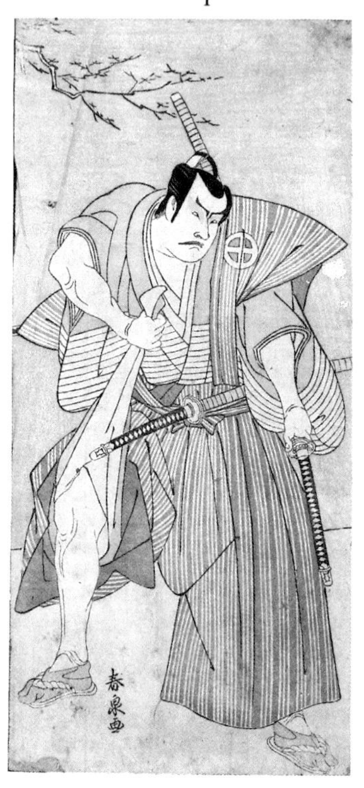

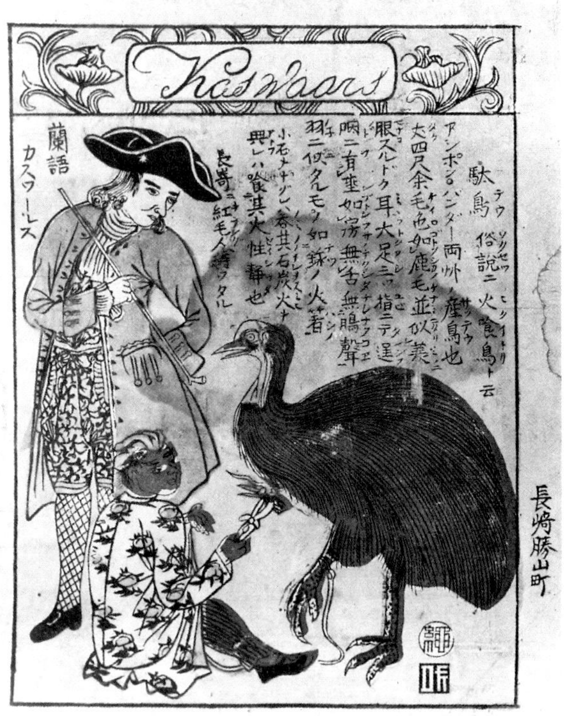

239 THE DUTCH SETTLEMENT AT DESHIMA, Japan, 1780,
woodblock print

227 BRIDGE OF BOATS AT SANO, Katsushika Hokusai (1760-1849),
Japan, ca. 1834, woodblock print

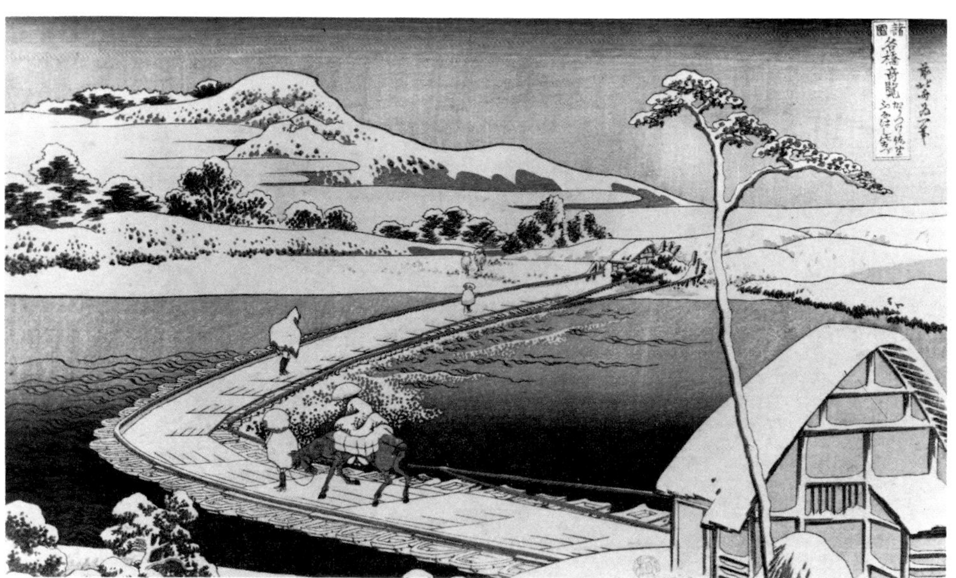

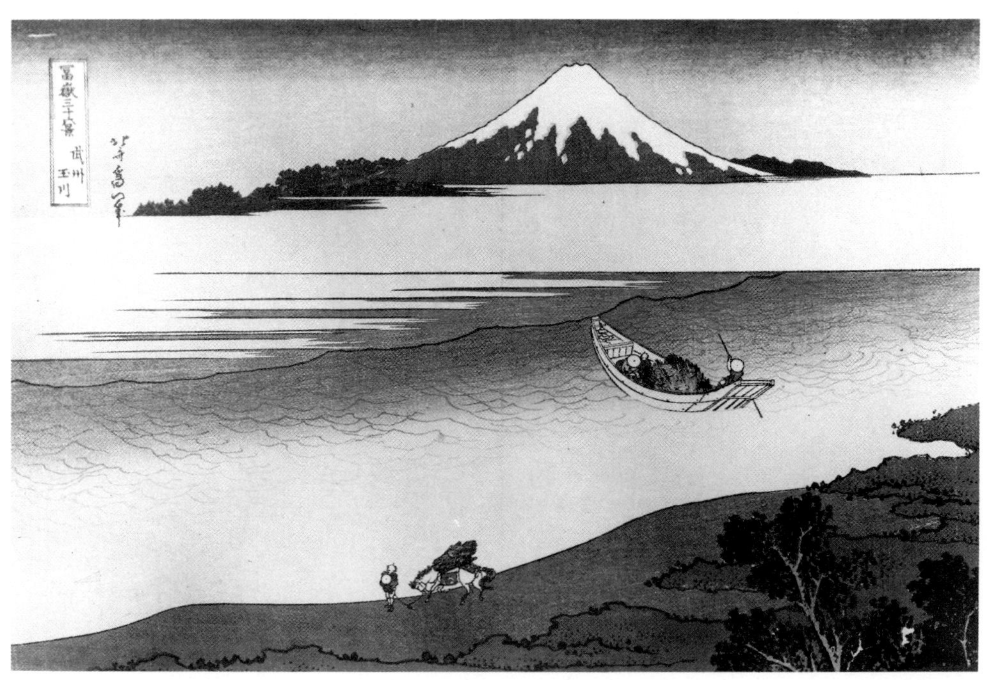

219   TAMAGAWA RIVER, Katsushika Hokusai (1760-1849), Japan 1823-
      1831, woodblock print

225   EVENING MOON AT SENKI, Katsushika Hokusai (1760-1849),
      Japan, ca. 1832, woodblock print

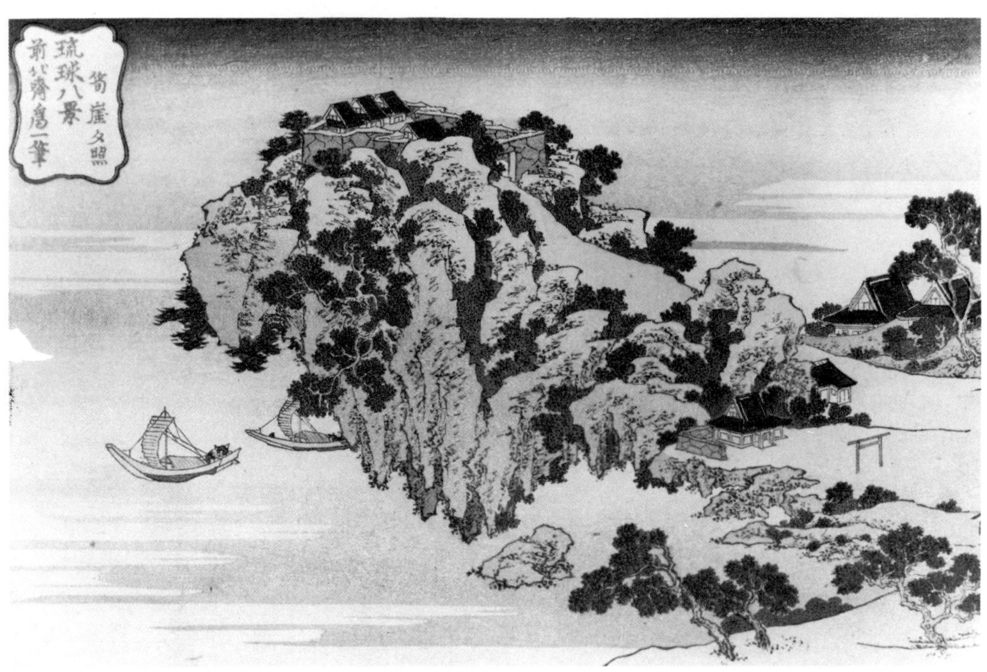

245 POEM-S, Haku Maki, Japan, mid 1960's, woodblock print

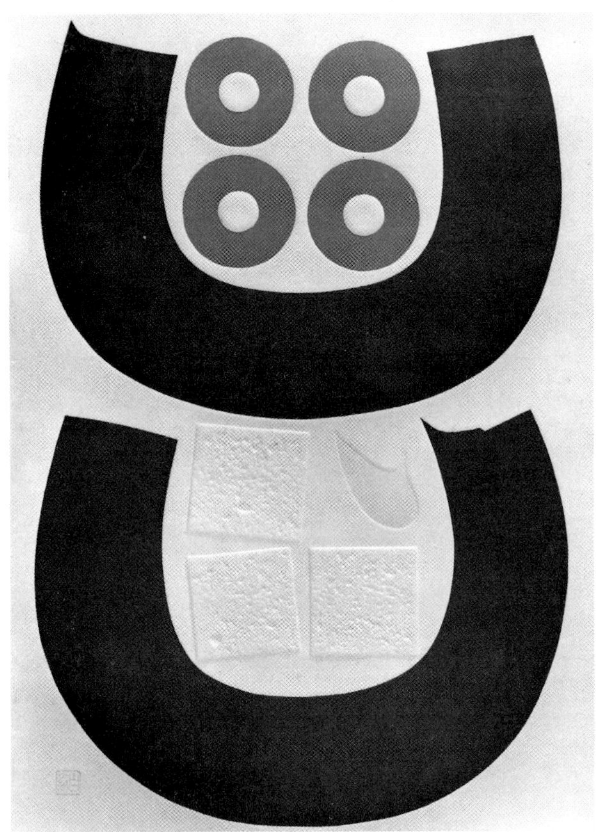

244 WIND IN THE MAPLE TREE,
Sasajima Kihei (1906-present),
Japan, 1961, woodblock print

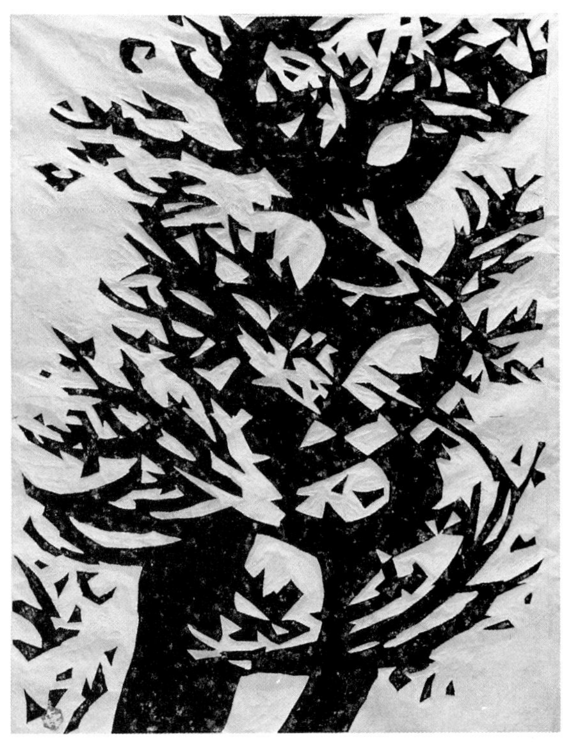

160

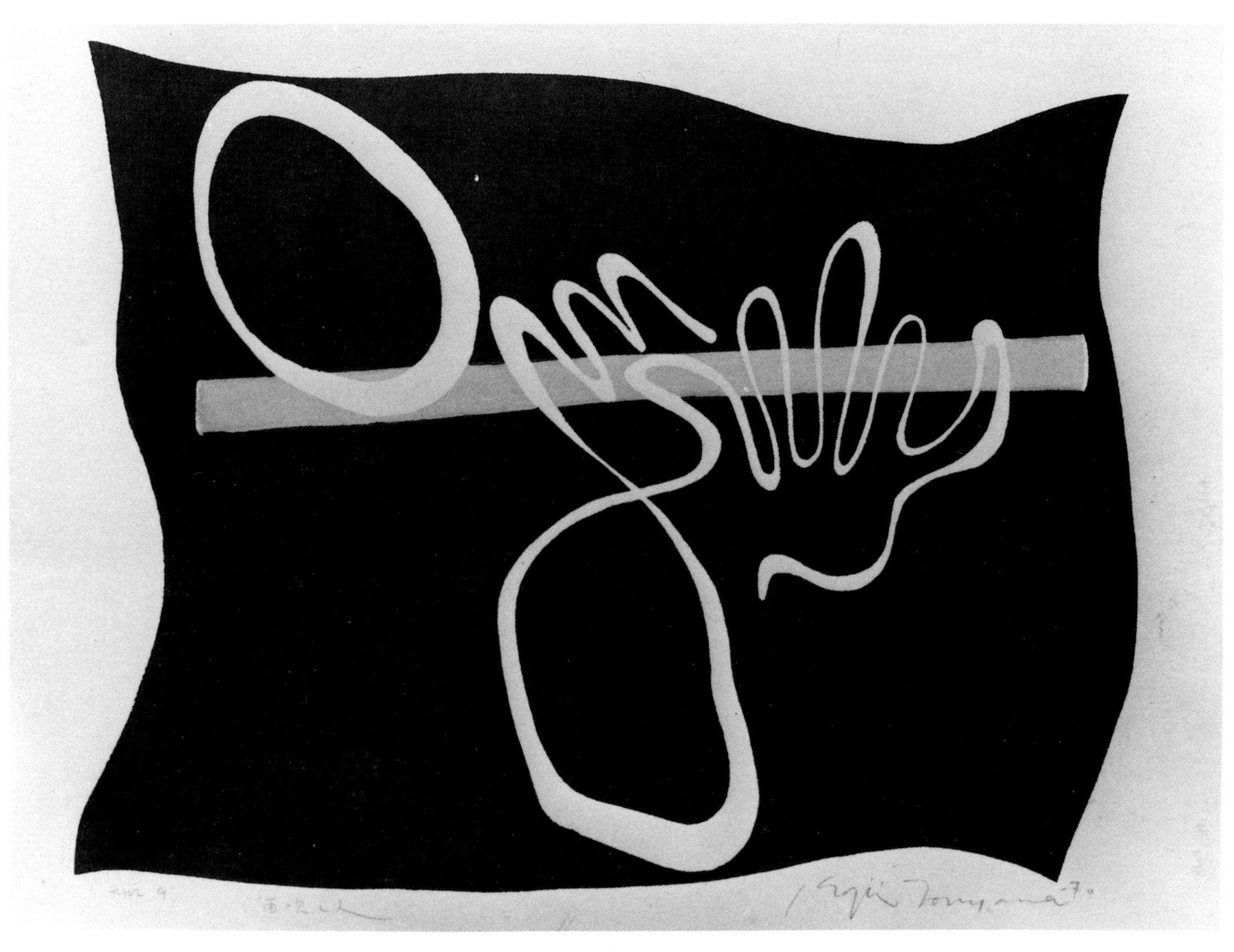

246 FLUTE PLAYER, Kōjin Toneyama (1921-present), Japan, 1970,
woodblock print